GW00985592

Victorian Buildings of London
1837–1887

VICTORIAN BUILDINGS OF LONDON

1837–1887

An Illustrated Guide

Gavin Stamp and Colin Amery

The Architectural Press · London

To Sir John Betjeman
Greatest friend and defender of Victorian buildings

First published in 1980 by The Architectural Press Ltd: London

© Gavin Stamp and Colin Amery 1980

ISBN 0 85139 500 7

All rights reserved. No part of this publication may be repro-
duced, stored in a retrieval system, or transmitted, in any form
or by any means, electronic, mechanical, photocopying, record-
ing or otherwise, without the prior permission of the publishers.
Such permission, if granted, is subject to a fee depending on the
nature of the use.

Filmset in 10/11 point Garamond
Printed and bound in Great Britain
by W & J Mackay Limited, Chatham

Sources and Acknowledgements

For a general survey of Victorian London, several books
may be highly recommended: Sir John Summerson's *The
Architecture of Victorian London* (1976) and *The Victorian
Rebuilding of the City of London* (1974); Priscilla Metcalf's
Victorian London (1972) and Donald J. Olsen's *The Growth
of Victorian London* (1977).

Several sources have been extensively employed and
quoted in the individual entries, notably C. L. Eastlake's
History of the Gothic Revival (1872), the *Ecclesiologist* (the
official organ of the Cambridge Camden Society, later the
Ecclesiological Society, 1839–68), the *Builder* and *Building News*, the principal mid-Victorian weekly architectural journals; T. F. Bumpus's *London Churches. Ancient
and Modern* (1907), B. F. L. Clarke's *Parish Churches of
London* (1966), H. R. Hitchcock's *Early Victorian Architecture in Britain* (1964), H. S. Goodhart-Rendel's *English
Architecture since the Regency* (1953) and, of course, Pevsner's *Buildings of England* for London. We also benefited
from access to the informative files of the Council for the
Care of Places of Worship.

For regrettably few areas of London, the recent vol-
umes available of the *Survey of London* have been extensively pillaged for their exhaustive research and the Victoria and Albert Museum's *Marble Halls*, edited by John
Physick and Michael Darby (1973) has been of considerable assistance, as was *The Houses of Parliament* edited by
M. Post (1976). For the later, Queen Anne architecture,
Mark Girouard's *Sweetness and Light* (1977) and Andrew
Saint's *Richard Norman Shaw* (1976) have been invaluable
and other useful biographies of Victorian architects
include Paul Thompson's *Butterfield* (1971) and Anthony
Quiney's *Pearson* (1979). For either their writings or for
their help, credit and thanks are also due to J. Mordaunt
Crook (on both the Reform Club and the British
Museum), Roger Dixon, Hilary Grainger (for informa-
tion about Ernest George), Peter Howell, Hermione
Hobhouse, Stefan Muthesius, John Physick (author of
The Wellington Monument), Margaret Richardson, Andrew
Saint, Alastair Service, Anthony Symondson, Nicholas
Taylor, David Watkin, Robert Thorne, Clive Wain-
wright and, above all, to Paul Joyce for his unstinting
generosity with information.

Note Many of the buildings described in this guide are private
property and not necessarily regularly open to visitors. Inclusion
here of a building does not imply right of access by members of
the public.

*Title page: Unexecuted design for the Royal Courts of Justice,
designed and drawn by Alfred Waterhouse, 1866. (The Royal
Institute of British Architects, London)*

Contents

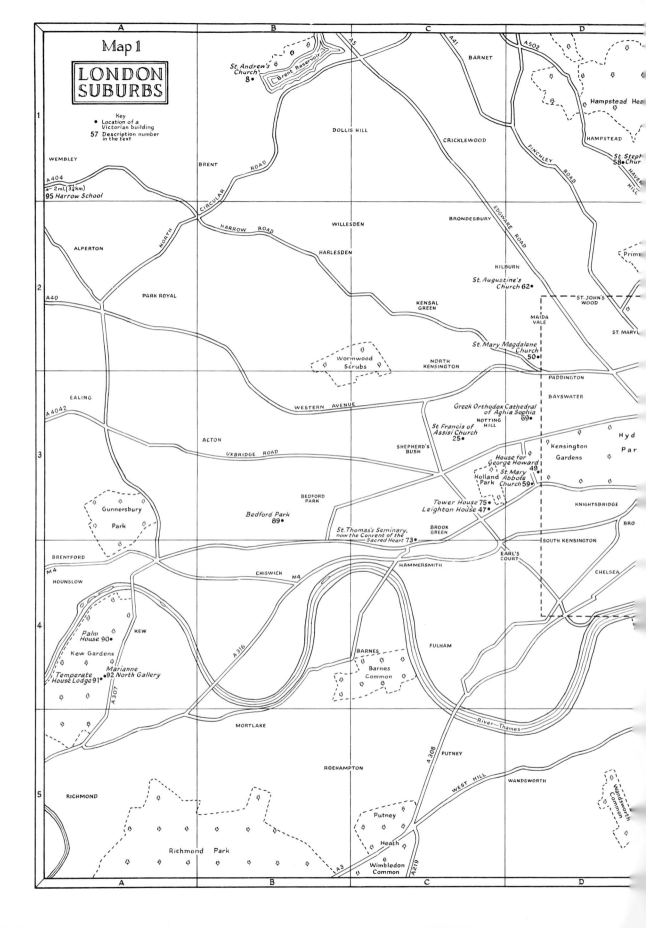

Map 1

LONDON SUBURBS

Key
● Location of a Victorian building
57 Description number in the text

A 404
← 2 ml.(3¼km.)
95 Harrow School

St. Andrew's Church 8●

Brent Reservoir

BARNET

A 5   A 441   A 502

DOLLIS HILL

CRICKLEWOOD

Hampstead Hea

HAMPSTEAD

St. Step 58● Chu

HAVER HILL

WEMBLEY

BRENT

CIRCULAR ROAD

NORTH

HARROW ROAD

WILLESDEN

HARLESDEN

BRONDESBURY

EDGWARE ROAD

FINCHLEY ROAD

ALPERTON

A 40

PARK ROYAL

KENSAL GREEN

KILBURN

St. Augustine's Church 62●

MAIDA VALE

St. John's Wood

St. Mary

St. Mary Magdalene Church 50●

PADDINGTON

Prim

A 4042

EALING

WESTERN AVENUE

Wormwood Scrubs

NORTH KENSINGTON

BAYSWATER

Greek Orthodox Cathedral of Aghia Sophia 69●

NOTTING HILL

St Francis of Assisi Church 25●

Kensington Gardens

Hy d Par

ACTON

UXBRIDGE ROAD

SHEPHERD'S BUSH

House for George Howard 49●

St. Mary Abbots Church 59●

Holland Park

Gunnersbury Park

BEDFORD PARK

Tower House 75●

Leighton House 47●

KNIGHTSBRIDGE

Bedford Park 89●

St.Thomas's Seminary, now the Convent of the Sacred Heart 73●

BROOK GREEN

SOUTH KENSINGTON

BRO

BRENTFORD

EARL'S COURT

CHELSEA

M 4

HOUNSLOW

CHISWICK

M4

HAMMERSMITH

KEW

FULHAM

A 316

Palm House 90●

Kew Gardens

BARNES

Barnes Common

Temperate House Lodge 91●

Marianne 92 North Gallery

A 307

MORTLAKE

River Thames

RICHMOND

ROEHAMPTON

A 308

PUTNEY

WEST HILL

WANDSWORTH

Wandsworth Common

Putney

Heath

Richmond Park

Wimbledon Common

A 3   A 219

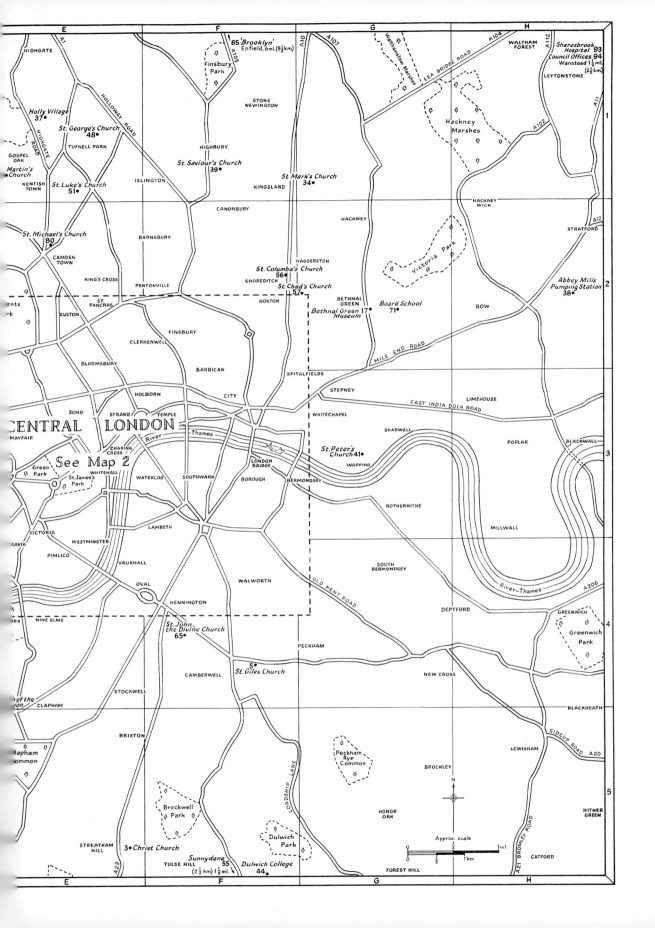

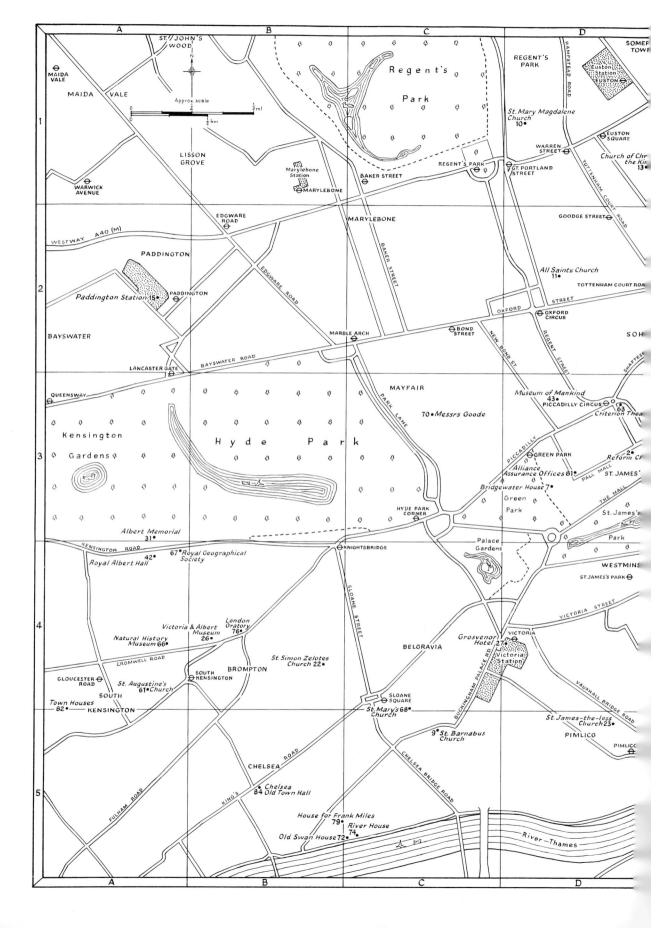

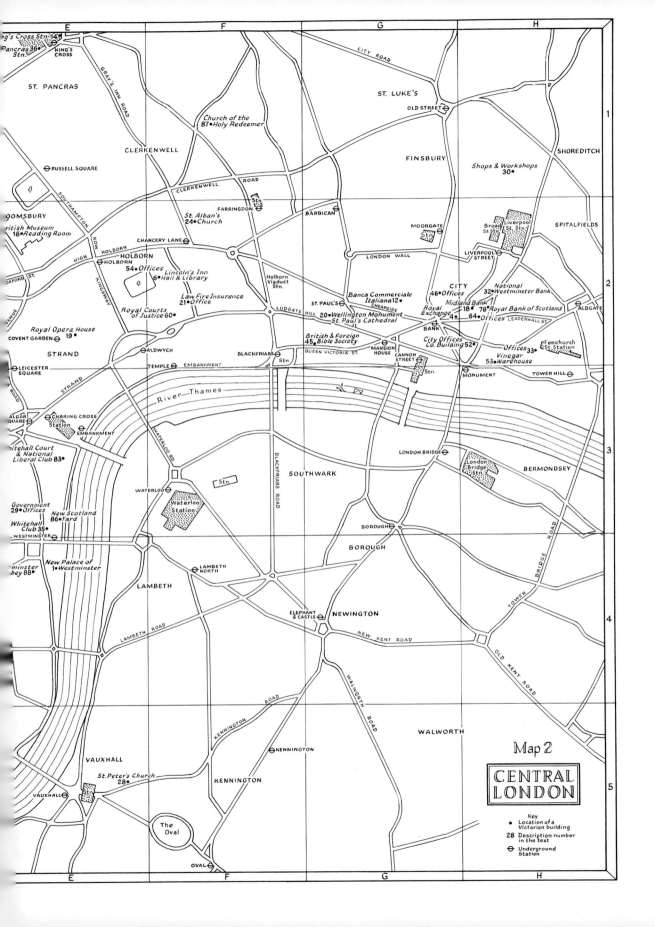

E F G H

ng's Cross Stn 45
Pancras 36
Stn.
KING'S
CROSS

CITY ROAD

ST. PANCRAS

ST. LUKE'S

SHOREDITCH

GRAY'S INN ROAD

Church of the
87•Holy Redeemer

OLD STREET

1

CLERKENWELL

FINSBURY

Shops & Workshops
30•

SPITALFIELDS

Russell Square

SOUTHAMPTON ROW

CLERKENWELL ROAD

FARRINGDON

Stn.

BARBICAN

MOORGATE

Stn.

Broad
St.Stn.

Liverpool
St.Stn.

LIVERPOOL
STREET

St. Alban's
24•Church

OOMSBURY

ritish Museum
16•Reading Room

CHANCERY LANE

LONDON WALL

CITY

HOLBORN
Holborn

Offices 46•

National
32•Westminster Bank

HIGH HOLBORN

Holborn

54•Offices

Lincoln's Inn
6• Hall & Library

Holborn
Viaduct
Stn.

ST. PAUL'S

Banca Commerciale
Italiana 12•

Midland Bank
18•

78•Royal Bank of Scotland

KINGSWAY

OXFORD ST.

Law Fire Insurance
21•Office

LUDGATE HILL

CHEAPSIDE

Royal
Exchange
4•

64•Offices

LEADENHALL ST.

ALDGATE

Royal Courts
of Justice 60•

ST. PAUL'S

20•Wellington Monument
St. Paul's Cathedral

BANK

Royal Opera House
COVENT GARDEN 19•

British & Foreign
45 Bible Society

City Offices
Co. Building 52•

Offices 33•

Fenchurch
St. Station

STRAND

ALDWYCH

MANSION
HOUSE

53•Vinegar
Warehouse

VENUE

LEICESTER
SQUARE

BLACKFRIARS

QUEEN VICTORIA ST.

CANNON
STREET

Stn.

TEMPLE EMBANKMENT

Stn.

Stn.

MONUMENT

TOWER HILL

STRAND

River Thames

ALGAR
QUARE

CHARING CROSS
Station

EMBANKMENT

WATERLOO RD.

LONDON BRIDGE

London
Bridge
Stn.

BERMONDSEY

3

hitehall Court
& National
Liberal Club 83•

BLACKFRIARS ROAD

SOUTHWARK

Stn.

Government
29•Offices

New Scotland
86•Yard

Waterloo
WATERLOO

Waterloo
Station

Whitehall
Club 35•

WESTMINSTER

BOROUGH

New Palace of
1•Westminster

minster
bey 88•

LAMBETH
NORTH

BOROUGH

BRIDGE ROAD

4

LAMBETH

ELEPHANT
& CASTLE

NEWINGTON

NEW KENT ROAD

TOWER

LAMBETH ROAD

WALWORTH ROAD

OLD KENT ROAD

KENNINGTON ROAD

WALWORTH

Map 2

VAUXHALL

KENNINGTON

CENTRAL
LONDON

St. Peter's Church
28•

KENNINGTON

Key
• Location of a
   Victorian building

VAUXHALL

5

The
Oval

28 Description number
    in the text

⊖ Underground
    Station

OVAL

E F G H

Introduction

This is a survey of a selected number of examples of Victorian architecture, in London, for the period 1837–87, rather than a complete guide to Victorian London. Such a selection is bound to be arbitrary, but the authors hope that the hundred or so buildings chosen for detailed study may be representative of the many strands and facets of the complicated phenomenon which was Victorian architecture.

The buildings have been chosen not for their curiosity value, but because they have considerable architectural merit. They are architecture rather than specimens of curious "Victoriana" or examples of engineering skill or purely utilitarian structures. It has been fashionable among certain writers to see more virtue in the engineering than the aesthetic achievements of the 19th century. In this book all the buildings are examples of what the Victorians considered to be architecture as an art.

Buildings cannot, however, be seen outside their context, both in the place they occupy in 19th-century architectural history and their part in the vast and expanding urban fabric of Victorian London. Each example selected has been put, as far as possible, in its architectural context, but the development of London in the 19th century—excellently surveyed in several books—can only be summarised here. The change in London during Victoria's reign was immense. In 1831 the population of London and its suburbs was 1,776,000; in 1901 it was 6,581,000. London became a city terrifying in its vastness and complexity, a fog-bound, awful phenomenon to Frenchmen like Gustave Doré, who represented the vigour, squalor and grim sublimity of London in his woodcuts. It was a city of extremes, of extreme wealth, of differing levels of civilisation; the biggest city in the world, the centre of government of the British Empire, and yet unplanned and with no central metropolitan governing authority. Yet much did happen in the course of Victoria's reign to transform London by the end of the century, a transformation in which architects played only a small part and which made London a very different city from, say, Paris or Berlin. In the words of G. M. Young, "The conversion of the vast and shapeless city, which Dickens knew—fog-bound and fever-haunted, brooding over its dark, mysterious river—into the imperial capital, of Whitehall, the Thames Embankment, and South Ken-

sington, is still the symbol of the mid-Victorian transition".

In 1837, when the young Victoria acceded to the throne, her capital was a Georgian city of stock bricks and new stucco. Her official residence, Buckingham Palace (which she never liked) was lately completed by the now disgraced John Nash; the Marble Arch still stood in front and Blore's mediocre façade existed as yet only on paper. Parts of London were ancient; many gabled plaster houses stood along the Strand and around the City, and the City itself was still largely as rebuilt after the Great Fire. It was the West End which was the pride of London: the regular gentlemanly terraces and squares of stock brick which lay between Holborn and the New Road (Marylebone and Euston Roads) and the famous metropolitan improvements—the one attempt to make London a little like Paris—carried out for his late, disreputable Majesty, King George IV, by his architect John Nash. Nash may often have built illiterately and badly in stucco, but his new Regent Street, Piccadilly Circus and Carlton House Terrace were boldly planned and smart. Trafalgar Square, with the new National Gallery on the north side, was slowly taking shape, and with no Nelson's Column, its scale was still civilised. The suburbs were growing with the "March of Bricks and Mortar" which Cruikshank satirised, but there were still green fields beyond Islington, Paddington and Walworth.

In 1887, when Victoria, Queen and Empress, celebrated her first Jubilee, London was built up beyond Hammersmith, Hampstead, Finsbury Park and Sydenham, and new streets of redbrick were growing in all directions. If in 1837, the colour of London was cream and grey, in 1887 it was becoming a city of redbrick and terra cotta. The City of London had been almost completely rebuilt once again and the capital could boast a large number of fine new public buildings.

In many ways London remained unchanged—Georgian London survived into the 20th century—and the extraordinary fact was that the capital, unlike the new cities of the midlands and the north, remained without any proper municipal authority. Local government was exercised by the old system of local boards and vestries and the City remained independent. Although the richest and biggest city in the world, London was very different from the Paris of Napoleon III who allowed M. Haussmann to give it its boulevards of uniform, sterile character. In the English tradition, private enterprise and vested interests reigned supreme, maintaining that complexity and diversity which was always the character of London, a diversity which extended also to architectural style.

There were, however, big improvements made in Victoria's reign, showing that, when really necessary, big things were possible. These were chiefly the achievement of the Metropolitan Board of Works, which reigned from

1855 until 1888. The body effected the few pieces of large-scale town planning: not straight streets, but necessary streets cut through for traffic, with no thought of visual or architectural unity after the swathe through old property had been made. These included Victoria Street (1845–51, ie before the MBW), Queen Victoria Street (1867–71), Shaftesbury Avenue (1876–86), the Charing Cross Road (1876–87), Garrick Street (opened 1861), Southwark Street (completed 1864), Northumberland Avenue (1874–6), Clerkenwell Road (opened 1878), and two great pieces of engineering: Holborn Viaduct (1863–9) and the Victoria Embankment (1864–70). The new streets were not beautiful; the curving street lines and the irredeemably mediocre new façades of, say, Shaftesbury Avenue are characteristic of both the best and the worst sides of Victorian London.

Another important area of Victorian improvement was the creation of public parks. Central London, of course, benefited from the ancient Hyde Park and St James's Park, but the expanding urban areas desperately needed "lungs" before all land was built over. Between 1842 and 1847 Victoria Park, in the East End, was created and Battersea Park was laid out after 1846. The long battle to retain Hampstead Heath for the enjoyment of Londoners was won in 1872 when it was bought by the Metropolitan Board of Works. Conversely, however, during the same years some of the old pleasure gardens, such as the Vauxhall and the Cremorne, in Chelsea, were closed because of their 18th-century tradition of sports and other vices.

The other important "lungs" in Victorian London, the cemeteries—Highgate, Nunhead, Norwood, Kensal Green, Abney Park, Brompton—were really creations of the 1830s, although their picturesque landscaping and buildings were sometimes not completed until the 1840s. The first, Kensal Green, was opened in 1833 and was a response to the insanitary and unsatisfactory conditions prevailing in old inner city burial grounds. All of these cemeteries, of course, contain magnificent examples of the Victorian monumental mason's art.

But the biggest change in London was achieved not by any authority but by private enterprise, in the shape of railway companies. When Victoria came to the throne, London's first railway, carried upon brick arches from London Bridge to Greenwich, had been open for a year. The recondite route from the City to Blackwall, boasting traction by cable, was opened soon after. In the first years of Victoria's reign the principal trunk lines reached London—Euston (1837): London and North-Western Railway for Birmingham, Liverpool and Manchester; Paddington (1838): Great Western Railway for Bristol and the West, on the seven foot broad gauge; Nine Elms (1838, extended to Waterloo in 1848): the London and South-Western Railway; and Shoreditch (1840) and Fenchurch Street (1841) for the east. These early lines amazed contemporaries by the glamour of steam and speed and the destructive and massive engineering works required in building the tracks, involving catastrophic changes such as are described in *Dombey and Son* (referring to Camden Town). After the "Railway Mania" years of the 1840s, the Great Northern Railway's east coast route to Scotland was opened from King's Cross in 1850. However, the 1860s were the years when London was really carved up by the railways. A new main line, the Midland Railway, came down to St Pancras and the southern companies—engaged in bitter internecine warfare—were flinging bridgeheads across the Thames. Victoria was opened in 1860, Charing Cross, on the site of the Hungerford Market, with its new bridge (replacing Brunel's suspension bridge) in 1864, Cannon Street in 1866, Ludgate Hill and the conspicuous bridge by Ludgate Circus in 1864. The North London Railway opened its extension to Broad Street in 1865.

In the same decade the first underground railway in the world was opened: the Metropolitan Railway from Paddington to Farringdon Street in 1863, built on the cut-and-cover principle chiefly along the routes of main roads. The Metropolitan District Railway was opened as far as Blackfriars in 1870 and the Inner Circle was completed, after big squabbles between the two companies and extensive works in the City, in 1884. Another important transport innovation was Shillibeer's omnibus that appeared on the streets in 1829. The knife-board bus came into general use in about 1849, and the London General Omnibus Company (not a monopoly) was formed in 1855; J. A. Hansom, architect, invented the horse-drawn "Patent Safety Cab" named after him in 1834.

The remaining large railway works in London were the extension of the Great Eastern Railway to Liverpool Street, opened in 1874 and the very late advent of the Great Central Railway at Marylebone in 1899. The construction of all these lines, with their associated branch suburban lines, which reached a pitch of frenzy in the 1860s, had two main effects on London. First, the railway encouraged the further growth of suburbs several miles from the business centre of London. Middle-class suburbs, whether villas in Norwood or Mr Pooter's Holloway, grew up on commuter railways. Secondly, parts of central London were transformed, as the railways demolished much poor property whose displaced inhabitants tended to gravitate to the East End of London.

As the poorest of London's railways, only the Great Eastern was really interested in expediting the compulsory cheap workmen's trains by promoting speculative building in east London. The area which was totally transformed was, however, the City of London. The City, rebuilt after 1666, was a densely populated residential area as well as being important for banking and commerce. In the first half of the nineteenth century, its

The Crystal Palace when re-erected on Sydenham Hill; perspective by J. D. Harding exhibited at the RA in 1854 (Royal Institute of British Architects, London)

population remained about static, but then the railways, together with rising land values, had a profound effect. Between 1851 and 1871 the residential population of the City dropped from 128,000 to 75,000 and in 1901 it was 27,000. The City was the one part of London almost totally rebuilt in Victoria's reign; the Georgian City which Dickens described disappeared, just as the Victorian City has largely disappeared in the next and catastrophic rebuilding since 1945.

From a distance, it seems that in the 1860s London must have been full of scaffolding and dust. Not only were the railways being built and new streets cut through, but a whole new array of public buildings were being raised—a new parliament house and central law courts, exchanges and markets, museums, concert halls, hospitals and schools. The religious revival of early Victorian England was more than just a reaction against the indulgent years of the Georges; it produced a new consciousness of poverty and degradation and added to the climate in which the Improver could work. If street and night life did, in fact, retain a Georgian vigour and a Regency rakishness well into Victoria's reign, as is clear from reading Henry Mayhew and the anonymous author of *London in the Sixties*, moral pressures militated against conspicuous vice and drove most of it underground. Furthermore, moral rebuilding was accompanied by physical rebuilding, even in the darkest East End of London. Men like Edwin Chadwick and Mayhew examined the problems of poverty (and came to very different conclusions) and philanthropists, like the Peabody Trust and the Industrial Dwellings Company, did much to alleviate bad conditions by building cheap tenement accommodation. Hospitals and schools were

built and London's appalling sanitation system was considerably improved. A concern for more than the material welfare of London's citizens produced not only churches but art galleries and museums. South Kensington is a monument to the Victorian faith in the benefit of culture and education.

The greatest and most famous expression of the Victorian sense of progress, of the possibilities of the improvement of mankind through the exercise of intelligence, ingenuity and peaceful free trade was, of course, the Great Exhibition of 1851. This, the first ever international exhibition, was held in Hyde Park in a remarkable prefabricated glass and iron structure, "a symbol of universal happiness and brotherhood of mystical significance", the glamour of which is best suggested by the name given to it: the Crystal Palace. So successful was this that Sir Joseph Paxton's building was taken down and re-erected, in an expanded form, on the top of Sydenham Hill in 1854 where it stood, as a popular entertainment centre and landmark, until the fire of 1936. Today the magical name is all that remains, although a few curious prehistoric monsters from the exhibition lurk around the boating lake in the park.

Many 20th-century historians have seen the Crystal Palace and the new architecture of iron and glass as the real achievement of the age, in contrast to the architecture of brick and mortar which was largely characterised by period revivals. There was good reason for some critics' indifference to and hostility to the Palace and it remains true that it had a negligible influence in the subsequent architecture of Victoria's reign. Morris and Ruskin disliked the rampant and vulgar materialism of the Exhibition and Ruskin felt that, impressive though Paxton's building was, it was irrelevant to the real problems of architecture. Indeed, the techniques of iron and glass construction—admirable for railway stations (of which the Victorians were not at all ashamed) or markets—have little more general application today than in the 19th century. In 1857 Ruskin lectured to architectural students that "if you are not content with a Palladio, you will not be content with a Paxton, and I pray you get rid of the idea of there being any necessity for the invention of a new style".

The 19th century was indisputably obsessed with *style*, as style was an inescapable problem in the design of a house, a church or a town hall. An unconscious tradition of building having ceased to exist, decisions about style could not be avoided, as the most intelligent architects realised. As Gilbert Scott observed in 1856, "the peculiar characteristic of the present day, as compared with all former periods, is this—that we are acquainted with the history of art . . . It is reserved to us above all the generations of the human race, to know perfectly our own standing-point, and to look back upon the entire history of what has gone before us, tracing out all the changes in the acts of the past as clearly as if every scene in its big drama were re-enacted before our eyes. This is amazingly interesting to us as a matter of amusement and erudition, but I fear it is a hindrance rather than a help to us as artists".

Several architects wished a new style to be invented, a style which, in the distant future, to Macaulay's New Zealanders visiting the ruins of London, would be clearly recognisable as *Victorian*. James Fergusson thundered that "the great lesson we have yet to learn before progress is again possible is that *Archaeology is not Architecture*" (1862). But the conspicuous fact is that the realised buildings (few enough in number) by forward-looking men such as Fergusson, Thomas "Victorian" Harris or Robert Kerr, are extraordinarily feeble, and have definite affinities with the Gothic or Italianate styles. The truth that architects cannot invent styles but that styles evolve from working in a tradition was fully appreciated by Ruskin, when he wrote, in the *Seven Lamps of Architecture* (1849), that

A day never passes without our hearing our English architects called upon to be original, and to invent a new style: about as sensible and necessary an exhortation as to ask of a man who has never had rags enough on his back to keep out cold, to invent a new mode of cutting a coat. Give him a whole coat first, and let him concern himself about the fashion of it afterwards. We want no new style of architecture. Who wants a new style of painting or sculpture? But we want *some* style . . . There seems to me a wonderful misunderstanding among the majority of architects at the present day as to the very nature and meaning of originality; and of all wherein it consists. Originality in expression does not depend on invention of new words; nor originality in poetry an invention of new measures; nor, in painting, an invention of new colours

. . . A man who has the gift, will take up any style that is going, the style of his day, and will work in that, and be great in that, and make everything he does in it look as fresh as if every thought of it had just come down from heaven. I do not say that he will not take liberties with his materials, or with his rules. I do not say that strange changes will be instructive, natural, facile, though sometimes marvellous; they will never be sought after as things necessary to his dignity or to his independence; and these liberties will be like the liberties that a great speaker takes with the language . . . the forms of architecture already however are good enough for us, and far better than any of us; and it will be time enough to think of changing them for better when we can use them as they are.

Once granted that a creative architecture depended upon tradition, there were two approaches to the past. One was that which was adopted in the Renaissance and which was attempted by the Gothic Revivalists after Pugin: to become proficient in the grammar and precise details of a past style, and then to allow it to evolve in response to contemporary needs once the discipline was mastered. The other, favoured more by the Classical School but evident in Gothic work after the 1850s, was eclecticism: to choose from different styles the best features and to combine them into a modern synthesis. And this eclecticism, of course, was the *raison d'être* behind the Queen Anne style of the 1870s and after.

Questions of style were central to Victorian architecture, even though it is clear that, after the 1870s, many critics and architects felt that Victorian architecture was a failure, that freedom from precedent—which was not frankly *gauche* or vulgar—had been insufficiently developed. But the buildings discussed in this book are taken at face value, on their own stylistic criteria; and not subjected to any *post-facto* moralism about what 19th-century architects should have done. One thing is certain: that 19th-century Gothic or Classical buildings need not worry us by seeming too literally archaeological, for they cannot but look Victorian. Victorian buildings, particularly in cities, are characterised by two possibly contradictory qualities. The first is the importance given to ornament, and particularly to legible symbolic and narrative sculpture. The second is that one of size, of overpowering scale, of the *sublime*, which seems to have been a response both to urbanisation and the massive works and power generated by industrialization. No Victorian, even the Gothic Revivalist, was unaware of the fact that he lived in the Age of Steam.

A Classical, or Georgian tradition in architecture survived in London well into Victoria's reign; the austerity of the Greek Revival was succeeded by the much richer "Greco-Roman" and by the panel-arched Italian Renais-

Richard Norman Shaw, New Zealand Chambers, Leadenhall Street, 1871–3. Demolished (National Monuments Record, Crown copyright)

sance style. While, however, distinguished designs were erected in the 1860s, a certain decline is evident from the high architectural standards of C. R. Cockerell or the young Barry. From the 1840s until the 1870s, the most interesting and remarkable talents associated themselves with the Gothic Revival, a style firmly entrenched in London from the Houses of Parliament rebuilding competition of 1836.

If any apology is needed for the large number of churches included in this guide, it is that religion and style were intimately connected in the middle of the 19th century. The early Victorian years were ones of religious revival and the 1840s to 70s saw the greatest period of church building in Britain since the Middle Ages, achieved entirely by finance independent of the state (unlike the results of the Church Building Acts of 1711 and 1819). In the 1870s, the peak years, eleven new churches were built on average in London every year. All denominations grew but, for architecture, the Tractarian Movement in the Church of England was most important.

The Oxford Movement, the attempt to revitalise the moribund Church of England by emphasising the Catholic aspect of it which had legitimately survived the Reformation, can be dated from 1833. It became (despite its founders) associated with the revival of Gothic architecture because of the Cambridge Camden Society (later the Ecclesiological Society), founded in 1839,

which wished to restore derelict or mutilated churches to their mediaeval glory and to build new churches on "correct" principles. These were chiefly derived from the writings of the Roman Catholic convert A. W. N. Pugin, who published *Contrasts* in 1836 and his *True Principles of Pointed or Christian Architecture* in 1841. The best period of Gothic must be chosen as a point of departure for future developments, and this was generally decided to be the Decorated of the late 13th century. Only Gothic was truly Christian architecture, and, absurd though that may be, it is significant that among Gothic Revival architects, Carpenter, Butterfield, Street, Brooks, Bodley, Pearson and Shaw were all convinced Tractarians. The attempt to bring religion into poor parts of London resulted in a number of Anglican churches with a Tractarian tradition being built which were conspicuous examples of that highly inventive and muscular Vigorous style of Gothic favoured by the *avant-garde* in the 1850s and 60s. Such buildings can now be seen as some of the principal artistic achievements of the Victorian age.

There was also the associated attempt to make Gothic a universal style, not just a style for churches. Despite the brave theories of Pugin, of Ruskin (whose writings were, directly and indirectly, responsible for some of the most strikingly original essays in the interpretation of Gothic) and of Scott, the attempt to use Gothic for hotels, government buildings and houses ultimately failed and Street's Law Courts were seen to mark the end of the secular Gothic Revival.

In the late 1860s arose a new eclecticism, the Queen Anne style, chiefly associated with domestic architecture. This was not, however, the creation of the remaining but disillusioned or wayward Gothics; the late 19th century saw a "renaissance of the Renaissance" as Goodhart-Rendell put it; "a Gothic game played with neo-classical counters".

The last decades of the 19th century saw this eclecticism turning into something more disciplined, as the English Renaissance was freed from the prejudice attached to it by Pugin and Ruskin; it was then seen as a *national* style eminently suitable, in particular, for public buildings. At the same time the Arts and Crafts movement, a valuable legatee of the Gothic Revival, turned more towards Georgian as the paradigm for domestic architecture.

What is true of the beginning and end of Victoria's reign is that a functional sense of style was paramount, that is, the idea that different styles were suitable for different building types. This was temporarily upset by the attempt by both Gothic Revivalists and some more eclectic architects to create a universal style for all buildings, but after the 1870s this orthodoxy broke down; it was again required that buildings should look like what they are.

Not all building types can be represented in this book and the impression may be given that the Gothic was used for *all* types of buildings and was to be seen as the dominant London style. In fact, despite the large number of significant Gothic Revival buildings, notably churches, the work of the Gothic men had less impact on the general look of London than that of the Classicists.

This is true of the main streets of the City and the West End, and particularly true of suburban development. Conspicuously, in the mid-Victorian growth of Kennington and Bayswater, the Georgian tradition of stuccoed terraces continued regardless of the Gothic Revival and only succumbed to the victory of redbrick and gables in the 1870s. The development of suburbs and the mid-Victorian stylistic modification of the standard terraced house to give it its characteristic segmental-headed, bay windowed form, typical of those streets determined by the local bye-laws, may be studied in many parts of London where the successive rings of growth may be identified. Large villas for the wealthier middle classes may still be found in a variety of types in such respectable areas as Hampstead and Belsize Park in the north, and Dulwich and Norwood in the south. However, with the exception of the consciously architect-designed Bedford Park, suburban houses are not examined in this guide.

Nor are the various forms of working-class housing discussed here, such as the Peabody tenements of the 1860s and 70s which still serve their purpose in many parts of London. Interesting as these may be for an historical perspective, such buildings did not rank high in the scale of "propriety" of Architecture as the Victorians understood it. But buildings by Henry Roberts, formerly architect of the Fishmongers' Hall who devoted his later career to philanthropic housing, should be mentioned, notably the dignified block of Model Houses for Families in Streatham Street, Bloomsbury, of 1850, and the Model Cottages erected in Hyde Park in 1851 (paid for by Prince Albert) and re-erected in Kennington Park.

The same is true of public houses, a type of building characteristically Victorian although usually in its present furnishings and arrangements a creation of the 1890s. For London pubs of the 19th century which were and still are legion, the reader must refer to Mark Girouard's *Victorian Pubs* (1975).

Victoria's long reign gives an apparent unity to a period conspicuous for its diversity and complexity. The adjective "Victorian" can no longer have any meaning applied as a generalization to both the 1840s and 90s, whether in respect of architecture, or politics, or intellectual life, and it is increasingly apparent that the 1870s were a great divide in the 19th century, in politics, in economic structure and, not least, in architecture. The other great divide, the 1830s, characterized by political unrest, religious revival, the Gothic Revival and the

Henry Roberts, Model Houses for Families, Streatham Street, Bloomsbury, 1850 (National Monuments Record, Crown copyright)

cataclysmic advent of the railways, nicely coincides with the beginning of Victoria's reign, but, although the century ended promptly in the political sphere, with the Boer War and the end of Victorian optimism and complacent insularity, 1901 is an unfortunate terminal date for architecture as there was no clear break then and the scene is confused.

In fact, with architecture there is a great unity in the period 1890–1914 and the 1880s seem a hiatus between the heady days of the Gothic Revival and the appearance of an Arts and Crafts architecture and the Wrenaissance. 1887, the year Victoria celebrated her Jubilee, is therefore taken as the terminal date of this guide: to have included the large amount of excellent London architecture of the 1890s would have unbalanced the attempt to give architectural coherence to the mid-Victorian period. The late 1880s is a satisfactory terminal date in other ways. A number of important mid-Victorian architects ceased to practice in that decade, owing to death or breakdown. Furthermore, the Metropolitan Board of Works was abolished in 1888, the year that the London County Council was created and gave London a unified authority for the first time. The same year saw the appearance of the buildings—by Brydon, Belcher and Shaw—which heralded the Classical Revival of the 1890s. London architecture after 1887 is surveyed in *London: 1900* (1978), edited by Gavin Stamp.

I
New Palace of Westminster
WESTMINSTER SW1

DESIGNED 1835-7
Charles Barry with A. W. N. Pugin
BUILT 1840-60

The New Palace of Westminster, to give the correct title of the Houses of Parliament, is not, strictly speaking, a Victorian building: indeed, its style of repetitive Perpendicular Gothic was regarded as old-fashioned by the middle of the century. Nevertheless, this monumental work—the first great Gothic Revival public building in the world and the largest and most complex structure yet raised—must be included as its slow continuing construction was the dominating fact in the early Victorian architectural scene. The designs, as executed, were not worked out until after Queen Victoria's accession and the building was not, in fact, finished until the 1870s, when its two creators were both dead and their children were squabbling about who *really* designed the Houses of Parliament.

The New Palace was of immense importance because of its influence: less because of its style than through its planning—of which no entrant in the future great competitions of the 19th century remained unaware. It was also of supreme importance owing to the tremendous impulse its construction gave to the building industry and to the trades connected with building—metalwork, woodwork, encaustic tile manufacture and architectural sculpture. This was because the Palace was not built in the thin, mechanical Gothic of the early 19th century but in a richly modelled, superbly detailed and convincing mediaeval manner, the result of the architect's colloboration with the brilliant and mad A. W. N. Pugin, who was the only man alive in the 1830s who could design such Gothic detail. The interiors of the Palace of Westminster are, in fact, the principal creations of that extraordinary designer and contain more of his designs for furniture, metalwork, decoration, floor tiles, etc than any of his churches and provide the only good example of his work to be seen in London. The execution of Pugin's sumptuous interiors gave employment to a whole range of craftsmen and firms, and from those newly acquired skills the next generation of Gothicists benefited. It may be

argued, however, that Pugin's obsession with detail could not have contributed to the artistic success of the building unless it had been disciplined by the practical, architectural genius of Sir Charles Barry (1795-1860), who had won the competition for the building in 1836 against ninety-six other entries.

Two years after the passing of the Great Reform Bill, the old, rambling Palace of Westminster caught fire, a conveniently symbolic conflagration which added to the mythological significance of the 19th-century idea of Progress. The buildings could have been patched up, but they had long been found inconvenient and the Reformed Parliament determined upon an impressive new building, such that London might vie with the great capitals of Europe. Parliamentary and professional objections to the establishment architect Sir Robert Smirke getting the plum job engendered the first great architectural competition in 19th-century Britain, the conditions for which, published in 1835, contained the significant stipulation that the style must be Gothic or Elizabethan.

This stipulation reflected the extent to which romantic, associational and national arguments had by now influenced the public's conception of architecture. Twenty years before no such stipulation would have been imposed and it would have been assumed that all design would be in the Classical taste; now the style must be "adapted to the Gothic origin and time-worn buttresses of our constitution". Pugin had yet to demonstrate that Gothic was the only style to be tolerated because it was both rational and Christian, but already it was widely regarded as being a national style and a symbolic expression of English institutions and liberties.

Indeed, all the competitors had to integrate into their designs one of the great mediaeval buildings of Europe: Westminster Hall, hallowed by great events in English history. Other ancient parts of the Palace survived the fire, including the structure of St Stephen's Chapel, a Perpendicular structure which had housed the Commons; this was swept away (the crypt was restored), "the destruction of this precious architectural relic is the single blot upon the fair shield of Sir Charles Barry", Gilbert Scott later wrote.

The clear logic of Barry's plan, arranged along several long axes, undoubtedly helped to secure him the commission, as probably did his skill in dealing with the immensely long river façade of the buildings. Instead of breaking it up into a number of picturesque units, Barry designed a long symmetrical façade, with repetitive detail derived from that on the adjacent Henry VII's Chapel, with twin towers at either end and a central range stressed by greater height. The result, especially after the modifications made to the design in *c.* 1841, which stressed the horizontals and raised the roof above the rich parapet, is immensely satisfactory in its position. Its

a *The New Palace of Westminster, early 20th-century photo-graph (National Monuments Record, Crown copyright)*

logic, repetitiveness and symmetry explain Pugin's famous comment, made when in a boat on the Thames, "All Grecian, Sir; Tudor details on a classic body".

However, Barry also appreciated that his building would almost always be viewed obliquely and he showed

b *Plan of the New Palace of Westminster; published in A. E. Richardson's* Monumental Classic Architecture, *1914*

himself to be a master of the picturesque by designing two towers, which were to become the great landmarks of London. The romantic skyline of the Palace was enhanced by other vertical features, principally the lantern and spire over the Central Hall, a feature required by the heating and ventilating expert, Dr Reid (who turned out to be as impractical as he was tiresome).

Barry's appointment having been confirmed, after inevitable controversy, the first work undertaken was the construction of the great River Embankment. The super-structure was commenced in 1840; the House of Lords

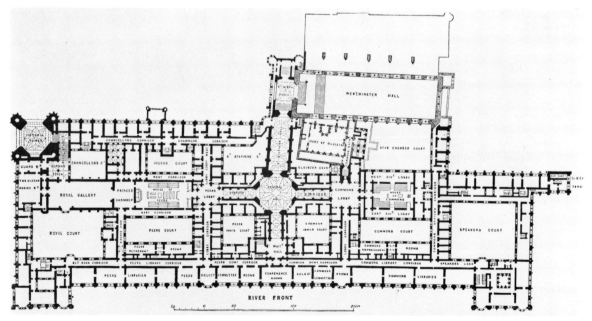

was ready for occupation in 1847, the Commons in 1850 (to secure better acoustics, its roof was then altered and lowered, to Barry's disgust, and re-opened in 1852); the Clock Tower, containing Big Ben was completed in 1858 and the Victoria Tower in 1860, the year of Barry's death. He had had to struggle for years against typical British parsimony and Parliamentary interference. That the building is as fine as it is is a tribute to Barry's diplomacy and toughness in executing his design; Pugin, as he himself knew, could never have coped with the job. However, he was vital in securing Barry's aim that the Palace should be a "sculptural memorial of our national history".

The two towers are both remarkable and decidedly 19th-century creations, owing little to precedent. The Clock Tower, with its overhanging clock faces and complex spire above, became one of the characteristic Victorian images, often repeated, and succeeded in becoming a national symbol; the prototype for this was possibly Pugin's tower design for Scarisbrick Hall. The Victoria Tower, a colossal structure, 336 feet in height, perhaps looks less tall than it is, as its architect was not aware of the subtle effect achieved by battering (slightly tilting back) the wall, which the mediaeval builder did. In some respects the Victoria Tower is a sort of proto-skyscraper, as it is divided internally by an iron skeleton of floors and columns. Also rather modern (in an art-historical sense), perhaps, are the elevations towards the Abbey, which, like Hardwick Hall, are "more glass than wall" with repeating bay windows.

Who designed the House of Parliament? When Pugin first executed details for Barry, in 1835–7, it was as a young Gothic draughtsman. He helped with the competition drawings (as he did with those by Gillespie Graham) and then assisted Barry in the drawings completed in 1837 used to secure estimates and measure quantities. The rough configuration of the interior, including the two debating chambers, was worked out at this time, Barry having re-worked most of Pugin's drawings. In 1844, harassed and criticised for delays in the building, Barry needed Pugin's help again.

By this time Pugin was famous, or notorious: the author of several important books and a conspicuously talented Gothic architect. In the end Pugin agreed to help Barry with drawings of Gothic details, and a successful collaboration ensued which continued until Pugin's untimely death in 1852. With frenetic industry, Pugin poured out sketches for all the details required for the elaborate interiors—designs for stained glass, hinges, tiles, tables, lights, even ink-stands and coal-buckets, of an imaginative and consistent mediaeval character of which Barry knew he was not capable, even if he had had the time to devote to them. Barry was, however, prepared to alter or modify Pugin's designs if he saw fit, possessing

that sense of scale and overall effect which was necessary; given the difficulties and differences between the two men, it was a singularly fortunate and fruitful collaboration.

Pugin's masterpiece is the House of Lords which survives in almost every detail. Its sumptuous furniture and decoration almost defy criticism. Pugin's other work in the Palace cannot be described here, nor can the other interiors. What does deserve mention are the murals, the result of a committee set up in 1841 to consider "the promotion of the fine arts of this Country in connection with the rebuilding of the Houses of Parliament". Because of the fresco technique used by, among others, William Dyce, the resulting patriotic historical murals were far from successful and not durable: the best are masterpieces, the two murals: the *Death of Nelson* and the *Meeting of Wellington and Blucher* painted by Daniel Maclise in the Royal Gallery. The work of mural painting extended, in the event, well into the 20th century.

After Barry's death, he was succeeded by his son E. M. Barry, who, before he was sacked in 1870 by A. S. Ayrton, the odious and parsimonious First Commissioner of Works, carried out several important works. These included the cloister and railings in New Palace Yard (1864–9), in a Gothic manner conspicuously different from that of Barry's father, and the decoration of the crypt of St Stephen's Chapel, and he began the decoration of the Central Hall. The erection of the railings signified the abandonment of Sir Charles Barry's plan of 1854 to enclose New Palace Yard with ranges of offices.

The external appearance of the Palace was completed by J. L. Pearson in 1884–8, who replaced Kent's and Soane's Law Courts on the west side of Westminster Hall (which had survived the fire). Pearson, with all the arrogance of Christian ecclesiology, ignored the "debased" Perpendicular of the surrounding buildings and designed a range of offices in a big-boned 13th-century manner. It was executed only after heated controversy fomented, in particular, by William Morris. Thanks, among others, to Ruskin, who described the Palace as "empty filigree", Barry's Perpendicular Gothic was utterly unfashionable by the time the building was finished.

James Fergusson called the Palace "perhaps the most successful attempt to apply Mediaeval Architecture to modern civic purposes which has yet been carried out". However, by the end of the century it was much preferred to the hard Middle Pointed buildings of the mid-Victorians: Ninian Comper praised Perpendicular as "the only style which is perfectly at home in our climate alike for buildings ecclesiastical and civil as witness the Houses of Parliament, alone amongst modern buildings".

In 1941 the House of Commons was gutted by an incendiary bomb. It was rebuilt in 1945–50 to the designs of Sir Giles Gilbert Scott (1880–1960), assisted

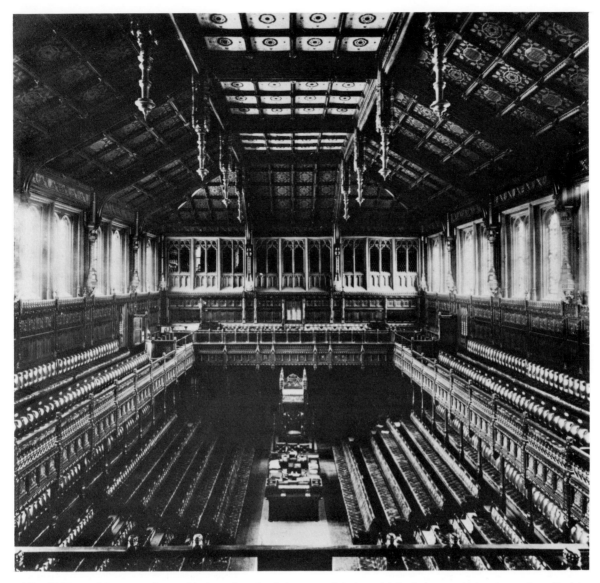

c *The old House of Commons, destroyed by incendiary bombs in 1941 (Department of the Environment)*

by his brother Adrian. The decision to rebuild the chamber on the lines of the old and in a traditional style was made by Parliament, conscious in a time of crisis of tradition and the effect upon parliamentary democracy of the size and shape of the destroyed chamber. Nevertheless, it has been criticised by, in particular, one famous historian, who considers that the British people deserved a new Chamber in a style "expressive of the present". Whether we would now be pleased with an austere International Style design, expressive of the age of Churchill and Attlee, is rather doubtful. Scott decided not to restore the work of Pugin and Barry, for which he may possibly be criticised, but to design in modern Gothic. Scott's Gothic is unfashionable, but it is neither derivative nor dull; it respects the character of the rest of the building while being a modern interpretation of the Gothic tradition. Scott designed in the spirit of Pugin: the ornament is varied and decorative and he tackled similar problems to Pugin's with equal inventiveness, designing such modern necessities as microphones and striplight "Neon-Gothic" fittings in the Gothic manner. As Scott's unstained oak matures, so the virtues of his Chamber become more evident. Within the walls of the Palace of Westminster almost the whole history of the Gothic Revival can be studied.

Map 2 E4

2
Reform Club
PALL MALL, SW1

DESIGNED 1839
Charles Barry
BUILT 1839–41

The Reform Club is the greatest—as architecture—of the clubs of Pall Mall; a great and sumptuous palace built for the luxurious enjoyment of liberal politicians. As the Club's historian, J. Mordaunt Crook, has written, "The Reform Club is in several ways unique: a private institution which has shaped the political history of this country, housed in a building of rare beauty and major architectural significance. The origins of modern party politics; the transition from Whiggery to Liberalism; the Renaissance revival in High Victorian architecture—all these are schemes embedded in the club's history".

The aristocratic and gaming clubs of the 18th century tended to be in the Piccadilly and St James's area. At the beginning of the 19th century, increasing demand from the affluent and influential middle class led to the establishment of new clubs and the new century saw a flowering of club life, with a variety of gentlemen's clubs becoming important both politically and socially. The Conservative Party Club was the Carlton; the Liberal Party had the Reform and, later in the century, the National Liberal Club (**83**).

In Pall Mall, first came the Athenaeum (Decimus Burton, 1827–30) at the corner of Waterloo Place. Next door soon rose the Travellers (1830–2), a stucco palazzo which first made Charles Barry's reputation. The adjoining site was taken by the Reform. It took its name from the Great Reform Bill of 1832, that reorganisation of the franchise which had been passed after a dangerous and tumultuous crisis. It gave representation to the new manufacturing towns of the Industrial Revolution and—symbolically, at any rate—gave power to the rising middle class. Radicals were not welcome in Brooks's, the Whig aristocratic club, so that Edward Ellice, MP and Whig party Whip at the time of the Reform Bill crisis, announced in 1836 "Well, gentlemen, we mean to start a club which will beat yours".

A competition was held for a grand new building in 1837. Barry, Blore, Cockerell and Sydney Smirke

entered; Barry won. His final designs were prepared in 1839 and the club was opened in 1841. Lord Macaulay wrote to Leigh Hunt that it was "a building worthy of Michaelangelo". Indeed, Barry created a Renaissance palace, developing the ideas he had first tried at the Travellers' next door; but the Reform was bigger and not of stucco, but stone. It was a very influential building and appealed to a public tired of the chilly austerity of the Greek Revival. Buildings like Smirke's British Museum might be imposing, but they were not comfortable or sympathetic. As Crook observes, "More than anyone it was Barry who replaced the Greek Revival of the Regency by High Victorian Italianate. Beginning as a Greek Revivalist, he quickly discovered the greater richness and flexibility of cinquecento Italy. The Travellers' Club began this architectural revolution, and the Reform Club completed it". What is strange is that, at the same time, Barry was hard at work on the Perpendicular Gothic style of the New Palace of Westminster. The French architect Hittorff (of the Gare du Nord) later said of Barry, with typical Gallic cultural arrogance, "it was only after he had built the Travellers' and Reform Clubs that we recognised in him a capacity truly unusual, joined to a quality rare among the English, I mean a predominant sentiment of 'Art'".

The inspiration for the exterior of the club is clear; "he thought of his old favourite, the Farnese Palace", wrote Barry's friend J. B. Wolfe. But the Reform is not a copy of the Roman original; it is of nine bays not thirteen, and the details are different. "Every design", according to Wolfe, "was conceived and indeed moulded into shape before he referred to a book or drawing—a mind like his was sure to be teeming with the stores of memory—the necessary pabulum of even the most creative genius. But he copied nothing . . .". The other conspicuously Italian feature is the great central court, a *cortile*, with an upper gallery and colonnade. At the Travellers' the courtyard was open, really just a light-well; at the Reform Barry had the sense to appreciate that the climate of London is very different from that of Rome. By covering the *cortile* with a vaulted skylight, the space is well used and becomes a saloon: one of the most splendid spaces in London. For this he "had visions of the Baptistry of St Peter's, and other gorgeous chapels at Rome and Florence. . . . He grieved at the necessity of employing imitations in paint or even scagliola—marbling, graining and all other 'impostures' disgusted him—nothing would content him but materials really precious, in fact, in his grandeur of ideas and his taste for splendour, he would not have disgraced the patronage of a Leo X or a Shah Jehan". Perhaps Barry had been seeing too much of Pugin, with his silly hatred of "shams"; Barry's "impostures" were necessary and the effect rich, convincing and excellent.

The upper floor is attained by a vaulted Grand Staircase

The Saloon of the Reform Club; steel engraving published in London Interiors, *c 1843*

opening off the saloon; the model for this was the Palazzo della Cancellaria, by Bramante. The dramatic effect of this was enhanced by mirrors, some only installed since the last war.

The other architecturally rich and satisfying rooms cannot be described here: they are all that a club's public rooms should be. Their original appearance, however, was a little different. The club was decorated to Barry's design in 1841, and the colours were much lighter and the upholstery red plush rather than leather. Further alterations were made in 1852–6 under Barry's direction, but the present appearance, with sombre, rich brown and gold dominant, was the result of a general refurbishment carried out by Barry's son, Edward Middleton, in 1878. The result is appropriate, comfortable, traditionally masculine and splendid.

To the club's credit most of this survives and nothing has been done to change it—no "good taste" redecorations such as have spoiled the Athenaeum. Mercifully, also, the Reform is still a club. Far too many of the Pall Mall club-houses have closed and been either demolished or let for other purposes.

Map 2 D3

3
Christ Church

CHRISTCHURCH ROAD, STREATHAM, SW2

1840–1
James William Wild

Christ Church, Streatham; etching by J. H. LeKeux

This church is a remarkable and successful curiosity, a curiosity in so far as it belongs to none of the mainstreams of development and style in the mid-19th century. It was disliked by the ecclesiologists, although admired by Ruskin. Nobody, indeed, has been quite sure in what style the building is designed: the *Ecclesiologist* (1843) called it "Romanesque of the South of Europe"; the *Art Journal* (1865), "Byzantine"; Bumpus (1907), "Italian Gothic"; Goodhart-Rendel (1953), "Eclectic Romanesque" and Pevsner, "rundbogenstil". Wild was evidently being eclectic, and successfully so, in a manner achieved by very few, that is, not an amalgam but a synthesis. Like Webb with No 1 Palace Green (**49**), he would have been pleased that critics were "unable to discover what actual style or period of architecture I have used".

But the design does have roots, not only in that Italian Romanesque, or early Christian, style fashionable in the 30s and 40s, but also in the German "round-arched style" characteristic of Munich, eg von Klenze's Ludwigskirche (1829–40) which had a painted polychromatic interior. Wild described his cornice as "Egyptian" and thought of the church as Byzantine, but the placing of the tower was as in an Italian Church. In 1840 he wrote that "it appears absolutely necessary that a church should have the appearance of solemnity and that the only means of attaining this attribute is by severe simplicity in design and by avoiding all appearance of having attempted more than could be accomplished" and, surprisingly, Ruskin praised the church in the *Stones of Venice* for the integrity of its brick style: "The church of Christchurch, Streatham, lately built, though spoiled by many grievous errors, (the ironwork in the campanile being the grossest), yet affords the inhabitants of the district a means of obtaining some idea of the variety of effects which were possible with no other material than brick".

The style and treatment of the brick are certainly original, and Bumpus was right to observe that it was "remarkable as being one of the earliest built in London to exhibit any intelligent departure from insular precedent". The tower is a bold composition of pilaster strips running the whole height which, with its batter, almost has a modern flavour of the 1920s. On the body of the church there are pilaster strips which become flush with the wall surface, and there is a curious and subtle ambiguity between the battered and vertical wall-planes. By giving his Romanesque arches a slight point, and with a pointed extrados of red brick, Wild gave the church a Moorish flavour as well as setting a fashion for a detail which appealed to certain architects in the 1850s.

The *Ecclesiologist*, of course, did not approve and asked "why were our own ecclesiastical styles deserted for forms which are at best imperfectly developed, and which are adapted only to the necessities of a burning climate?"

The interior is in a basilican, or early Christian, plan with an apse; each bay of the round-arched arcade being subdivided to carry a gallery. The stairs are iron, which would not have pleased the Gothic purists.

James William Wild (1814–92) was a pupil of Basevi and was recommended for the job by the Bishop of

Winchester for "his powers of design, originality and accuracy of estimate"—rare qualities, indeed. Exotic as Christ Church is, Wild did not go on his travels in Asia Minor and Egypt until 1842. He became an expert on Arabian art and was Curator of the Soane Museum from 1878 until his death. He designed an Anglican Church in Alexandria in Egypt and his St Martin's schools, Covent Garden (1849, destroyed) were an influential and pioneering example of the secular use of Gothic.

Wild supervised the architectural decoration at the Great Exhibition of 1851 and was very friendly with Owen Jones (1809–74) who decorated that structure, and also the interior of Christ Church. This, together with Arthur Henderson's scheme of 1924–33, has been largely obliterated except for the ceiling of the apse. Much of Lavers & Barraud's stained glass was destroyed in the Second World War; two windows by Walter Crane (1891) survive in the north aisle. The mosaic panels in the apse are Italian of *c.* 1900.

Map 1 E5

4
Royal Exchange
CITY, EC3

1841–4
William Tite

The old Exchange burned down in 1838 and the City authorities planned to remove some adjoining properties so that a new Royal Exchange could dominate the open space between Soane's Bank of England and Dance senior's Mansion House. The competition for this new building was one of the most disgracefully managed of all 19th-century competitions—which is saying a great deal—and the most unsatisfactory as it deprived London of the possibility of having a monumental building by the most distinguished, scholarly and imaginative of all early 19th-century Classicists, C. R. Cockerell. This is especially unfortunate now that all Cockerell's London commercial buildings have been lost, the last, the Sun Assurance Office (97) behind the Bank of England, being destroyed, quite inexcusably, as recently as 1971.

Cockerell detested competitions, but in that one of 1839 (assessed by Smirke, Barry and Hardwick), he in fact designed the entry submitted by H. B. Richardson. This did not come in the first five owing to absurd disputes over the estimated cost. By 1840 it was decided that only Cockerell's, Donaldson's and Mocatta's designs were within the estimates. A second competition was held in which Cockerell's only competitor was William Tite, as the other parties had withdrawn, considering that the arrangement was unfair to Cockerell. Tite was involved as he had been asked by Cockerell to give a second opinion on the cost of his design; he was also a friend of the chairman of the committee of the Graham Trustees, who were responsible for the rebuilding. Cockerell prepared a huge model of his design; Tite persuaded the committee that it would be unfair for them to see it as he had not made one. In the final round the odious and well-connected Tite secured the commission.

Cockerell's design was widely regarded as a magnificent thing. It was a development of his preoccupation with the triumphal arch theme, but expanded to six bays rather than four. He saw it as appropriate to the site in view of the surrounding distinguished church buildings and so as to complete the "Forum Londinium". As David

a *C. R. Cockerell's unexecuted design for the Royal Exchange (Royal Institute of British Architects, London)*

Watkin has written, Cockerell's design was "one of the great triumphs of his career and hence of the whole of nineteenth-century architecture . . . he was not content to clap a conventional portico on the Exchange behind but was concerned with integrating structure, function and adornment into one triumphal whole".

Tite's deep portico is indeed conventional and clapped on to the building behind, but it is at least a grand

b *The Royal Exchange as built; early 20th-century photograph published in A. E. Richardson's* Monumental Classic Architecture, *1914*

composition which makes the space in front seem like a Forum, an effect which benefited from the creation of Queen Victoria Street in 1867–71. The portico, with its noble Corinthian columns, fine Roman lettering and sculpture in the pediment by Westmacott junior, is modelled on that of the Pantheon in Rome. Tite's side elevations are much less satisfactory and are stiff and undistinguished essays in the Renaissance tradition. The excellent arched chimneys Tite employed were a favourite motif of Cockerell's, who, of course, took them from Vanbrugh. A fine feature is the Baroque spire at the east end of the building, a design reminiscent in character of a City church and of the tower Cockerell planned on his building.

The interior of the now largely useless Exchange is an arcaded courtyard with offices above which, until 1880, was open to the sky. Behind the richly modelled arches are a series of large historical paintings on the outer walls, the early 20th-century ones, eg that by Brangwyn, being rather better than the Victorian efforts.

Sir William Tite (1798–1873) introduced himself wherever possible; the son of a City merchant he was twice PRIBA and from 1855 sat as MP for Bath (in which capacity he waged war on Scott's Gothic design for the Government Offices). Not all his work was Classical; he designed a rather repulsive church at Gerrard's Cross in a polychromatic brick Italian Byzantine style. He is reported to have said to the Prince of Wales, "I inherited a fortune, I married a fortune, and I have made a fortune", to which the Prince made the obvious reply "Lucky man".

Map 2 G2

5
St Giles

CAMBERWELL CHURCH STREET, SE5

FIRST DESIGN 1841
FINAL DESIGN 1842
George Gilbert Scott & William Bonython
Moffatt
BUILT 1842–4

🙕 🙔

This was the building which first established the young and ambitious George Gilbert Scott (1811–78) as a serious and correct Gothic Revival architect.

The ramshackle mediaeval church of Camberwell was completely destroyed by fire in 1841. A competition was held for a new building assessed by Edward Blore, the antiquary and Surveyor to Westminster Abbey. The winning design was by Scott and Moffatt but this, with its ambitious groining in terra cotta, was thought to be too expensive by the parish and a less expensive design was built in 1842–4.

Scott later recalled that "the pains which I took over this church were only equalled by the terror with which I attended the meetings of the committee . . . the then incumbent was the Rev J. G. Storie, a remarkable person. He was a man of remarkable talent, and personal and moral prowess, the most masterly hand at coping with a turbulent parish vestry I ever saw. His only great fault was that he was a clergyman, instead of, as nature intended, a soldier or a barrister . . .".

Scott further noted, with characteristic and unashamed self-confidence, that "he [Storie] was determined to have a good church, and so far as his day permitted, he got it", and he described St Giles as "the best church by far which had then been erected", which was doubtless true as, with its correct late 13th-century style, cruciform plan, tower and spire and a decently big chancel of three bays, it was one of very few churches designed by architects other than Pugin which satisfied the archaeological and liturgical criteria of the Cambridge Camden Society. Indeed, the *Ecclesiologist* called it "one of the finest ecclesiastical structures of modern days", and it is certainly an improvement upon the earlier mediocre churches of Scott and Moffatt, such as Christ Church, Turnham Green, W4 (1841–3) and St Mary, Hanwell, W7 (1841). The improvement resulted from Scott's becoming aware of the *avant-garde* tendencies in the Gothic Revival and he later wrote, in

tones which suggest the great moral fervour of the High Gothic Revival, that "this awakening arose, I think, from two causes operating almost simultaneously: my first acquaintance with the Cambridge Camden Society, and my reading Pugin's articles in the *Dublin Review* . . . Pugin's articles excited me almost to fury, and I suddenly found myself like a person awakened from a big feverish dream, which had rendered him unconscious of what was going on about him".

St Giles was actually improved in the course of construction: "my conversion to the exclusive use of real material came to its climax during the progress of this

St Giles, Camberwell; original engraving of interior showing galleries, since removed

work, and much which was at first shown as of plaster was afterwards converted into stone". The structure is of Smeaton and Caen stone. Nevertheless, there are elements about the church which are rather pre-ecclesiological. Not only did St Giles have the picturesque or rather useless transepts (for a small parish church) but it sported that most objectionable feature of Georgian times: galleries, since removed. The furnishings were a little mean; the seats were made with Pratt's patent carving machine.

The stained glass is of some interest. There is glass by Lavers and Barraud and also by Ward and Nixon, but the east window glass was designed by John Ruskin and Edmund Oldfield, both members of the building committee, after a design by Ward and Nixon had been rejected. Ruskin, who lived nearby, was then (1844) in France studying the 13th-century glass at Chartres and he wrote to Oldfield making suggestions about the east window. The glass was made by Ward and Nixon and put in at intervals, giving a variation of tone in the same colours. Canon Clarke observes of this window that "it is really good, and makes the two windows by Comper look amateurish in comparison." The interior of the church was whitened by Comper after the Second World War. He also coloured the reredos.

St Giles, Camberwell was one of the last jobs Scott undertook with William Bonython Moffatt (1812–87), with whom he had originally entered into partnership in 1834 to compete for building the new Union workhouses. It is often assumed that Scott (or, rather, Mrs Scott) cynically abandoned his partner once he was set on a firm career as a Gothicist (in 1844 Scott won the competition for the St Nikolaikirche in Hamburg), but in fact Moffatt was a difficult and arrogant man: "he was also extravagant", Scott later noted in his (unpublished) "Recollections", "keeping four horses, and one thing with another all our practice lead rather to debt than to laying by money. Besides this, the great Railway speculation mania was just then coming on and Moffatt was severely bitten, so much so as to be absolutely wild" and he was severely stung in the crash of 1846. In 1860 Moffatt was arrested for debt (he had been involved in speculative housing in Norwood), and Scott helped him over legal fees and with further donations later. Scott designed St Matthew, Great Peter Street, SW1, in 1845 still in partnership with Moffatt; but the church was not built until 1849–50 and, sadly, was gutted by an arsonist in 1977.

Map 1 F4

6
Lincoln's Inn Hall and Library
LINCOLN'S INN, WC2

1843–5
Philip and Philip Charles Hardwick

1871–3
George Gilbert Scott

The new 19th-century buildings at Lincoln's Inn are in the brick Tudor style which was particularly favoured for collegiate work. Examples may be found at Oxford and Cambridge, usually designed by architects who were not of the ecclesiological Gothic persuasion, for Tudor, although appropriate, was considered by many as the most debased period of mediaeval art. At Lincoln's Inn, architects known for their Classical work were employed.

The Inns of Court, like schools and colleges, were expanding in the 19th century, and in 1840 Philip Hardwick (1792–1870) was asked to design temporary courts, to extend the Stone Buildings and to design a new hall and library. The Stone Buildings, of 1774–80, were completed, in the style of Sir Robert Taylor, at the south end of the west range in 1843–5.

The new Hall and Library were planned on a large scale on a new site by Lincoln's Inn Fields. Both Hall and Library are on first floor level, above service accommodation. The Hall, running north–south along the east side of the Fields and the west side of the Inn, has its "principal entrance . . . on one side, following the example of nearly all the Ancient Halls in this country" and this is approached up an impressive external staircase. The style of the Hall, Tudor, in diapered red brick with stone dressings, is taken from the old Gatehouse by Chancery Lane and is the "Collegiate style of Architecture . . . of the period towards the end of the sixteenth century before the admixture of Italian architecture". The side walls are buttressed; there is a large window at the south end between the twin tower, and at the north end bay windows. The skyline is particularly fanciful, with rubbed brick chimneys, a lantern and an elaborate pinnacle on the gable. The interior has a hammerbeam roof and a screen at the south end. On the north wall, behind the high table, is a large fresco, *The Lawgivers* by George Frederick Watts (1859).

a *Hardwick's original perspective drawing of the Hall and Library at Lincoln's Inn, 1842 (Royal Institute of British Architects, London)*

b *Lincoln's Inn Hall and Library in 1956 (National Monuments Record, Crown copyright)*

The lower Library is connected with the north end of the Hall, but runs east–west. It is in the same style. Throughout there is great attention to detail and a conspicuous *panache* in handling the detail motifs of mediaeval architecture in a romantic and picturesque manner. "P.H." and the date are worked into the pattern of black brick diapers in the brickwork.

Philip Hardwick was known for his excellent Classical work: Goldsmiths' Hall in the City (1829), the City

Club, Old Broad Street, EC2 (1832) and the wickedly destroyed great Propylaeum at Euston Station (Euston Arch 1838, **96**).

At Lincoln's Inn he was taken ill soon after the work began and the buildings were completed by his son, Philip Charles Hardwick (1820–90): "the crowning features and all the fittings were carried out from his designs". Much of the detail may also be due to J. L. Pearson, who was employed to do the working drawings in 1842 and was briefly in control in 1843 when both Hardwicks were ill. Pearson later recalled that "Mr Hardwick placed the whole thing unreservedly in my hands, and afterwards never interfered with my work . . . I superintended almost daily the building until it was all covered in".

P. C. Hardwick went on to do other works in Tudor and Gothic styles, such as Madresfield Court, Glos, and the new Charterhouse School, Godalming, Surrey. Perhaps he was happier with Classical work: he designed the Great Western Hotel at Paddington (**15**) and, with his father, one of the most magnificent of grand Victorian rooms, the now destroyed Great Hall at Euston. At Lincoln's Inn, P. C. Hardwick designed the new Gateway to Lincoln's Inn Fields, south of the Hall, and the Stewards' block, to the north-west.

By the 1870s the Library was found to be too small. A plan to lengthen it three bays to the east was instigated by E. B. Denison (later Sir Edward Beckett, author of the anti-architect *Book of Building*; later still, the execrable Lord Grimthorpe, the destroyer of St Alban's Abbey), who had been called to the Bar at Lincoln's Inn in 1841. Denison called in Gilbert Scott, with whom he had worked at Doncaster and Scott extended the building in the Hardwicks' style. Much work to the interior was done by Scott. Scott also designed a separate range of buildings in a rather more pedantic version of Tudor to the north of the Chapel. Doubtless Denison (the designer of the bell Big Ben) interfered as much as possible with Scott's work, as he always thought he knew much more about architecture than any architect. In 1881–4, the 17th-century Chapel was extended by Beckett. Scott had prepared a design, but Beckett had associated with him another architect, Samuel Salter, and Salter rebuilt Wyatt's ceiling. Beckett hated antiquarian prejudice in favour of old buildings. In 1890 he wanted to have down the Chancery Lane Gateway and its adjoining chambers. This vision was realised seventy years later when these ancient structures were completely rebuilt.

Map 2 F2

7
Bridgewater House
CLEVELAND ROW, SW1

DESIGNED 1845
Charles Barry
BUILT 1847–54

Bridgewater House—rebuilt by Lord Francis Egerton, 1st Earl of Ellesmere, the brother of the Duke of Sutherland—was one of the last aristocratic houses (as opposed to *nouveau riche* palaces) to be built in the West End, and one of the very few to survive today.

It is built to the north of Stafford House, now Lancaster House, which was begun in 1825 by Benjamin Dean Wyatt (and has a staircase of 1838 by Barry), which had been leased by the future Duke of Sutherland in 1827. In 1840 Barry had proposed balancing Stafford House with another palace on the north of a widened Cleveland Row, continuing the line of Pall Mall to Green Park where the vista would be terminated by Marble Arch, re-erected with flanking colonnades. Barry was at this time working on the completion of Nash's work in Trafalgar Square; he continued Pall Mall East in front of the National Gallery on an embanked terrace and laid out the fountains and double staircase.

By 1845, when new designs for Bridgewater House were prepared, Sir Charles Barry had moved from his early Greek Revival phase to a suave and influential exploitation of the Italian Renaissance style in palazzi like the Travellers' and Reform Clubs. Bridgewater House heralds a later phase of his Classical work, which his son described as exhibiting "greater freedom of treatment and a desire for greater richness of effect", but others have seen it as exemplified by increasing coarseness and eclectic vulgarity typical of such mid-Victorian Classicism. Barry himself called his style "Anglo-Italian" and said of the design, "this will I think be a very grand mansion, but one that will excite much animadversion on account of its style as being far from a pure one". Nevertheless, Bridgewater House is nobly scaled and has a classical discipline which makes it greatly superior to much mid-Victorian Classical work.

The Cleveland Row façade has the nine bays and the palazzo character of the Reform Club, but the ground floor is rusticated and has a projecting rusticated porch.

South elevation of Bridgewater House, c1845 (Royal Institute of British Architects, London)

Under the heavy cornice, the square windows are separated by raised panels, but rather surprisingly, Barry did not go further and put ornament in these. The skyline is enlivened by balustrade (none at the Reform), urns and rather coarse chimneys, the ones at the corners continuing the line of the quoins of vermiculated rustication. On the Green Park façade, the end bays, with Venetian windows, are emphasised by being framed in pilaster strips of rustication.

Barry was assisted in making the designs by his son Charles and pupil Somers Clarke. Building began in 1847 and the carcase was complete by 1849. The picture gallery was open in time for the Great Exhibition but the house was not ready for occupation until 1854.

The glory of the interior was almost an afterthought and not designed until 1849: a top-lit central hall, as at the Reform Club. This rises through two storeys and is surmounted by a superb ceiling of bevelled glass panels in which sculpture, ornament and function are completely integrated. The nymphs and cherubs were carved by John Thomas and Richard Westmacott, junior.

The hall is surrounded on two floors by a corridor which sports elaborately decorated saucer domes. In 1857 the 2nd Lord Ellesmere employed the German artist of Göttzenberger, a pupil of Cornelius, to paint a series of murals depicting the Muses and Virtues on the walls of the hall. These were said to be somewhat lascivious and not at all approved of by Barry. They are now covered with cleverly marbled boards.

The once-splendid picture gallery—designed for the Orléans collection acquired by the last Duke of Bridgwater from the Palais Royal after the French Revolution—was gutted in the last war. The rest of the house was restored in 1948–9 by Robert Atkinson and Partners.

Barry made extensive alterations and additions at Cliveden, Bucks, for the Duke of Sutherland very much in the same style, shortly after Bridgewater House was completed.

Map 2 D3

8
St Andrew
OLD CHURCH LANE, KINGSBURY, NW9

1845–7
Samuel Daukes

St Andrew as it was when it stood in Wells Street, Marylebone; an illustration published in the Builder, *1847*

The inclusion of this building might at first seem perverse, as Kingsbury, Middlesex, consisted of little more than fields for the whole of Victoria's reign, and now it is quintessential inter-war semi-detached land. But St Andrew is remarkable, both in itself and also because it must be the first example of a Victorian building *taken down and re-erected*. This was because of its fame as a High Anglican church in the 19th century.

St Andrew began life as St Andrew, Wells Street, in Marylebone, just around the corner from where All Saints, Margaret Street, would rise. Its architect was Samuel Daukes, or Dawkes (1811–80), whose Gothic work is seldom very sympathetic; he also designed the now ruined Witley Court. Daukes, being a little old fashioned, used a style which offended against the orthodoxy of the Cambridge Camden Society. The *Ecclesiologist* commented in 1847 that "we must protest vehemently against the style, which is Third-Pointed [ie Perpendicular]. We can hardly say how sorry we are at its adoption in a structure which aims so much after correctness. It is, however, good of its sort, and the architect deserves great credit for the bold and honest manner in which he has dealt with his most unmanageable site . . .".

The church began to become really interesting during the incumbency of the Rev Benjamin Webb from 1862 until his death in 1885. During these years the church became a model of High Anglican worship—but never as "high" or extreme as All Saints around the corner. As Webb was the co-founder of the Cambridge Camden Society and editor of the *Ecclesiologist*, it was to be expected that he would bring in the very best designers to enrich the interior.

G. E. Street designed the reredos, which was carved by Redfern between 1865 and 72: "We feel sure that if the Reredos of St. Andrew's were in any foreign church, it would be marked by Baedeker with a star, and everyone would go to look at it, even though the church were darker than St. Andrew's, and the street dirtier than Wells Street" (1897). Street also designed the wrought-

iron chancel screen (1865) and the marble font (1878). The font cover was by J. L. Pearson (1887) who also designed the sedilia and canopied arch in the sanctuary (1888).

William Burges designed the litany desk (1867) and the monument to the second incumbent, James Murray, which is a recessed tomb, carved by Nicholl, and exhibited at the 1862 International Exhibition. The Sacristy was decorated by G. F. Bodley in 1881. The lectern—in place in 1847—was by Butterfield. Much of the stained glass was by Clayton and Bell, but the great east window, *c.* 1851, was designed by Pugin and executed by Hardman. The wooden galleries were embellished after 1872 with paintings by Clayton and Bell, that is, with saints designed by Alfred Bell. In short, St Andrew was a treasure house of the best mid-Victorian ecclesiastical design and would today be much more celebrated if still standing on its central London site.

In 1932 the church was demolished but, as specified in an Order in Council of 16 August, 1932, every stone was numbered. St Andrew had become redundant owing to the depopulation of the neighbourhood but, because it had been a fashionable and much-loved church, there was sufficient influential and sentimental concern about its fate to produce the enlightened decision to rebuild it out in a new suburb. The Archdeacon of Hampstead wrote that "I am very anxious that those who feel most keenly the loss of this Church, should be comforted by the worthiness of its successor".

In these years, some Wren churches—victims of the Bishop of London's plan for the City—were rebuilt in new suburbs, but none so faithfully as Daukes's church. A site was chosen next to Kingsbury old church, a tiny ancient building now much too small. St Andrew was carefully reconstructed in 1933–4 under the direction of the architect W. A. Forsyth. It was re-consecrated by a former Bishop of London, who said that it had "dropped from heaven" into Kingsbury.

In the rebuilding changes were inevitably made; the plan was made regular and new windows put in the walls—originally the church had been fitted into an awkward confined urban site. Some wall decorations were lost, but almost everything which could be salvaged, including monuments, paintings, and stained glass (some of which was later lost in the war), was carefully re-used, even Bodley's decorations in a much enlarged sacristy and vestry. The result is remarkably faithful to the character of the old St Andrew, the product of a period which, in 1933, was far from fashionable. Anglo-Catholic piety was more conservative than ever architects or historians would have been at the time. St Andrew, with its ragstone exterior and country-looking tower and spire, seems much more at home in the suburbs than ever it can have in central London: Butterfield, unlike Daukes, knew how to build in a truly *urban* manner.

Map 1 B 1

9
St Barnabas
PIMLICO ROAD, SW 1

1847–50
Thomas Cundy II

This church is, perhaps, the most interesting of several "correct", "ecclesiological" churches of the 1840s, built of ragstone (other conspicuous examples are St Stephen, Rochester Row, SW 1 by Benjamin Ferrey, 1847–50, and the church of St Thomas of Canterbury, Rylston Road, SW 6, 1847–9 by Pugin). St Barnabas differs, however, by being in the Early English lancet style (Early Pointed) rather than the much approved Decorated (Middle Pointed).

St Barnabas, Pimlico was founded by the Rev W. J. E. Bennett as a mission church in the poor part of his parish of St Paul, Wilton Place, Knightsbridge, SW 1. The architect was Thomas Cundy II (1790–1867), Surveyor to the Grosvenor Estates. It is said that Cundy was influenced by William Butterfield in the preparation of the design; certainly it is a much more competent essay in Gothic than his earlier St Paul (1840–3) which has a wide galleried nave—everything the ecclesiologists hated (since improved by a chancel and screen by Bodley, 1891). The connection between Cundy and Butterfield may well have been the latter's friend and sometime partner, the Goth Henry Woodyer (1816–96) who was possibly associated with Cundy.

St Barnabas is a complete religious collegiate establishment. South of the church, with its tall north-west stone tower and spire, is a long clergy house, and to the north, running along the Pimlico Road, is a school. All, like the church, are carved out in gloomy ragstone.

Bumpus observed that "these buildings cannot be considered worthy of the church to which they are attached, and with which they attempt uniformity by identity of form rather than by plasticity of spirit— by a repetition of Lancet windows rather than by success in grasping that intermediate character between ecclesiastical and domestic architecture, which all such buildings should possess".

The foundation stone was laid by Dr Pusey in 1847 and the church was consecrated by Bishop Blomfield in 1850. Soon afterwards Blomfield had occasion to complain

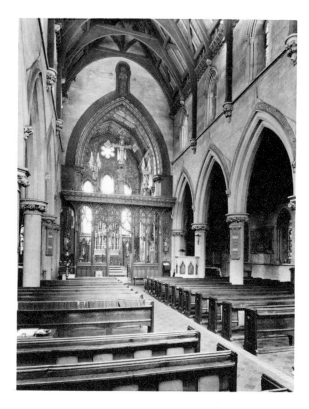

a *St Barnabas, Pimlico; interior looking east in 1979*
(*Architectural Press*)

b *Detail of the south wall of the chancel of St Barnabas in 1967*
(*National Monuments Record, Crown copyright*)

about the "historic" ceremonial: as may be assumed from the connection with Dr Pusey, St Barnabas was intended for Tractarian services and from the beginning there was a double daily choral service. The clerical composer and organist, Sir Frederick Gore Ouseley, who was on the staff, gave the organ and established a choir school in the collegiate buildings. All this was asking for trouble in the year when Lord John Russell, the Whig Prime Minister, promoted the Ecclesiastical Titles Bill to counter the re-establishment of a Roman Catholic hierarchy in Britain and "No-Popery" riots were fomented against "Papal Aggression". In 1850 and 51 disgraceful scenes were organised in St Barnabas which eventually resulted in the resignation of Bennett. The offending ceremonial included merely such practices as lighting candles on the altar, changing altar frontals in accordance with the seasons, etc, which were commonplace by the end of the century; at this stage, such ritualistic innovations as incense and Eucharistic vestments were unthinkable. Such was the struggle the determined clergy of the Oxford Movement had to make to revive the liturgical dignity of the Church of England in the face of violence and the riots at St Barnabas were a prelude to the troubles at St Alban, Holborn and St George-in-the-East.

Originally, in 1850, St Barnabas was "the most complete and sumptuous church dedicated since the revival", quoting the *Ecclesiologist*, that is, there was a separate raised chancel, a wooden chancel screen with a cross, stalls, metal gates and painted decoration and Latin texts, stained glass by Wailes. In the course of the 19th century, the Anglo-Catholic tradition maintained at St Barnabas demanded richer fittings. There were more stencilled decorations by C. E. Kempe, W. Tower and Comper, a crypt chapel by Bodley and a sacrament house by J. N. Comper, a reredos and an organ by Bodley (1893), a Lady Chapel off the south aisle by Comper "and furnished in what that gentleman considers the true English mediaeval style" (Bumpus, ie English Perpendicular), a baptistery by Frederick Hunt (1902), a new screen by Bodley (1906) and a new east window glass by Comper, replacing that by Wailes (1953).

The church was very smart at the turn of the century. Comper was married here in 1890 and Aubrey Beardsley attended its services—until he Poped.

Map 2 C5

10
St Mary Magdalene
MUNSTER SQUARE, NW1

1849–52, 1883–4
Richard Cromwell Carpenter

The first stone of this church was laid in 1849, the year All Saints, Margaret Street (11), was begun, and with which building it should be compared. Both churches were designed as models for Tractarian Anglican worship in towns, and the architects of both were the most favoured protegés of the Cambridge Camden Society. But whereas Butterfield, at All Saints, threw off the restraints of archaeology, Carpenter remained loyal to English precedents.

St Mary Magdalene was founded by the Rev Edward Stuart, a rich curate of the nearby Christ Church, Albany Street (a building of 1837 in the Commissioners' church tradition by Pennethorne—its utter dissimilarity emphasises the profound change effected in church architecture in the 1840s by the ecclesiologists). St Mary was built in a corner of what was then called York Square, an area which had rather come down in the world owing to the proximity of the Cumberland Barracks and its associated brothels. It was Stuart's resolve to build a church "as nearly perfection as the handicraft of man, the skill of architects, and the experience of ecclesiastical art could make it".

The exterior is not prepossessing. It has never received the planned tower and spire on the south side, and the Kentish ragstone—so favoured by the early ecclesiologists and by the Broad Church throughout the mid-century—becomes wretched in the London atmosphere. Street, in an essay of 1851, "On the Proper Characteristics of a Town Church", recommended brick, of which material All Saints is, of course, built.

It is the interior which tells: tall, spacious and elegant. As Francis Bumpus observed (1907), it is "thoroughly imbued with a devotional spirit; while the faint odour of incense, which always seems to pervade the interior, informs the visitor of the type of worship customary there". Carpenter designed a "hall church", that is, with nave and aisles of almost equal height, and no clerestory. The chancel, nave and south aisle were completed in 1852, the north aisle not until 1883–4 but to Carpenter's

designs. The *Ecclesiologist* described it, in 1852, as "the most artistically correct new church yet consecrated in London". Carpenter used the style which the Camden Society, Pugin and Ruskin all thought of the best period of mediaeval art, ie Decorated Gothic, (Middle-Pointed) when the Geometrical style of tracery was just turning into Flowing. With its piers of four clustered shafts, graceful arches, fine window tracery and white plastered walls, the building is very English in style; with its generous sanctuary it was ideally suited for the more elaborate form of Anglican worship favoured by the Tractarian.

Richard Cromwell Carpenter (1812–55) died young, and survived his contemporary, Pugin (whom he knew) by just three years. Like Pugin, he was an early and

Carpenter's original design for St Mary Magdalene, Munster Square, showing the unexecuted tower and spire; lithograph published in the Ecclesiologist, *1850*

scholarly enthusiast for mediaeval architecture and much favoured by the Cambridge Camden Society. He designed St Paul, Brighton (1846–8, completed by his son, R. H. Carpenter) and the splendid chapel at Lancing College, Sussex (begun 1854). He also designed Lonsdale Square, Islington, N1 (1842–5).

Carpenter died just at the moment when the enthusiasm for foreign Gothic, polychromy, and more "vigorous" styles was supplanting English mediaeval ideals, but, after about 1870, architects tended to return to English ideals, and a church like G. F. Bodley's Holy Trinity, Prince Consort Road, Kensington, SW7, built over half a century after St Mary Magdalene, is extraordinarily similar to it in its tall, spacious character and its plan, if a little later in style. Norman Shaw, who worshipped at Munster Square for forty-two years, much admired it and described it, in 1902, as "the *beau idéal* of a town church. In general aspect it is very restful, and is entirely free of all affectation in design".

The stained glass in the east window, since destroyed, was designed by Pugin and executed by Hardman; other surviving glass is by Clayton and Bell, and Heaton, Butler and Bayne. Unfortunately, the church has never received the wood screen which was intended, but later architects have respected the character of the building. As Canon Clarke observed, "there are no baroque altars of the naughty twenties". The rood beam (1903) and parclose (side) screens (1906) were designed by J. T. Micklethwaite; the reredos by Sir Charles Nicholson (1933); and the paintings in the sanctuary were begun in 1867 by Bell and Almond.

Map 2 D1

I I
All Saints
MARGARET STREET, W1

1849–59
William Butterfield

All Saints fulfils a very precise dream. It was designed as a model church for the Cambridge Camden Society to provide, in a perfectly ordered architectural setting, for all the needs of ritualistic worship. The Society chose a young architect to realise these needs, William Butterfield, then just over thirty. Alexander Beresford-Hope and Sir Stephen Glynne of the Ecclesiological Society supervised the project. It was A. J. Beresford-Hope who was the key figure; he was both a major benefactor of the new church and a highly knowledgeable student of church architecture.

At a time when new churches were being built of crudely laid Kentish rag stone it is hard to imagine the originality of Butterfield's conception as it must have appeared to people in 1849. A redbrick church of great height on a difficult site, and one full of rich and rare ornament, must have seemed quite astonishing. Today it remains a building of extraordinary impact.

Butterfield was certain of his mission "to give dignity to brick" and his architectural convictions gave the church a powerful visual vocabulary for the delivery of its Divine message. Significantly it was Dr Pusey who laid and blessed the foundation stone on All Saints' Day in 1850. As a founder of the Oxford Movement he saw new churches as important bulwarks of the faith against the rising tide of secularism—to be built and seen in areas where the working classes remained untouched by religion. All Saints now stands, in Sir John Betjeman's words, as "a Tractarian oasis among furriers", but when it was built Margaret Street was described as an area of, "dirty shops and dingy private dwellings . . . where children never washed". Butterfield was just the right architect to build for this missionary spirit; he believed in objective architecture, in buildings that were not sermons but expositions of the creed. The pioneers of the Oxford Movement hoped to recapture some of the spontaneity of early Franciscan Christianity, and the new All Saints must have seemed like a triumphant shout of riotous praise.

a *All Saints, Margaret Street; view from the east in 1943 (National Monuments Record, Crown copyright)*

From the tall tower with its lead and slate spire to the masterly arrangement on an awkward site of church, clergy house and choir school, it is clear that the effect of this building is achieved by massing and scale. The consistency of the decoration and the sheer vigour of the constructional polychromy are the outward signs of the birth of High Victorian Gothic architecture. As the walls of All Saints were rising, Ruskin's *Stones of Venice* appeared (the first volume in 1851, the other two in 1853) and Butterfield's work was inevitably seen in the light of an incipient Italian Gothic revival. But it is important to remember, as one is drawn through the tight courtyard between the dramatic walls of red and black bricks into the darkly sumptuous interior, that this church is a very original work of genius. Butterfield probably never built another building that has quite the emotional intensity of All Saints; his chapel at Keble is a much calmer, more certain Te Deum. For thirty years Butterfield kept the portfolio of working drawings for All Saints behind his chair in his study, always influencing his work as though he knew that it was his masterpiece.

The influences are easy to see. The great spire is based upon St Mary's Church at Lübeck, the high exterior of the choir is drawn from Freiburg im Breisgau and the vaulted interior of the chancel is influenced by the upper church of St Francesco at Assisi (which Butterfield much admired). The essential structure is English Middle Pointed, while the internal structural decoration owes much to Ruskin's writings about the aesthetic possibilities of different materials, that, "beauty and effect of colour shall arise from construction and not from super addition".

The original Tractarian plan ensured that the altar, raised high, was visible from all parts of the church and that the chancel should be the richest part of the church. This is indeed the case. The east wall with its dramatic reredos—tiers of blue and red figures under gilded canopies—make the altar appear enthroned and surrounded by the Saints. The painting of the reredos was originally completed by William Dyce. He placed the twelve Apostles around the central wider panels where the subjects are, rising up from above the altar; the Virgin and Child, the Crucifixion and high up Our Lord in Majesty surrounded by the Saints. Dyce's frescoes suffered greatly from the London atmosphere and were replaced by paintings on canvas by J. Ninian Comper in 1909; during 1977–8 these have been cleaned again (by John Larkworthy) and also Comper's decoration of the groined roof (originally designed by Dyce).

There is a marked contrast between Butterfield's tiled and patterned wall surfaces and the quality of decoration in the chancel. Critics have said that Butterfield's lavish polychromy went too far, indeed the patron of the church, Beresford-Hope, disagreed violently with his chosen architect. He referred to the "clown's dress" with which Butterfield had "parricidically spoilt his own creation". Eastlake wrote of the interior of All Saints that, "there is evidence that the secret of knowing where to stop in decorative work had still to be acquired". Time and other critics have been more kind, but Butterfield will always remain one of those architects who divides critical opinion. He has been attacked for this "aesthetic sadism" while the Jesuit poet Gerard Manley Hopkins loved All Saints for its "beautiful and original style".

Hopkins was right: there is so much originality inside this relatively small space. The short broad nave with its three wide bays has a dignity and proportion that belies its size. The height is about seventy feet, the roof ridge and the chancel only a little lower seen through a graceful and wide arch. The nave is separated from the aisles by three arches supported on clustered shafts of polished red Peterhead granite. The capitals are carved from Derbyshire alabaster. Ruskin believed that the carving was unequalled in modern times, while Hopkins was moved by what he called the "touching and passionate curves of the lilyings". Hopkins was in fact so moved by All Saints that when he was on a visit to Tintern Abbey, he stood in

37

b *The interior of All Saints as first completed; woodcut published in the* Builder, *1859*

the rain contemplating the ruins and being reminded of Butterfield!

The rich and noble tracery that fills the side arches in the choir is made of marbles from Devon and Cornwall and the chancel floor continues this richness with a dazzling series of patterns in red, yellow, brown, white and blue tiles. In many respects the chancel looks its best during the altar stripping ceremonies of Holy Week when Butterfield's vision is clearly revealed. The long wall of painted tile pictures in the windowless north aisle has caused much controversy. The pictures are simple, almost childishly innocent views of the Christian story. The Nativity with its happy beasts has all the tenderness

of "Away in a manger". The wall paintings were designed by Butterfield, those on the north wall in 1876, on the west in 1887 and the tower wall in 1891. These tile paintings, being later, do employ the bright apple greens and maroons that are not quite in keeping with the harder jewelled effects of the tile patterns over the arcades. One object calls out for special attention, and that is the pulpit. It contains the essence of so many of Butterfield's ideas on pattern and decoration. It is made of several decorative marbles; grey Derbyshire fossil, warm brown Sienna, fresh Irish green and sharp red Languedoc. The whole strongly patterned pulpit is raised up on a cluster of pink granite columns.

All Saints has a rich collection of stained glass. Beresford-Hope selected Henri Gerente, a refugee from revolutionary France, and a distinguished artist. Sadly he died in 1849 and his brother Alfred took over the work. His great west window is modelled on the 14th-century Jesse window at Wells Cathedral. Gerente's glass was a failure; Beresford-Hope particularly disliked the "cabbage green" of the west window. Much of Gerente's work was replaced, the windows in the south aisle and the south and east windows are by O'Connor and the remainder by Gibbs.

The rich gilded reredos of the Lady Chapel in the north aisle is by Comper (1911), as is the great hanging pyx (1930); in a typical late Gothic, it is much more archaeological and literal than Butterfield's work, but not unworthy of the church (which cannot be said of the screen in the south aisle, by F. King, 1962).

Comper greatly admired the proportions of Butterfield's church, but he reflected the late Victorian incomprehension of the mid-Victorians when he wanted to remove the polychromy and bring out the architectural forms by whitening. Mercifully this never happened (as it did elsewhere). But Butterfield is so strong that the problem of interpretation, or mis-interpretation of his intentions remains. Sir John Summerson, in 1945, wanted to see Butterfield as a sort of *naif*, a narrow intense action builder, whose "first glory . . . is his ruthlessness . . . How he hated 'taste'!" Paul Thompson, in contrast, explodes the myths and denies Butterfield deliberately set out to achieve "ugliness", but, with his colours, wanted the House of God to be cheerful and gay. Neither view seems wholly right, or wrong. Certainly Butterfield was one of Lethaby's "hards" and his buildings are "real" enough. It is a tribute to his imaginative genius that All Saints is still a building which provokes, amazes and impresses.

Why is All Saints, Margaret Street so important? It is because it showed that intelligent historicism could produce a totally original building that is not pedantically stilted. It is also important because it is fundamentally simple and yet experimental (literally experimental in the introduction of cast-iron girders in the clergy house). As an amalgam of English and foreign influences it is important. It is possible to see in this church a dazzling reflection of the coloured interiors of the churches at Orvieto or Assisi, yet it is also a profound reflection of the catholic side of the English nature and its brilliance was recognised at the time of its consecration. The architect George Edmund Street wrote in 1859, "I cannot hesitate for an instant in allowing that this church is not only the most beautiful, but the most vigorous, thoughtful and original among them all".

Map 2 D2

12
Queen's Assurance Company, now Banca Commerciale Italiana
42 GRESHAM STREET, EC2

1850–2
Sancton Wood

This is a dignified commercial building of a common early Victorian Italianate type, but the quality of its details and general configuration raise it above the average. The Gresham Street and King Street façades have a palazzo quality, but, because of its situation the corner is stressed and, on the first and second floor, but not the ground and the third, is taken by a curve. Each storey is successively reduced in height and importance before the heavy cornice is reached, in the correct Classic manner.

Certain features of the building are characteristically Victorian, however. The large windows of the ground floor have segmental heads on haunches which rest on Tuscan columns, the first example of this common mid-Victorian window form. The first floor windows are of a form which, although having precedent, seems somehow more Victorian than Renaissance, that is, a pediment above and round-headed window.

Sancton Wood (1816–86), a pupil of Sir Robert and Sydney Smirke, is, perhaps, best known as a railway architect. His best-known stations are Cambridge, for the Eastern Counties Railways, an elegant Italianate arcade in brick of 1845, and the more elaborate Kingsbridge Station in Dublin, of 1845–61.

Map 2 G2

The Queen's Assurance and Commercial Chambers; woodcut from the Builder, *1852 (Royal Institute of British Architects, London)*

13
Church of Christ the King

GORDON SQUARE, WC1

1850–4
John Raphael Brandon

Catholic Apostolic Church (Church of Christ the King); interior looking east (National Monuments Record, Crown copyright)

This church has been since 1963 the University Church of London University but it was built as the Catholic Apostolic Church. It was the Irvingites, followers of the Scots Presbyterian preacher-in-tongues Edward Irving (1792–1834), who called themselves the "Catholic Apostolic Church". They were governed by a college of "apostles" and the congregations were adept at speaking in tongues. The last member of the college of apostles died in 1902 since when there have been no more ordinations. The other Catholic Apostolic Church in London remains in use by them and is a fine, but little-known, church by J. L. Pearson, standing in Maida Avenue, Paddington (1891–3).

The Gordon Square church was started in 1851 and opened by twelve "apostles" in 1853; the architect was John Raphael Brandon (1817–77). He wrote a learned treatise with his short-lived brother: *An Analysis of Gothic Architecture* in 1847, and his skilful copying of the Gothic is evident here. The building has never been completed according to the original plans. Today the nave, choir, east chapel and transepts are extant but neither the additional two bays of the nave nor the central tower with a 300 foot spire were built. It was John Belcher, a practising Irvingite, who prepared a modified design to complete the building in 1900. Eastlake described the church as "one of the largest and most imposing modern churches in England . . . its internal length is 212 ft; width from North to South of transepts 77 ft. . . . built of Bath stone with groined chancel and presbytery". It is the height of the nave that is the most striking feature of the interior. It soars to ninety feet, about thirteen feet less than Westminster Abbey. The nave roof is a fifteenth century hammerbeam which looks slightly odd over the pure 13th-century arcade and triforium. Any originality, that is, lies not in any style but in the imaginative combination of different precedents. The corbels in the nave are carved (not until 1895) and they show the works of Creation, the sun, moon, stars, wheat, trees, fish, eagle, lion and lamb and at the crossing the figures of Adam and

Eve. The corbels of the tower piers represent the beasts of Ezekiel's vision.

The most interesting feature of the church is the open tracery to the present Lady Chapel, an elegant tripartite screen in the Decorated style. The Lady Chapel was originally used as the "English Chapel" where mass was celebrated for the English "tribe" as opposed to the Church Universal. The glass in the chapel by Gerrard and Gibbs shows the life of Christ and scenes of the Creation and it replaces stained glass by Ward and Nixon. The tiles are excellent originals as they are in the choir.

Particularly striking features of this church are the "angels" throne and the seven lamps that still swing before the altar according to Catholic Apostolic practice. The sanctuary lamp is by A. W. N. Pugin and the great tabernacle is by Brandon. The "angels" throne, which looks like a bishop's throne, was used by the "angel" during especially solemn celebrations; it was not completed according to the original specifications and looks rather squashed as a result. It is very difficult to explain what the Catholic Apostolic Church was. The extreme nonconformist ritualism of the Irvingites amazed and shocked people in the 1850s; it resulted from a curious revelation which was vouchsafed to one of the "apostles" when in Rouen Cathedral, "those are the vestments in which the Lord would have His priests serve before him", that is, full blooded Tridentine Roman Catholicism. Thus by 1850 the Catholic Apostolic Church was up to all sorts of Continental tricks—Latin vestments, incense, reservation, full confession—of a sort which High Anglicans would not dare try for half-a-century. The door to the confessionals can still be seen in the south aisle.

The Irvingites were very rich; most of the adherents were respectably middle class and they had to pay a tenth of their income to the Church. As a result a number of huge and splendid Catholic Apostolic Churches were raised. Where is all that money now? Today the apostles are long dead and there are few adherents. Since 1963 this church has been leased to the Anglicans as the University Church of Christ the King. It is quite unaltered; trendy Anglican destructiveness is forbidden by the lease.

Poor Raphael Brandon; in 1877 he cut his own throat in his chambers in Clement's Inn, which he had designed. The life of a Victorian architect was not without its tensions. Pugin and his son both died mad, as did Sir Gilbert Scott's son. Others took to the bottle, and a few committed suicide. There was so much passion in that complex, intense, tortured, pious age; fortunately, a great deal of that passion went into architecture.

Map 2 D1

14
King's Cross Station
KING'S CROSS, N1

1851–2
Lewis Cubitt & Joseph Cubitt

King's Cross is the terminus of the Great Northern Railway, the second, east coast, railway route to the north, opened in 1850 in time to accommodate many of the vast numbers who descended upon London to see the Great Exhibition the following year.

The station building was opened in 1852. It was conspicuously different from the now-destroyed triumphal gateway to Euston down the road (1837), for it was a palpably cheap and unpretentious structure, built of London stock bricks, which was erected quickly and which proclaimed that it was a railway station, no more. The engineer to the GNR was Joseph Cubitt (1811–72) and he was assisted in the architecture by a relation, Lewis Cubitt (1799–1883), one of the Cubitts, the great speculative builders of Belgravia.

The station is of the double-sided type, characteristic of the 40s and 50s, with one side intended for arrival and one for departure, with the booking halls and waiting rooms placed along this latter side. Each side was covered by a big transparent arched roof (originally of laminated timber, but replaced by iron by the 80s) of 71 foot span. These roofs are expressed externally by two huge glazed arches on the principal elevation, with a clock tower in between. As a Classicist, the architect was able to give these elements a simple but effective bold architectural treatment; he depended, as he said, "on the largeness of some of the features, the fitness of the structure for its purpose, and a characteristic expression of that purpose". Certainly it has an Italianate dignity and grandeur of style which are shared by those early stations spared by British Rail.

When clever intellectuals and men of taste laughed at Victorian architecture, it was fashionable to admire King's Cross for its functional simplicity, especially in comparison to the ornate Gothic St Pancras (36) next door. In fact the designer of King's Cross did not attempt all the functions achieved by St Pancras. The double-sided station was soon found to be inconvenient once more than one departure platform was necessitated by

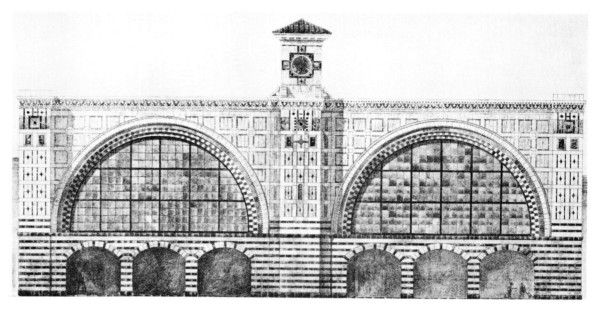

a *King's Cross Station, elevation of façade with proposed facing in marble designed by A. C. Dickie and published in the* Builder, *1905*
b *Departure of the Scotch Express at the turn of the century, from John Pendleton,* Our Railways, *1896*

increased traffic, and the extra platforms could only be reached from the end of the station, which was only a screen wall. Indeed, there was no point in expressing the shape of the train sheds on the façade when that end of the building is the logical place for the necessary booking halls and offices, or a hotel as was done at the Gare de l'Est in Paris, built in 1847–52 from the design of François Duquesnoy, the principal prototype of the "head station". At King's Cross, the Great Northern Hotel is a detached building, in a mean Italian style, while at St Pancras the Midland Hotel is placed in a sensible position and integrated into the whole station.

Map 2 E1

15
Paddington Station
PRAED STREET, W2

Station and train shed
1852–4
Isambard Kingdom Brunel and
Matthew Digby Wyatt

Great Western Hotel
1851–3
Philip Charles Hardwick

I. K. Brunel's 7 foot broad guage tracks to the west were opened in 1838 from Bishop's Bridge Road. It is fortunate that the Great Western Railway waited a few years before building a proper terminus as the result is one of the masterpieces of the heroic period of station building.

Paddington Station is one of the structures of the 19th century which confounds Ruskin's denial of the merit of any iron architecture, in his hatred of industrialisation and railways. It impresses, not because of its engineering

b *Paddington Station; interior of train shed as depicted by William Powell Frith in* The Railway Station, *now in Royal Holloway College*

a *Great Western Hotel, Paddington; perspective by P. C. Hardwick, 1851 (Royal Institute of British Architects, London)*

audacity, but because it is a very beautiful shape: three big "naves" of elliptical form, the centre wider than the others, and the spaces unified by the two "transepts" of equal height.

There is also a good, if strange, fusion between form and decoration. Isambard Kingdom Brunel (1806–59), "the last Renaissance man", had a powerful architectural sense as well as being an engineer of imaginative genius, which may be seen in the engineering works on the main line to Bristol, such as the Wharncliffe Viaduct at Hanwell and the bridges over the Thames between Twyford and Didcot. At Paddington he worked in with his friend Matthew Digby Wyatt (1820–77), an accomplished writer and designer in many fields but whose architecture often shows the weakness of a catholic eclecticism. He had, however, an enthusiastic appreciation of modern things and of the possibilities of iron, which made him an ideal collaborator. Wyatt designed the excellent decorative treatment of the ironwork, the shape of the iron columns (which, with their brutal rivets, might seem to anticipate Otto Wagner) and the swirling iron decoration in the glazed end arches. He also designed the architectural treatment of the buildings on the south, departure side: especially the highly eclectic fenestration in the transepts. The original colour scheme of the station was proposed by the illustrator and designer Owen Jones (1809–76) who had coloured the Crystal Palace.

Paddington, like King's Cross, was a "double-sided" station, but with more than one platform on each side. It is now difficult to appreciate that, originally, the inner platforms were attained by retractable bridges across the tracks, for there was no concourse at the east end of the platforms. The station hotel abutted directly against the tracks, and the arriving passengers went straight out into Praed Street. The fourth span of the train shed was most sympathetically added in 1909–16.

The Great Western Hotel, with its principal frontage in Praed Street, masks the station proper. It was designed by Philip Charles Hardwick (1820–90), son of Philip Hardwick who designed the Euston Arch (96). The younger Hardwick was considerably more eclectic than his father: he was happy to use Gothic, as at Lincoln's Inn. At this important luxury hotel he adopted a fashionable French Second Empire style, with its pavilion roofs, a style which also appears at J. T. Knowles's Grosvenor Hotel (1860–1) at Victoria (27). The Great Western Hotel has been much spoiled by alterations made in the *Jazz Moderne* style favoured by the GWR in the 1930s.

Map 2 A2

16
British Museum Reading Room
GREAT RUSSELL STREET, WC1

1854–7
Sydney Smirke

The principal English monument of the Greek Revival, the severe Ionic stone quadrangle of the British Museum, was rising to the designs of Sir Robert Smirke (1781–1867) between 1823 and 1857. Ill health forced Smirke's retirement in 1845 and some of the interiors of the Museum, and the lodges and the richly ornamental cast-iron railings were completed by his younger brother, Sydney Smirke (1799–1877)—"little Sid".

The older Smirke's reputation much suffered from the time taken to complete the Museum. By the 1840s the austere and archaeological Greek of twenty years before could not be more unfashionable, and Robert Smirke's great internal quadrangle was particularly disliked. It did not last long: in 1852 it was decided to fill it in with a large new Reading Room and bookstacks planned by the Keeper of Printed Books (the Principal Librarian in 1856), the Italian, Sir Anthony Panizzi (1797–1879) to contain the rapidly expanding number of printed books.

Panizzi's first scheme did not envisage the single dome; this was designed in 1854. There were precedents for circular libraries, the Radcliffe Camera at Oxford, for instance. Another was a project for a Circular Royal Library in Paris, prepared by B. Delessert in 1835. The immediate inspiration for Smirke's design, however, was a scheme prepared for the British Museum in 1848 by William Hosking (1800–61), Professor of Architecture at King's College, London.

Hosking proposed a masonry structure in the Classical style inspired by the Pantheon in Rome. The genius of Smirke's design was its construction: a framework of cast-iron ribs supporting brick arches. Smirke employed for an institution of learning the new technology being evolved for railway stations. Again there were precedents: Henri Labrouste employed cast-iron columns supporting visible and decorated arched iron ribs for the reading room of the Bibliothèque Sainte Geneviève in Paris (1843–50), and J. B. Bunning's now destroyed Coal Exchange (98) in the City had a circular domed and galleried hall of iron and glass (1846–9).

The Reading Room, and the attendant corridors connecting it with the old north and south wings, and the bookstacks in the spaces left between the circle and the rectangle containing twenty-five miles of shelves for 1,300,000 books, was rapidly constructed and opened in 1857. Its metal construction and the complicated system of heating and ventilation were much admired. Each desk contained warming pipes and air vents and an elaborate system of ventilation was worked out, introducing fresh air through a system of pipes below the floor. The dome itself had three skins. The inner space, between the brick vaulting and the internal decorated surface, was designed to carry away used air, a process accelerated in summer by "steam pipes" at the top of the dome, while the outer space, between the brick and the upper covering, acts as an insulator in both summer and winter. The windows and lantern were all double-glazed.

All in all, the technology would seem to be more sophisticated and more efficient than that employed in the much vaunted glass and metal History Library in Cambridge (1964–8). The floor was raised on brick arches and was covered in a sound-absorbing material. Smirke designed the chairs, Panizzi the iron bookshelves and the solid padded wooden reading desks, which radiate from the centre.

The dome exceeded in size those of St Peter's, Rome

b *The interior of the Reading Room in 1943 (National Monuments Record, Crown copyright)*

and St Paul's Cathedral. At 140 feet, it was beaten only by the Pantheon (143 feet) but, whereas 7500 square feet of masonry abutment supported that great dome, only 200 square feet were needed in Bloomsbury. It is with regard to architectural treatment that the Reading Room is open to criticism. Smirke made no attempt to make his dome consistent with the neo-Greek of his brother's building, but the iron ribs demanded a treatment different from the coffering of a Roman or neo-Classical dome. The ribs, quite rightly, are stressed, but their junction with the side walls and galleries is unhappy. The crude brackets where the curve of the dome begins were to support statues standing in front of the ribs; below, the ribs continue and cut through the unbroken curve of galleries and bookshelves, and the protuberance is vainly concealed by false book-spines and shelves. Furthermore, although Smirke said that "it was Michael Angelo's cupola of St. Peter's which suggested the present lines" and the spaces between the ribs were to be divided into panels and painted by the great Alfred Stevens (never executed), the round-headed windows were filled with Lombardic tracery, typical of mid-Victorian eclectic work. Smirke's "best work was the outcome of his collab-

a *The British Museum Reading Room under construction in 1855 (British Museum)*

oration with other architects", thought Albert Richardson, "his great failing was indecision; he had neither the inspiration nor power for recasting historical Classic *motifs* into new forms. In consequence his buildings reflect a conflict of taste".

With his brother, Robert, Sydney Smirke designed the Oxford and Cambridge Club in Pall Mall (1836–7); with George Basevi he designed the Conservative Club in St James's Street (1843–5), an association terminated by the latter's unhappy descent from scaffolding on Ely Cathedral owing to his having his hands in his pockets. Smirke's own unaided efforts included the Carlton Club in Pall Mall (1847–56, destroyed), putting another storey on Burlington House and adding the Academy Schools and Exhibition Galleries in 1867–74, and putting the portico, dome and wings on the Royal Bethlem Hospital in Lambeth (now the Imperial War Museum) in 1838–46, a building, originally of 1812–15, where, among famous architects, A. W. N. Pugin and G. G. Scott, Junior were both obliged to spend a short time.

It is hard not to agree with J. M. Crook's judgement on Sydney Smirke that he was "a first-class second-rate architect" and with his sound observation that "we learn more about the generality of mid-Victorian architecture by studying the leaders of the profession—men like T. L. Donaldson, Sydney Smirke and Sir William Tite, orthodox and often dull—than by analysing the eccentricities of rogue elephants like E. Buckton Lamb and J. Basset Keeling. To get a balanced picture we must look at the insiders as well as the outsiders".

At the time of writing it is still planned to move the British Library to the site of the old Somers Town Goods Yard in the Euston Road, so that Smirke's efficient and comfortable Reading Room may ultimately become redundant, which will be a loss for architecture and for scholars.

Map 2 E2

17
Bethnal Green Museum
BETHNAL GREEN, E2

1855–6
C. D. Young & Co

1872
James William Wild

The structure of the Bethnal Green Museum is the re-erected greater portion of what was derisively known as the "Brompton Boilers"—the first home of the South Kensington Museum, later the Victoria and Albert Museum (26).

The Department of Science and Art had been founded in 1852. In 1855 Parliamentary permission was granted to erect an Iron Museum on the ground owned by the Commissioners of the 1851 Exhibition in South Kensington. It was to be an economical, possibly temporary structure (£3000) as an expensive and inefficient war was then being waged in the Crimea. The distinguished engineer Sir William Cubitt was asked to supervise the erection of the building, but the design and construction were the work of C. D. Young & Co, a firm who specialised in exporting pre-fabricated iron buildings to the colonies.

The structure was completed in 1856 and the South Kensington Museum opened in 1857. Among the exhibits was temporarily housed the "Architectural Museum", the collection of architectural casts and fragments assembled thanks largely to the energy of Gilbert Scott.

The building was not popular with the public. Although its basic form—a central "nave" flanked by side "aisles" with galleries—was derived from the Crystal Palace, the structure was smaller and had none of the glittering novelty of the 1851 Great Exhibition building. Besides, the Crystal Palace was a temporary structure for a utilitarian purpose; a museum demanded something more imposing, a masonry structure of architectural dignity. Iron and glass structures had become associated in the public mind with temporary buildings or utilitarian structures like railway stations. Historians often condemn the Victorians for being interested in style and not developing a truly modern

"The Brompton Boilers" as they stood in South Kensington from 1856 until 1867 before being re-erected in the East End as the Bethnal Green Museum (Victoria and Albert Museum)

architecture of iron and glass, but it should be remembered that glazed structures are not suitable for all purposes, certainly not for domestic architecture. The South Kensington Museum only had skylights along the tops of the naves and low along the walls because the Crystal Palace had suffered from extremes of heat and cold.

The most absurd aspect of the Museum was its façade facing Cromwell Road. The problem of ending a structure of repeated modules had not been resolved and the three bays were simply faced with corrugated iron. Not surprisingly the Museum buildings were derisively called the "Brompton Boilers". The Prince Consort, who had taken a close interest in the project, had the façade painted in green and white stripes and an iron *porte-cochère* was added (shipped, unaccountably, from Scotland) but it was not enough. Permanent masonry buildings for the Museum were erected to the designs of Francis Fowke and in 1867 the greater part of the Brompton Boilers were dismantled, the last few bays surviving until Aston Webb's Cromwell Road front to the Victoria and Albert Museum was built in 1899–1909.

The iron museum was not wasted, however. As part of a project to bring Art to the deprived East End of London, it was re-erected in Bethnal Green, thereby incidentally demonstrating the economical merit of pre-fabricated architecture. The site had been purchased in 1869 by local residents, who transferred it to the Lords of the Committee of Council on Education for a local museum. But this time the iron and glass was clothed with a decent and reassuring masonry façade, designed by James William Wild (1814–92), the architect of Christ Church, Streatham (3), who was connected with the South Kensington Museum (26). Like the Streatham church, this façade has a Germanic flavour and in its *rundbogenstil* (round-arched style) and polychromatic brick it has the character of the early 19th-century rational architecture of Schinkel or Klenze. Like the façade of King's Cross Station, it has the merit of appearing to do no more than conceal an iron shed behind—if that is a virtue.

The Bethnal Green Museum was opened by the Prince and Princess of Wales in 1872. For the first three years of its existence, the Museum housed Sir Richard Wallace's paintings and works of art, which are now in the Wallace Collection. Of architectural interest today is the present collection of dolls' houses. Of particular historical interest are two collections of furniture banished by the Victoria and Albert Museum from South Kensington. The first comprises several extravagant pieces of furniture exhibited at the exhibitions of 1851 and 1862 of the sort which—according to the standard interpretation—appalled visitors like William Morris because of their bad design. German furniture made of antlers suggests that Morris had a point.

The second is a batch of Continental *art nouveau* furniture—the Donaldson bequest—which was offered to the Victoria and Albert Museum in 1901 to the fury of artists like Norman Shaw and E. S. Prior, who criticised the objects for bad design and craftsmanship and their decadent style. They were objects which offended the canon of the Gothic Revival and the Arts and Crafts tradition. Inspection suggests that Shaw also had a point.

Map 1 G2

18
City Bank, now Midland Bank
THREADNEEDLE STREET, EC2

1856
William and Andrew Moseley

For its new premises on the corner of Finch Lane, the new joint-stock City Bank emulated the high standard of Classical design achieved by early 19th-century commerce and commissioned a very distinctive building.

Although, like many other City premises this is a four-storey Italianate building with a heavy top cornice, the City Bank was much more Mannerist in style than many of its contemporaries, notably in the complex rustication on the ground floor and, above all, in the design of the entrance on the corner. The door is flanked by two rusticated Doric columns which support an entablature which breaks back before curving around the corner; above this a semi-circular lunette window with a concave rusticated voussoir which also takes the curve, and above this a very mannered segmental pediment sheltering a richly carved garlanded cartouche. All this clever detail is not weakened by being executed on a curve, as often is the case.

The architects were two brothers, William and Andrew Moseley. William Moseley (1799–1880) designed several pre-ecclesiological churches in Sussex and several lunatic asylums, including those at Hanwell (1839), Wandsworth (1839–41) and Clerkenwell (1845–6). His most famous building was the once celebrated "monster" Westminster Palace Hotel, now destroyed, opposite Westminster Abbey in Victoria Street, which boasted the first lifts in London.

Map 2 H2

The City Bank, Threadneedle Street, in 1979 (Architectural Press)

19
Royal Opera House
BOW STREET, WC2

1857–8
Edward Middleton Barry

The Royal Opera House is entirely a Victorian building. Sir Robert Smirke's severe Neo-Classical theatre of 1809 burnt down in 1856. The Opera House was re-opened in 1858, having been rebuilt from scratch in just six months, a considerable achievement in design and organisation.

The architect was Edward Middleton Barry (1830–80), Sir Charles Barry's second son. His theatre was very different from Smirke's (it was smaller and oriented differently), although the general configuration of a big rectangular building with a portico in Bow Street was the same. Instead of Smirke's four-column Greek Doric portico, Barry raised a hexastyle Corinthian portico above a basement, which forms the principal entrance.

a *The Royal Opera House, Covent Garden; woodcut from the* Builder, *1857, showing exterior with the Floral Hall to the south (Royal Institute of British Architects, London)*

However, it is not a particularly imaginative building in style or plan. The Victorians were superb in the creation of railway stations or churches, but the theatres are not especially remarkable (until the end of the century) and look abroad and to the past for inspiration. Perhaps conventional public attitudes to the theatre ensured that

b *Interior of the Royal Opera House in 1944 (National Monuments Record, Crown copyright)*

the Royal Opera stayed in a back street in Covent Garden rather than holding a prominent site; certainly compared with the sophistication in planning, circulation and services of the near contemporary Opera in Paris, designed by Garnier, the Royal Opera House is a provincial work. Victor Glasstone pertinently observes that Barry's Palladian design is "a very fair copy" of von Knobelsdorff's 18th-century Staatsoper in Berlin; but he also points out that the Royal Opera House is "the oldest and quite the most beautiful surviving Victorian theatre in Britain".

The auditorium is Barry's triumph, being both rich and delicate in its decoration, making an interior as intimate and festive as a theatre must be. The balconies have cream and gold fronts, enlivened with garlands and sensuous angels, a scheme perhaps French in style. Certainly the delicacy of the early 19th century is retained, as in the decoration of the ceiling. Here Barry triumphantly unified the great space with a huge saucer dome, like one of Soane's, stretched and magnified.

In the niches either side of the portico are figures of Melpomene and Thalia by Rossi; one decorative feature from Smirke's theatre was re-used: the long frieze by Flaxman placed high behind the portico. The portico itself was elegantly disfigured late in the century when the crush bar was extended outwards by a sort of conservatory.

E. M. Barry died a disappointed man; the son of a successful architect he was cruelly denied success in his own career. He was dismissed from the Palace of Westminster and, having jointly won the Law Courts competition, he was fobbed off with rebuilding the National Gallery, a project which was never realised.

Barry was certainly versatile. Right next to the Opera House is the Floral Hall, a prefabricated cast iron building designed by Barry and built at the same time as the theatre. It stands on a site made available because Smirke's auditorium ran along Bow Street but Barry's new one is on axis with the portico. For opera-goers, Barry provided Palladian; for selling flowers, Barry created a most playful and elegant structure on the theme of the Crystal Palace. It stands in contrast both to the Opera House and Charles Fowler's severe granite Tuscan market buildings placed in 1830 in the centre of the Covent Garden *piazza*. Now redundant, like the other Market buildings, the future of the Floral Hall is uncertain. One recent imaginative project envisaged reproducing and continuing its prefabricated structure so as to make an extension to the Opera House.

Map 2 E2

20
Wellington Monument
ST PAUL'S CATHEDRAL, EC4

DESIGNED 1857
Alfred Stevens
BUILT 1858–1912

In the centre arch on the north side of the nave of St Paul's stands the finest piece of 19th-century sculpture: the Monument to the Duke of Wellington. It is included here because it is as much architecture as sculpture. Its designer, Alfred Stevens (1817–75) was one of few Englishmen to have been trained in Rome and to have drawn his inspiration from the Renaissance: his art transcended all distinction between architecture, painting and sculpture. An unstable and improvident genius, tragically few of Stevens's designs were ever executed and he is represented in London only by the Wellington Monument and his fireplace in Dorchester House (1856–8), now in the Victoria and Albert Museum. It is little short of miraculous that Stevens's design for the Wellington Monument was ever executed, in view of the bureaucratic muddle and indifference and his own unreliability. Remarkably, for Britain—thanks to the strong support of a number of discerning individuals—the greatest of Englishmen was commemorated by the *magnum opus* of the greatest of 19th-century sculptors. It is sad that the Monument is not better known.

The Iron Duke and A. W. N. Pugin both died on 14 September 1852; "by singular coincidence", wrote Pugin's biographer, "on the same day, in the same country, and within a few miles of Ramsgate, died also the greatest man this country has produced, the Duke of Wellington". There already was a memorial to Wellington, a colossal and unhappily proportioned statue by Matthew Coates Wyatt, placed on the top of the Constitution Hill Arch in 1846, against the wishes of its architect, Decimus Burton. Always unpopular, it was finally removed in 1883 and ended up at Aldershot.

The Duke was buried in the crypt of St Paul's. In 1856 it was announced in Parliament that the government intended to erect a monument in St Paul's and that a competition would be held. Quarter-sized models were to be produced for a monument to go in an arch on the north side of the nave. No judges were named, which increased public suspicion that, as so often, the competition would be a sham. In 1857 it was leaked that the Italian Baron Marochetti was working on a design, which did not observe the rules of the competition as he thought he would get the commission. "Our national art-patrons like their pictures from abroad. It would appear that we have no sculptor in England worth a national commission."

Eighty-three models were displayed in Westminster Hall in 1857. The judges were the Marquess of Lansdowne, Dean Milman, Lord Overstone, General Sir Edward Cust, W. E. Gladstone and C. R. Cockerell, the Surveyor to St Paul's. W. Calder-Marshall came first; Alfred Stevens sixth; but nobody was satisfied with the result, and Cockerell had withdrawn from making the final selection (very likely because he was dissatisfied with the result and because he had championed Stevens's design. Cockerell had employed Stevens in Liverpool). A row raged at exactly the same time as the controversy over the Government Offices (29). In 1858 it was announced that Lord John Manners, the new Tory First Commissioner of Works, had discussed the matter with the new Cathedral Surveyor, F. C. Penrose, and that Penrose had chosen no 18: the model by the almost unknown Alfred Stevens. At the same time, Penrose recommended a new site, in the south-west chapel. The appointment was confirmed by the Cathedral authorities.

Stevens had, by 1858, little executed work to his credit. He had spent nine years in Italy and been a pupil of Thorwaldsen; later he designed a railway carriage for the King of Denmark, stores for Messrs Hoole of Sheffield in 1849, and some exterior sculpture for St George's Hall, Liverpool. Because of the change of site, Stevens was asked to make a full-size model, which he agreed to do, and he proposed to make the monument for £6000 less than the sum originally proposed by the government, which was £20,000. The seeds of disaster lay here, as, for the next seventeen years, Stevens was constantly short of money and asking for more.

The model did not appear for years, despite repeated demands for completion from the Office of Works. Stevens was making a more elaborate model than expected, so that it could be cast in bronze, and he had not simplified his original design, although he had accepted a lower price. The model was ready for viewing in 1867, and was accepted but the Dean of St Paul's disliked the equestrian group at the summit.

Work went ahead on the monument. Unfortunately, in 1869 the detestable A. S. Ayrton assumed the office of Finance Commissioner and began to persecute Stevens as he persecuted all architects working for the government in his single-minded belief that his Liberal duty was to save public money. As almost all of the £14,000 had been paid to Stevens and there was little to show for it, Ayrton attempted to remove the monument from Stevens's con-

a *Lithograph showing the lying-in-state of the Duke of Wellington in Chelsea Hospital in 1852; the funeral arrangements were designed by C. R. Cockerell*

trol. In 1870 his contract was terminated. In 1871 the architect L. W. Collman was engaged to complete Stevens's design. In 1875 Stevens, ill and in financial trouble, suddenly died. His monument—without the equestrian figures—was completed in 1877 with the help of his pupil, Hugh Stannus. Stevens had managed to have his revenge—the face of Falsehood in the lateral group "Truth plucking out the tongue of Falsehood" was modelled on that of Ayrton.

Lavinia Handley-Read wrote that "the blind and cruel treatment of Alfred Stevens by church and state became a legend, a stick to beat English philistinism and a solace to the unsuccessful, but he was not forgotten as the different groups of his admirers were apt to believe". The Monument was not yet finished and during the next four decades other artists succeeded in getting it completed.

In 1894 the Monument was moved from its inconvenient position in the south-west chapel to under an arch

was *architecture*, a complex tall structure in sympathy with the building in which it was placed, scaled so that the upper cornice, on which the rider and horse stand, is at the height of the springing of Wren's arches.

The basic scheme, of an arched canopy supported on free-standing columns over a sarcophagus, is that of earlier monuments, such as those to Queen Elizabeth and Mary, Queen of Scots in Westminster Abbey. But Stevens made the architecture more complex so that the arch carries an upper stage and projects laterally. The treatment of the segmental pediment proclaims one major source of influence—Michelangelo—an architect admired by Cockerell but who was not to be a source of inspiration again to English architects until the turn of the century.

Inside the colonnade the bronze sarcophagus seems to be floating, and it is composed as architecture: resting on a complex base of trophies and pedestals, the mouldings and curves beautifully drawn. There is no clear division between architecture and sculpture: the lateral groups—palpably inspired by Michelangelo—of "Valour and Cowardice" and "Truth and Falsehood" rest on plinths but, although they are full of expressive movement, they seem inseparable from the composition. Proudly riding over all is the man and horse: compared with all other such groups in London, surely the most lifelike and vigorous. Stevens, as a man of the Renaissance, knew how to integrate all the trappings of pomp and war into a sumptuous but disciplined style: the garter, placed like a Classical garland against the upper plinth; the lettering of the names of the battles around the base—all are superb. Round the monument are railings with lions, modelled by Stevens.

The Wellington Monument is the finest addition made to the Cathedral in Victoria's reign when it was a deeply unfashionable building. Gothic Revivalists sneered at its false domes and the upper wall which, they thought, was a sham as it concealed the flying buttresses to the nave vault (in fact, these screen walls help buttress the dome) and most Victorians found the grey and grave Classical interior cold and colourless. In 1858 Dean Milman decided that something must be done to improve its appearance. Stevens was approached in 1862 by Penrose and he produced a Michelangelesque scheme for the treatment of the dome. In 1864 one of the spandrels was filled with Stevens's figure of Isaiah carved out in mosaic by Salviati. Three other spandrels of prophets were filled in 1888 after Stevens's designs (the four Evangelists are by Watts). In 1875 William Burges prepared a scheme of mosaic and marble decorations, which was as extravagant as it was destructive to Wren's architecture. In the event, the vaults of the choir were covered in mosaic in the 90s, by Sir William Richmond, an artist who misunderstood the qualities of Classical architecture and the importance

b *The Wellington Monument in St Paul's Cathedral; photograph of 1903 when a cast of Stevens's equestrian group was placed in position (Victoria and Albert Museum)*

of the nave, as originally planned, thanks to the efforts of Lord Leighton, PRA. There remained the crowning feature of the design: the equestrian group of the Iron Duke on his horse, for which Stevens's model existed. D. S. MacColl, future Keeper of the Tate, energetically lobbied and, after more protracted arguments about, among other things, whether Wellington should be riding towards or away from the High Altar, a group modelled by John Tweed was fixed in position in 1912.

Was it worth all the effort? Comparison between Stevens's monument and the other competition entries of 1857 emphasises its qualities. The other designs were almost all statues of the Duke standing on pedestals flanked by martial or allegorical figures. Stevens's design

of subtleties like lettering as much as Stevens appreciated them.

In view of the sad fact that so little of Stevens's designs were ever executed—such as those for the domes of the British Museum Reading Room and St Paul's—John Physick's final judgement on the Wellington Monument should be remembered. Stevens "received a large sum of public money and had produced almost nothing but a plaster model; time and time again he gave successive Commissioners of Works assurances that all was going well . . . It is hardly surprising that, after some ten years or so of delay, the Office of Works at last lost patience and demanded more positive action. If the Office of Works had not taken a firm stand, in all probability the Wellington Monument would have been yet another scheme which Stevens did not bring to fruition, and the finest work of sculpture produced in this country during the 19th century would have been lost".

Map 2 G2

a *Bellamy's perspective of the Chancery Lane façade 1858 (Royal Institute of British Architects, London)*

21
Law Fire Insurance Office
114 CHANCERY LANE, WC2

1858–9 AND 1874–6
Thomas Bellamy

"We see in this building how wisely Mr Bellamy was guided by Italian art, and could rise to the level of Palladio and the other distinguished masters of the great school," remarked Professor T. L. Donaldson after his friend's death. It would be more accurate to say that Bellamy here rose near the level of Cockerell, for this is one of the most refined Renaissance buildings of the mid-Victorian years and the subtleties of its Classic detail reflect that master's lifelong concerns.

The Chancery Lane end was built first. Its façade is of three bays with a prominent central entrance raised up above a flight of steps so as to allow the basement storey to be well lit. Each floor is carefully scaled in diminishing size and this careful proportioning even extends to the crisp Mannerist rustication, which becomes less bold as the building rises. The façade is of the palazzo type; the Order is only expressed in the porch, which is given delicacy as well as refinement by relief panels on the *antae* within the Roman Doric columns. These are complex arabesques, carved by C. S. Kelsey, which incorporate firemen's helmets and other appropriate devices.

The interior, since altered, was remarkable for its soundproof double-glazed screens with an embossed pattern on one sheet of glass. Bellamy wrote a pamphlet on fireproof construction. He was here assisted in the supervision of the job by the architect Thomas Pownall.

The Bell Yard façade of the building was Bellamy's last work, and was built as Street's Law Courts were rising opposite in a very different style. Bellamy's 1874 perspective for this front shows a single storey building but it is, in fact, of three. More arabesques and the elaboration of the three ground floor arched windows make it seem more typically Victorian than the Chancery Lane front, but it is again a tribute to Cockerell, particularly to his Bristol Bank of England branch office which also has flanking *antae* breaking forward at the extremities of the façade. Another favourite Cockerell motif was lions' heads on the Doric cornice. Bellamy's smooth walls are here enlivened by neat reliefs in the antique manner, but of firemen's helmets and hatchets rather than Roman helmets and swords. Firemen's heads even peep out of some of the capitals.

Donaldson described Thomas Bellamy (1798–1876) as "a purist to excess". He did not build much and his principal surviving works are the old Town Hall at Hitchin (1839) and a wing at Corsham Court (1848) which employs iron girders and concrete. A pupil of David Laing, he had the misfortune to marry young and to discover on his Continental honeymoon that his new wife was going insane. "This calamity saddened his whole existence" and made him reticent and reserved, and in later years he could never be persuaded to go abroad. In 1876 on his deathbed, Bellamy was visited by the Secretary of the Law Fire Insurance Office who told him a handle was needed for the door in the new Bell Yard front. "Mr Bellamy begged him not to buy one ready made. Within a few days he sent Mr Bell a drawing done by his own hand, on his sick bed, beautifully designed, and which was, of course, duly executed and fixed. The same earnest, scrupulous worker to the end."

Bellamy's building forms part of a most distinguished group of Classical architecture. Immediately to the north is Vulliamy's Greek Ionic Law Society of 1831 and beyond that, on the corner of Carey Street, the extension of 1902–4 designed by Charles Holden: a building which really does rise to the level of Palladio, if not Michelangelo. Thanks to Holden, both the Law Society buildings now have railings which sport Alfred Stevens's lions, or "cats".

Map 2 F2

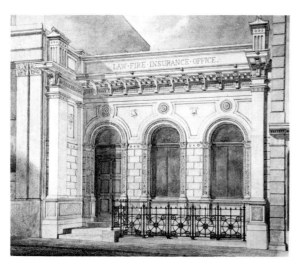

b *Bellamy's perspective of the Bell Yard façade 1874 (Royal Institute of British Architects, London)*

22
St Simon Zelotes
MILNER STREET, SW3

1858–9
Joseph Peacock

This church is one of the more interesting examples of what Goodhart-Rendel characterised as "Rogue" architecture, in this case, Rogue Gothic. Architects like Peacock and E. B. Lamb (qv St Martin, Gospel Oak, 40) were affected by the mid-Victorian desire for a "new style" and were in conscious rebellion as much against Gothic archaeology as against the dullness of the 18th century. They also were unaffected by the serious developments of the High Church party (Butterfield, Street, etc), although they appropriated the motifs used by the "hard" Gothicists and used them with ostentatious licence—to the fury of the *Ecclesiologist*.

Goodhart-Rendel wrote of Lamb and Peacock that "the two knew how to provide places of architectural entertainment for Sundays without either profanity or popery", and of St Simon Zelotes, that "Peacock was determined that no visitor should be dull for a single moment".

The exterior is of ragstone (abandoned by Street et al for urban sites) and is conspicuous for over-buttressing and the odd shapes of window tracery. The west elevation, with its "vigorous" motif of a buttress above a porch bisecting the west window (pinched from Butterfield's St Matthias, Stoke Newington), its *vesica piscis* and bellcote, seem unnaturally and absurdly stretched upwards.

The interior has a perverse plan which is difficult to describe. The two easternmost bays of the nave once had galleries (removed in 1896). The arches of the nave arcades change in height and there are most oddly shaped arches between aisles and the side chapels. The window tracery is mannered, especially that of the east window where it is largely blocked by carved foliage. Peacock employed constructional polychromy internally with exposed bands of red and black brick.

The position occupied by such creatively vulgar architecture in both the popular world and the artistic élite of the Victorians is well brought out by two contrasting contemporary quotations. The *Illustrated London News* called St Simon "one of the most original and beautiful of the many churches which have been built of late years in the metropolis", while the *Ecclesiologist* commented that "altogether we fear this building will be no gain to art".

The church and vicarage cost £7000. Peacock's building may be further contrasted with the dignified economy of J. F. Bentley's Roman Catholic Church of St Mary, Cadogan Street—at the other end of Moore Street from St Simon—built in 1877–9 of stock brick and stone in the Early English style.

Not much is known of Joseph Peacock (1821–93). He later designed St Stephen, Gloucester Road, SW7 in 1864 (since altered and now much Higher in churchmanship from St Simon). A much later building, the Church of the Holy Cross, Cromer Street, WC1, of 1887–8, is interesting, decent and of brick. Peacock became less tiresomely original in later years, but some of the fittings here come from his St Jude, Gray's Inn Road, now demolished, which was very extreme.

Map 2 B4

St Simon Zelotes, Chelsea; woodcut from the Illustrated London News, *1859 (*Illustrated London News*)*

This church was Street's first church in London. After All Saints, Margaret Street, it is the building which proclaimed that the Gothic Revival need not be tied to archaeological precedent but could be novel, original and creative. George Edmund Street (1824–81) was already conspicuous for the imaginative and careful excellence of his ecclesiastical and domestic work in the diocese of Oxford and his group of buildings at All Saints, Boyne Hill, Maidenhead (1854–7) of polychromatic red brick and stone, were much admired. In 1855 he published *Brick and Marble Architecture in Italy*.

St James-the-Less was built in memory of their father for the Misses Monk, three daughters of the Bishop of Gloucester and Bristol. Street later built (in 1879), for these ladies, the one house in Cadogan Square which is not Queen Anne in style. At the time the church was designed (1859), the enthusiasm for foreign Gothic was growing and, as Eastlake later observed "in no instance was this revolt for national style more masked than in the church of St. James-the-Less". But the design is not to be accounted for in terms of foreign sources; in its materials, its proportions and in its style, the church is an original creation by the man who, more than any other, was the creator of the "Vigorous style", that highly creative phase of the Gothic Revival which concentrated on mass, on the integrity of the wall-plane, and on a disciplined originality of composition. The *Ecclesiologist*, who, by 1861, was obliged to approve of such buildings, noted that Street "has stepped beyond the mere repetition of English mediaeval forms, to produce a building in which a free eclectic manipulation of parts has been grafted upon a system of polychromatic construction, having its basis in the fact that London is a brick town", a consideration which Street had stressed back in 1851 in his lecture "On the Proper Characteristics of a Town Church".

Everything about the exterior proclaims that reaction against pettiness in favour of muscularity—"vigour and go": the heavy curved wall of the apse accentuated by

George Frederick Watts—and its numinous atmosphere of darkness and richness. Unlike the nave, the chancel is groined in brick, the vaulting being curved round the un-English apse.

The sanctuary demonstrates Street's decorative ability, with inlaid marble and much mastic decoration incised in the stonework. The windows, like the painting on the nave ceiling, were by Clayton and Bell. The nave is lighter, in contrast to the rich and dark and sacred sanctuary, so that the congregation could read their books. Further light is let in by the two tall dormer windows in the clerestory by the chancel arch, designed to illuminate the painting and which adds to the careful picturesque quality of the exterior. The phase of the Gothic revival combined both tough stylised detail and naturalistic carving; the pulpit was richly carved by Farmer and the capitals of the columns and other sculpture by W. Pearce.

Street had a great interest in the crafts. It is not

a *St James-the-Less, Westminster; perspective from the east drawn by Street, published in the* Ecclesiologist, *1859* (*National Monuments Record, Crown copyright*)

massive buttresses, the simple plate tracery, the parts of the building being clearly separate sculptural forms. St James-the-Less is entered under the detached tower which is Italian in inspiration, although its strange short spire is somewhat Germanic. This was praised by Eastlake ("If Mr. Street had never designed anything but the campanile of this church—and its Italian character justifies the name—it would be sufficient to proclaim him an artist. In form, proportion of parts, decorative detail, and use of colour, it seems to leave little to be desired") and it meets the conditions Ruskin laid down in the *Stones of Venice* for a fine tower, which "shall verily stand in their own strength; not by help of buttresses nor artful balancings on this side and on that. Your noble tower must need no help, must be sustained by no crutches, must give place to no suspicion of decrepitude. Its office may be to withstand war, look forth for tidings, or to point to heaven: but it must have in its own walls the strength to do this".

The interior continues the character of the exterior. Unlike Butterfield's All Saints, or, indeed, Street's later churches in London, the overall impression is of weight, not height. The arcades—of notched polychromatic brick in all their obvious integrity—rest on squat granite columns, of "barbaric bulk". The plan is pure Tractarian: nave and aisles, and a very separate chancel, made distinct by the chancel arch—painted with a large early fresco by

b *St James-the-Less; woodcut of the interior published in the* Builder, *1862*

surprising that William Morris, Philip Webb, Norman Shaw and J. D. Sedding were all in his office in the 1850s and 60s, and he took a particular care over ironwork. The canopy over the font and, especially, the "tulip" wrought-iron railings to the east of the church (by James Leaver, 1866) are particularly fine.

The church makes a group with the school (1864–6; extension at west end of the church by A. E. Street, 1890). Originally the church was hidden from the Vauxhall Bridge Road as it was built in a poor area to redeem shabby Pimlico. The *Illustrated London News* commented at the time that it "rises . . . as a Lily among weeds". Now, perhaps, it is more like an old rose among floribundas as it has become the centre and the stylistic key to the Lillington Gardens Estate, designed by Darbourne and Darke and begun in 1961.

Map 2 D5

24
St Alban
BROOKE STREET, HOLBORN, EC1

DESIGNED 1859
William Butterfield
BUILT 1861–2

St Alban was gutted in the Second World War, but quite enough remains to justify inclusion here and to show the power and quality of Butterfield's design for what was one of the most famous Anglo-Catholic churches of 19th-century London.

St Alban, like many of the great 19th-century churches, was a slum church, built to bring the glory and consolations of religion to desperately deprived areas of cities. The site, in the middle of a notorious "Thieves' Kitchen" tucked away behind High Holborn and Gray's Inn Road (the social pattern of 19th-century London was still intricate and complex) was bought by Lord Leigh and the building paid for by the Rt Hon J. G. Hubbard, MP (afterwards the 1st Lord Addington).

Francis Bumpus thought that "architecturally considered, St. Alban's, Holborn, may be styled a *via media* between the dignified severity of St. Matthias, Stoke Newington, and the gorgeousness of All Saints', Margaret Street. Perhaps we see Butterfield at his highest level in St Alban's". As with All Saints (11), the building was hemmed in by, and had to dominate, surrounding buildings, so, as at All Saints, there is no east window but a blank east wall, again covered by paintings, here originally by H. Styleman Le Strange. The general plan is similar to All Saints—a nave and aisles with generous clerestory, a structurally separate chancel beyond a low chancel arch, a high timber collar-braced roof.

As at All Saints, the interior was a systematic essay in the architect's characteristic structural polychromy, almost every exposed brick surface mechanically patterned in coloured brick, stone, terra cotta and incised mastic.

The great difference in plan compared with All Saints was at the west end, where Butterfield placed a tower with short transepts containing both a narthex and a baptistery. This is connected with the nave through an arch, whose height and magnificent proportions excited the admiration of contemporaries. For the body of the church through this arch was visible, the two west windows and the font, with its (later) tall cover by Comper, in between.

This west tower is the remarkable feature of the church—a solid brick structure of uncompromising and dominating form which originally rose above small houses and which, until recently, proclaimed amidst gloomy Peabody tenements the presence of a very special church. It is a remarkable design: brick—appropriate in a city—banded in stone; a saddleback roof with a broken profile; a tall stair turret with blank tracery rising between the two west windows with Geometrical tracery. All this seems in accord with the vision of Butterfield as a stern, uncompromising Tractarian, with "a vision of ugliness".

But it would, perhaps, be a mistake to overemphasise the aggressively original element in Butterfield's work. Always there were precedents, precedents chosen with an informed and developed sensibility to achieve a definite artistic vision, qualified by his sense of "propriety", and St Alban was a slum church. The tower of St Alban is based on that of St Cunibert, Cologne (a German inspiration also lay behind the external appearance of All Saints and St Augustine, Queen's Gate), and the proportions and style of the interior—Butterfield's favourite Middle Pointed—were derived from Tintern Abbey. The comments of the Church of England paper, the *Guardian*, in 1863—the year the church was consecrated by Bishop Tait—should be borne in mind: "It is an English Church, for the worship of the Church of England, and built in a thoroughly English style. It is such as an English mediaeval architect might have built, if he had to consider the needs of our own times and the ritual of our own church. Men cry out for a new style, and perpetrate eccentricities in a desire for originality. . . . A man of genius can speak to the heart in the old native style of architecture".

It was, indeed, the ritual which brought most visitors to St Alban—whether to participate or to object, for the church became one of the most famous of Anglo-Catholic shrines and rows about Ritualism punctuated the first few decades of the parish's existence and revolved around the saintly Fr Mackonochie and his curate, Fr Stanton. As the late Canon Clarke observed, "there were prosecutions for illegal ceremonial; and certainly some things were done at St. Alban's which it would be hard to defend on the basis of the ornaments rubic—e.g. 60 candles on and around the altar at Christmas 1863. But almost everyone agreed that there was evangelistic fervour as well".

It was inevitable that St Alban should receive gorgeous furnishings over the years which both enhanced and obscured Butterfield's conception: an enormous triptych altarpiece by Garner, a hanging rood, chapel of St Sepulchre and the chapel added to the south-west transept to the memory of Mackonochie (1890) by C. H. Mileham;

a *St Alban, Holborn; view from the west drawn by Beresford Pite published in the* Builder *in 1884 after the surrounding slum buildings had been demolished (National Monuments Record, Crown copyright)*

font cover and Stanton Chantry by J. N. Comper.

All were damaged or perished in 1941—save the Mackonochie chapel—when the church was gutted by bombs. Fortunately it was scheduled for repair and did not go the way of so many war-damaged Gothic Revival Masterpieces which were the victims both of the unthinking condemnation of Victorian architecture by contemporary good taste and the implicit hostility of the Church of England hierarchy to the centres of Anglo-Catholic worship. But there was controversy over how St Alban should be rebuilt.

In 1945 Sir Giles and Adrian Gilbert Scott were commissioned to prepare designs, one for a complete restoration and one for a modern restoration. The work actually devolved upon the younger brother, Adrian Gilbert Scott (1882–1963). The Scotts were officially in collaboration with the octagenarian John Ninian Comper (1864–

1960) as "Architect for the Interior Restoration". Comper had been the church's architect. He prepared a design himself and, in the event, partially restored his Stanton chantry in the south aisle; this, with its recumbent effigy by Thorneycroft, now lacks its metal canopy. Comper seems to have fallen out with the incumbent, Fr Ever, and it was Adrian Scott who designed the temporary church in the ruins in 1949.

The designs made by the two architects are very revealing about the attitude of 20th-century Gothic Revivalists to their Victorian forbears; both knew better than Butterfield even though, at the time, with historicist architecture under attack from the young modern generation, the safest policy would have been to respect Butterfield in all his integrity. Comper's rejected design restored Butterfield's detail and proportions, but he hated the structural polychromy and proposed a whitened interior with a characteristic gilded baldachin and a new east window. The authority for this was Tintern, as Butterfield had been inspired by it. Comper felt himself to be a superior colourist to Butterfield, although he appreciated the vigour of his architecture; he also had proposed whitening All Saints, Margaret Street.

Adrian Scott, on the other hand, felt that his design must be modern—modern Gothic—as he was not a restorer, nor an archaeologist but an *artist*. In this he followed his brother who had reacted strongly against what he thought was the uncreative archaeology of Victorian Gothic. (Curiously, Comper wrote to Giles Scott in 1950 that "I shall always have the happiest remembrances of our association over St. Alban's, Holborn, and am proud that, though a 'restorer', you can still recognise me as a fellow artist".) Therefore, although in 1956 he considered a complete restoration, the church which was re-opened in 1961 was completely new between the west tower arch and the sanctuary. What is curious is that the new interior is a modern version of the great model church of the late Victorian period—G. F. Bodley's St Augustine, Pendlebury, Lancashire (1870–4)—and is a tribute to the abiding power and relevance of that masterpiece. Scott swept away Butterfield's damaged walls and arcades, raised the outer walls (not, of course, following the polychromatic brick patterning) and removed the clerestory and raised the chancel arch. Instead there are internal buttresses, pierced by tall passage aisles, and a big waggon roof. The organ was placed in the west gallery, marring the north-westward vista. Typical of the Scotts is the Hopton Wood stone dado around the walls. Scott's design for an elaborate reredos was not executed. Instead the church is dominated by a peculiarly strident and repellent mural by Hans Feibusch which covers the east wall.

St Alban is not as Butterfield intended, but it still is a church full of interest and restored in the Gothic spirit and it is a mercy that it did not go the way of Pearson's St John, Red Lion Square, or the younger Scott's St Agnes, Kennington, as it might so easily have done.

Butterfield's clergy house still survives on the north-west corner of Brooke Street, an austere building whose polychromatic brickwork respects the street-line; the church is reached through an arch which leads into a narrow courtyard. Next door, the white painted brick building with shutters was designed by Halsey Ricardo (c. 1907), and the island block in the square is an attractive piece of early LCC housing.

Map 2 F2

b *St Alban, Holborn; woodcut of the interior looking east, published in the* Builder *in 1862 (Royal Institute of British Architects, London)*

25
St Francis of Assisi
POTTERY LANE, NOTTING HILL, W11

1859–64
Henry Clutton & John Francis Bentley

This was a small, humble mission church built by the newly founded English branch of the Oblates of St Charles in the (then) notorious slums of Notting Dale.

The original building, consisting of nave, north aisle and apsidal chancel, was built in 1859–60 to the design of Henry Clutton (1819–93). It is a good example of the severe French 13th-century style favoured by the architect; the style was doubtless increased in severity by the demand for economy and the church is built of London stock brick and fitted onto an awkward site.

Clutton's work was conspicuous for its French influence. Between 1851 and 56 he was associated with William Burges and in 1856 their design won the competition for a new cathedral at Lille, a victory (albeit abortive) which both emphasised the international quality of English Gothic architecture at the time and inaugurated the phase of the Revival which was strongly affected by early French styles. In the event, Burges built more in the style than Clutton, who became a Roman Catholic in 1858 and who was never able to take advantage of Cardinal Manning's promise to design the new Westminster Cathedral.

Clutton's assistant from 1857–60 was the young John Francis Bentley (1839–1902), who supervised the erection of this church, and was eventually to design the Cathedral. He was launched on his independent carrer—having just refused a partnership with Clutton—by being asked to add to the church by the Oblate in charge, Fr H. A. Rawes. These additions included a baptistery, Lady Chapel, presbytery, school and internal decoration and fittings.

Bentley's baptistery (1861) is the most celebrated addition, noted by Eastlake in his *History of the Gothic Revival* (1872) "as the production of a young architect then little known to fame, was much admired. There is a breadth and simplicity about the design which distinguished it from previous work, as well as from much that was executed at that time. In the character of the capitals, the treatment of the font, and other details a tendency to

depart from English tradition may be noted". The first person to be baptised in the new baptistery was the architect himself, who, on his reception into the Roman Catholic church in 1862, took the additional name of Francis. The font itself was installed in 1862, its cover, with its elaborate counterweight, was designed by Bentley in 1865 for a thank-offering for his reception into the Catholic Church. The baptistery was not fully completed until 1907–10.

Because of the confined site, the Lady Chapel was ingeniously added by Bentley by prolonging the north aisle round the apse. The alabaster Lady Altar, with paintings on slate by Westlake, was installed in 1863.

Bentley had met the painter N. H. J. Westlake (1833–1921) in 1859; he gave him the job of painting the side panels of the Altar of St John the Evangelist (between two columns in the Lady Chapel) in 1861. Westlake later recalled that while Bentley "was ingrained with early ideas when first I met him. I, on the contrary was 'nuts' on the Italian *quattrocenti*". This altar has elaborate work in marble, glass mosaic and mastic inlay; the carving was by Thomas Earp.

The fittings throughout the church show Bentley's

St Francis, Pottery Lane, Notting Hill; woodcut of the baptistery published in Eastlake's Gothic Revival, *1872*

great interest in the detail and materials of church furnishings and all the crafts. The High Altar, 1863, has inlaid marble and glass mosaic, mastic in alabaster and a painted reredos. The Stations of the Cross were by Westlake, 1865–70, who, in 1872–3, decorated the walls and ceiling of the sanctuary (which only survives in parts). The stained glass in the baptistery was designed by Bentley and installed in 1872; other windows were designed by Bentley in collaboration with Westlake and made by the firm of Lavers & Barraud, with which Westlake was connected. Altogether the interior of St Francis is remarkable (these days) for the completeness and excellence of its furnishings and fittings.

The presbytery was built in 1861–3 in a French style based on the house of Jacques Coeur at Bourges—a favourite subject for English architect sketchers. Clutton had built Minley Manor, Herts, in 1858–62 in an early French château style. The school was originally designed by Bentley and replaced later, probably by Bentley. This interesting and charming group of church, school and presbytery is a good example of the integrity of High Victorian Gothic when built cheaply, and it retains much of the old atmosphere of Notting Hill now that the surrounding area has become trendy.

Map 1 C3

26
South Kensington Museum, now the Victoria and Albert Museum
CROMWELL ROAD, SW7

1856–84
Main Quadrangle
DESIGNED 1860
Francis Fowke, Godfrey Sykes and others

Cromwell Road Entrance Range
FIRST DESIGN 1891
BUILT 1899–1909
Sir Aston Webb

The Huxley Building, Exhibition Road, SW7
1867–71
Henry Scott and James William Wild

The South Kensington Museum was the nucleus of the "culture centre" which now stretches from Kensington Gore to the Cromwell Road. This was a Germanic concept, imported and actively promoted by Queen Victoria's German husband, Albert, Prince Consort (1819–61). Albert was a man of high seriousness to whom, and to whose ideas the English—especially the "swells" of the aristocracy—were not at all sympathetic. He was, however, possessed of vision and determination and, as President of the Commissioners of the Exhibition of 1851, was instrumental in the realisation of the project in its Crystal Palace in Hyde Park.

Albert was well aware that Britain was slowly losing her industrial ascendancy over other European countries and that standards of design needed to be improved—design, that is, not associated with the academic, humanist ideal but concerned with the commercial requirements of craft and industrial processes, an attitude infinitely more relevant to early 20th-century Bauhaus approaches to design than ever was William Morris and Ruskin's concern with the humanity of the craftsman. In

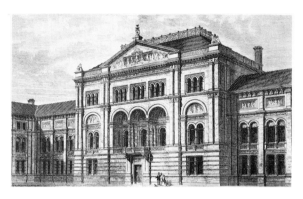

this endeavour to improve technical art education, Albert was assisted by the painter William Dyce, like him powerfully influenced by the German "Nazarenes", and, above all, by Sir Henry Cole (1808–52), first and greatest director of the South Kensington Museum. Cole, in building up the collections, was not just assembling another High Art Museum, but putting before art students and manufacturers a variety of objects of the highest quality for edification and for emulation, a purpose which is often forgotten today. Hence the collections of old furniture, ceramics, metalwork and needlework from both Europe and the Orient, which were complimented

a *Courtyard of the South Kensington Museum; woodcut published in the* Builder, *1870 (Royal Institute of British Architects, London)*

b *Plan of the Victoria and Albert Museum (The Survey of London, redrawn with the permission of the controller of Her Majesty's Stationery Office)*

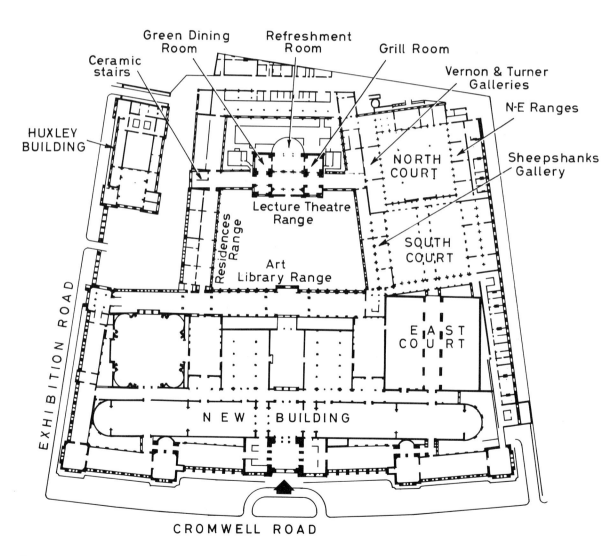

by purchases of the best examples of contemporary work.

The South Kensington Museum also promoted a style, and a type of architecture, a result of the fact that the Government's Science and Art Department was responsible for the design and erection of its own buildings. The key figure again was Cole, who preferred engineers and decorative artists, whom he could influence, to professional architects, whom he profoundly distrusted. Cole's principal agent was the sapper, Captain Francis Fowke (1823–65) of the Royal Engineers, who became architect and engineer to the Department in 1856. Fowke was responsible for the South Kensington buildings being a curious mixture of modern technology and decorative detail; in aesthetic matters he was happy to be advised by a formidable battery of artists and experts. Beresford-Hope in 1857 described the Museum's "cheerful appearance midway between the National Society's Repository and the Soho Bazaar".

The South Kensington style was a sort of Lombardic Renaissance carried out in brick and the new terra cotta. The complexities of its evolution, together with the elaborate history of the Museum's buildings, are superbly analysed in the *Survey of London*; suffice to say here that it was a Germanic style, a variant of the *rundbogenstil* employed by, say, Gärtner in Bavaria, and promoted in Britain by Prince Albert and another German, Gottfried Semper, who had been exiled after the events of 1848 and taught technical processes in the Department in 1852–5. There were also important English promoters of this style which was intended to be a compromise between Gothic and Classic, notably Matthew Digby Wyatt, Owen Jones and J. W. Wild—architect of Christ Church, Streatham (3) who assisted Fowke's successor, Henry Scott.

There were more immediate influences on Fowke, such as Richard Redgrave, the Department's art superintendent, the decorative artists James Gamble and Reuben Townroe and, above all, Godfrey Sykes (1824–66), an informal pupil of Alfred Stevens. The author of the *Survey of London* observes that Sykes "clothed Fowke's ingenious but rather uninspiring compositions with the craftsmanship and humanist idealism of the Renaissance as taught by Stevens—much more in the mood of late-19th-century connoisseurship than of mid-19th-century revivalism. In fact it was this spirit of connoisseurship in the decoration which helped South Kensington to avoid the Battle of the Styles".

The Museum stands on land purchased by the 1851 Commissioners. In 1853 Prince Albert promoted a scheme to move the National Gallery to a complex of museums in South Kensington. The Department of Science and Art, established in 1852 at Marlborough House, moved there in 1855; the Museum opened in 1857. The earliest buildings were extraordinarily utilitarian—haphazard—and temporary, eg the Iron Museum, or the

"Brompton Boilers" (the Bethnal Green Museum, 17); indeed for many years the Museum seemed to grow with no coherent plan and for over forty years presented to the public gaze bare brick walls and sheets of corrugated iron.

The earliest building which still survives (inside the east side of the main quad) is Fowke's Sheepshanks Gallery of 1857–8. North of this come the Vernon and Turner Galleries 1858–9. East of these arose structures of iron and brick, the north court and south court (1861–2). The south court in structure is like a railway station train shed of the time but over the next few years it was elaborately decorated and Sykes's treatment of the ironwork was much admired. The present debased jazz-modern restaurant occupies one of the two "sheds" which are now so cut up and concealed that Leighton's spirit frescoes of "Peace and War" in the lunettes are only to be viewed in narrow first floor corridors. South of south court are the great cast courts, raised in 1868–73 to the designs of Fowke's successor Lieutenant Colonel Henry Scott, assisted by J. W. Wild, and decorated by Moody.

The principal architectural display in the Museum is the main quadrangle. This was envisaged in 1860 as part of Fowke's scheme for slow growth; here the decorative South Kensington style, in red brick, terra cotta and mosaic, may best be studied. The west side came first in 1862–3; the most important north side in 1864–6. Here, below the central pediment is an arcaded loggia with terra cotta columns designed by Sykes in the early Renaissance style. There are also mosaic Lunettes by Townroe, terra cotta detail modelled by Gamble, and great bronze doors—installed in 1869—designed originally by Sykes and modelled by Gamble and Townroe.

Because of indecision over executing several schemes by Fowke and his successor, the south side remained open for several years until filled in 1879–84 by the Art Library Range, a meaner version of the Fowke-Sykes manner. The east side consisted of the gaunt polychromatic brick exterior of the Sheepshanks and Vernon and Turner Galleries until decently clothed in 1901 by Aston Webb who made an exemplary copy of the opposite range.

The Museum also had some remarkable interiors commissioned from contemporary artists which survive on the north side of the quadrangle. The New Refreshment Room and the Grill room are both splendid examples of glazed ceramic interiors. The Grill Room, of 1865–c. 1873, was largely the work of Edward Poynter; the New Refreshment Room in 1866 was decorated by Sykes and completed by Gamble with majolica by Mintons, Hollin & Co. It now also boasts the chimney piece carved by Alfred Stevens for Dorchester House. Next to these glazed, colourful and washable spaces is a contrast: the Green Dining Room, commenced by the new firm of Morris, Marshall, Faulkner & Co, and decorated in

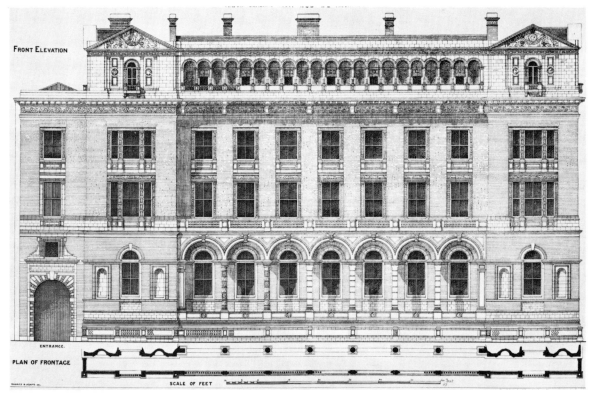

FRONT ELEVATION

ENTRANCE.

PLAN OF FRONTAGE

SCALE OF FEET

c *The Huxley Building, Exhibition Road; elevation published in the* Building News, *1876*

1866–9, ie designed by William Morris, Philip Webb and Edward Burne-Jones (and spoiled by unnecessary redecoration in 1978).

Right through the 1860s and 70s Cole commissioned decorative work from the best contemporary artists: Leighton, Watts, Pickersgill, Val Prinsep. Some of their work may still be discovered, but most was systematically destroyed or covered up in 1910–14 by order of the Director, Sir Cecil Harcourt Smith who was of a generation which held the mid-Victorian in the very lowest esteem. The attempt to destroy the majolica staircase decorated by Moody at the west end of the north range (up to the Lecture Room) provoked a petition of protest from a number of architects and artists. It is now to be hoped that more of the mid-Victorian decorations may be uncovered.

The long entrance range along Cromwell Road was not built until 1899–1909 when the name of the Museum was changed to "Victoria and Albert". Aston Webb's designs for the New Building were chosen in 1891 by Waterhouse after a limited competition. Work was then stopped by Gladstone's last Government in 1892 (the Liberal governments had constantly opposed expenditure on the Museum, perhaps reflecting the considerable dis-

trust of the Treasury for South Kensington). Webb's final design, in a strange eclectic Continental Renaissance style, was prepared in 1902–3. As with the rest of the museum red brick was used, but Portland Stone instead of terra cotta, which was now rather old fashioned, although Webb had been a master in its use. The great corona above the main entrance in Cromwell Road contains absolutely nothing.

The Huxley Building in Exhibition Road is rightly now part of the Museum again—rightly, as it was designed for the Science and Art Department, but when it was being built in 1867–71, it was transferred to what became the Royal College of Science and Professor T. H. Huxley had a teaching laboratory there. The building is the finest example of the South Kensington style: it presents to the street a massive but elegant façade on which an upper terra cotta arcaded gallery in the Sykes style sits above a disciplined composition of brick and terra cotta. Henry Scott was the artist, with Cole and Redgrave as consultants, and J. W. Wild took an important role in the design.

Map 2 B4

27
Grosvenor Hotel
VICTORIA STATION, SW1

1860–1
James Thomas Knowles

The Grosvenor Hotel (run by a private company until 1977) was built in connection with the new Victoria Station at the end of the recently completed Victoria Street. The temporary station was opened in 1860. The line from the Thames—the Victoria Station and Pimlico Railway—was built on the Grosvenor Canal basin and enabled the southern railway companies to cross the river in central London for the first time.

Victoria Station is a perfect architectural expression of the competitive commercial spirit which got Britain's

a *The Grosvenor Hotel, Victoria Station; exterior published in the* Building News *in 1863 (Royal Institute of British Architects, London)*

railways built, for it is not one station but two, and until 1923 there was no connection between them at all. On the right (west) was the London, Brighton and South Coast Railway station, entirely rebuilt in 1898–1908. On the left the London, Chatham and Dover Railway station (a poor line, popularly known as the "London, Smash'em and Turnover") whose new baroque façade (1907–9, A. W. Blomfield, architect) was erected to compete with the Brighton side's rebuilding. But the remainder of the Chatham's side is the structure opened in 1862; a fine, elegant train shed of two spans using the crescent-truss, and the original stock-brick Italianate station buildings on the west side.

The Grosvenor Hotel was built next to the Brighton side. It was not the first station hotel in London, but the first of a new type. As the *Builder* observed in 1860, "it is only recently that the idea has occurred to enterprising minds to connect with the chief termini hotels equal to the demand of the traffic on the lines, adapted for the reception of the middle and the higher classes, and even more commensurate with the importance of London than the best 'Railway Hotels' are with that of provincial towns".

The hotel was designed on a magnificent scale and must have dominated the area around when first built: a solid oblong of brick, with the ends of the big façade (262 feet) firmly stressed and surmounted by four French pavilion roofs still topped with their balls and spikes. The building is a characteristic example of a type of architec-

b *The Hall of the Grosvenor Hotel in 1910 (National Monuments Record, Crown copyright)*

ture which seemed to be able to resolve the still-raging "Battle of the Styles". Critics had observed how secular Gothic was learning from the Renaissance by using strong horizontals with deep cornices, etc, while buildings in the Classical tradition were becoming more arcaded than trabeated and were employing richer naturalistic ornament and much more picturesque outlines. The Grosvenor Hotel is Classical ("a modification of the Florentine-Italian"), with its regular windows, symmetry and heavy modillion cornice; but in its rich surface decoration and elaborate curved and dormered pavilion roof, it has definite affinities with contemporary Gothic designs.

On the exterior, white Suffolk brick is relieved by Bath stone and coloured Portland cement. All the railings and balconies are elaborately moulded and there are extravagantly carved friezes and garlands which obey Ruskin's dictates by representing wild flowers, vine leaves, etc. On the first and top floors the verdant spandrels to the arched windows are further elaborated by medallions containing portrait busts of famous contemporaries: Queen Victoria, the Prince Consort, Lord John Russell, Lord Palmerston, etc. All the carving was carried out by Daymond & Son.

The architect of the Grosvenor Hotel, James Thomas Knowles (1806–84) is often confused with his famous son of the same name (1831–1908) who was knighted. The latter founded the Metaphysical Society in 1869 (which often met in the Grosvenor Hotel) and the journal the *Nineteenth Century* in 1877, which he edited. He contributed the design of the Ruskinian friezes to his father's design and gave up architecture in 1883.

Several other London buildings survive in this elaborately ornamented coarse brick style of "the most

c *Details of the exterior published in the* Building News *in 1863 (Royal Institute of British Architects, London)*

advanced portion of the Italian School of Architecture". Knowles designed the two big terraces on the north side of Clapham Common, SW4 in 1860 and, with his son, the Thatched House Club at the south-west, bottom end of St James's Street in 1862, which makes a painful contrast with Norman Shaw's smooth Classical Alliance Assurance of 1901–5 next door.

The Grosvenor Hotel clearly had an influence on the design of the Langham Hotel, at the bottom end of Portland Place, by Giles and Murray, 1864: "a High Victorian monster, dash, big and grim, in a Trecento style" as Pevsner describes it, and which has never been fully restored after bomb damage. The Grosvenor is, therefore, in its way an important building and Summerson writes that it "magnificently typifies its period. In its massive uniformity it inherits something from Barry's school, in the naturalistic whimsicality of its detail it echoes Ruskin, in its deliberate coarseness it speaks for the age of steam. Still much as it has always been, it is one of the representative monuments of Victorian London".

Map 2 D4

28
St Peter
KENNINGTON LANE, VAUXHALL, SE11

DESIGNED 1860
John Loughborough Pearson
BUILT 1863–4

When Pearson's original design of 1860 was exhibited at the Royal Academy the following year, the *Ecclesiologist*, that arrogant mouthpiece of High Church Gothic orthodoxy, commented that "we have seldom had a more important design—or one more thoroughly satisfactory—than this before us".

When built to a less ornate design in 1863–4, the church was regarded as the ideal of what a town church should be, as it depended for its effect on its grandeur, simplicity of materials and height above the surrounding houses and, with its unbroken roof line, strong brick walls, apse and simple 13th-century French Gothic style, became a model for Brooks's churches and many others.

a *St Peter, Vauxhall; east elevation from the set of contract drawings, 1863 (Royal Institute of British Architects, London)*

67

ment is concentrated into the carving and into the fittings, such as the alabaster and mosaic reredos—a remarkable period piece. Indeed there is no other Anglo-Catholic church in London in which the austere and dignified sanctuary arrangements of the 1860s have been allowed to remain.

Pearson would not be so severe again, but, as may be seen in St Augustine, Kilburn (62), he never lost his sense of the majestic possibilities of brick walls and vaulting. Nor did he ever lose his clear sense of proportion. Many of Pearson's churches were designed on basic geometrical principles and St Peter is based on the Golden Section, evident in the ratio of internal height (to the springing of the vault) to width.

The parish was created in a part of south London made shabby by the closure of the Vauxhall Gardens. The founder, the Rev Robert Gregory, wanted a sort of social centre, of church and school. First came the school, behind the site of the future church, the foundation stone of which was laid in 1860. The art school here became important and developed links with Doulton's pottery works nearby. In Kennington Lane, to the left of St Peter is the orphanage, to the right is the vicarage which is palpably a late Georgian house improved by Pearson by adding a gabled attic storey.

Map 2 E5

b *Woodcut of the interior of St Peter published in Eastlake's Gothic Revival, 1872*

John Loughborough Pearson's (1817–97) career in church design fell into three phases: his early work was rather strictly ecclesiological English Gothic, then he moved into a Vigorous interpretation of French Gothic, in the 1860s, before building his masterpieces of the 70s and 80s: tall, spacious churches in his favourite French 13th-century style which depend on their complex plans and vaulted spaces for their effect. St Peter, Vauxhall is the urban masterpiece of the middle period. The exterior is striking for its noble simplicity and unbroken roofline, the wall sweeping round unbroken into the apse, and the west end of massive buttresses rising above the narthex, between the windows of tough plate-tracery (the tower and spire on the north side were never built). The interior was the first vaulted throughout in masonry since the early days of the Gothic Revival (St Luke, Chelsea, 1820–4, by James Savage). Butterfield, Street et al, all favoured the wooden roof: but Pearson was to become the master of the brick vault. The great walls, on their arcades with strange rectangular carved capitals, and the rest of the vaulting are broken only by the purely liturgical chancel arch before sweeping round into the apse. The interior, like the exterior, is of unashamed brick: orna-

29
Government Offices

PARLIAMENT STREET, DOWNING STREET,
ST JAMES'S PARK AND
KING CHARLES STREET, SW1

1861–74
George Gilbert Scott, partly assisted by
Matthew Digby Wyatt

Foreign and India Offices

FINAL DESIGN 1861
BUILT 1863–8

Home and Colonial Offices

BUILT 1870–4

The building of the Government Offices was the principal engagement of the "Battle of the Styles", and was a long-drawn-out saga of muddle, politicking and compromise in which the victor, Scott, emerged with his honour tarnished. After agreeing to design in the "pagan" Classical style that Pugin and Ruskin abominated, Scott lost his moral position as a leader in the Gothic Revival which he had enjoyed since the mid 40s.

The whole hilarious story of Scott's battle with the old Whig, Lord Palmerston, cannot be told in full here. To summarise, not one competition but three were announced in 1856: one for the Foreign Office, one for the War Office on the adjacent site, and one for the general treatment of the Whitehall area. This was asking for trouble. In 1857 it was announced that Coe and Hofland had won the Foreign Office; H. B. Garling the War Office, and a Frenchman's general plan was thought best. Scott, who came third for the Foreign Office and was unplaced for the War Office, thought that "the judges, who knew amazingly little about their subject" were prejudiced against Gothic design.

Palmerston then set aside the results of the competition and appointed James Pennethorne as architect, a non-competitor, who had prepared designs in 1855. At this the architectural profession, and Scott, felt "at liberty to stir" and lobbied the government. In 1858 Palmerston fell and a new Tory administration appointed a Select Committee to look at the matter, and which appointed

Scott architect. Palmerston remarked that a horse which came second in both races had taken the stakes.

The War Office had tired of the affair and dropped out, but the India Office came in with its architect, Matthew Digby Wyatt (1820–77) who agreed to collaborate with Scott, whose new Gothic design was published in 1859.

But now other architects—the Classicists—were aggrieved and Palmerston, assisted by William Tite and Professor Donaldson, attacked Scott's appointment. In May 1859 Lord Derby's government fell "and my arch-opponent became once more autocrat of England". Palmerston sent for Scott and told him "in a jaunty way that he could have nothing to do with this Gothic style, and though he did not want to disturb my appointment, he must insist on my making a design in the Italian style, which he felt sure I could do quite as well as any other". When Scott and his supporters remained adamant, Palmerston toyed with making Garling—who had been an original winner—the real architect.

Scott was alarmed and so upset that he had to take a holiday where he decided upon compromise as "to resign would be to give up a sort of property which Providence had placed in the hands of my family". He produced a design in a sort of Italo-Byzantine style—"a variety of Italian, as little inconsistent with my antecedents as possible . . . Byzantine, in fact, turned into a more modern and usable form". Though, incredibly, Burns, Fergusson and Cockerell all approved of it, Palmerston did not: "neither one thing nor t'other—a regular mongrel affair—and he would have nothing to do with it either".

It must be Italian (or, unthinkably, resignation): "I made up my mind . . . bought some costly books on Italian architecture, and set vigorously to work to rub up what, though I had once understood pretty intimately, I had allowed to grow rusty by twenty years neglect". His design was approved in 1861. The Foreign and India Offices, at the St James's Park end of the site, were built in 1863–8. The Home and Colonial Offices were built at the other end in 1870–4, Parliament Street then being widened to the width of Whitehall.

The irregular St James's Park façade, with its tower, is not the work of a formal Classicist, but its picturesque configuration was first suggested by Wyatt, who was entirely responsible for the elaborate Italianate Durbar Court of the India Office at the south-west corner. Scott's elevations have a small-scale richness of detail and sculpture which was more the work of a Gothicist. There is sculpture by Armstead, Philip, Protat and Raymond Smith, and touches of polychromy in the roundels on the pilasters. The principal Parliament Street elevation is marred by the omission of the corner towers and the central porch, pruned as an economy by Ayrton, the First Commissioner of Works who also made Street's life difficult at the Law Courts.

a

b

c

d

e

a *Scott's unsuccessful competition design for the Government Offices, 1856; perspective showing the War Office in Parliament Street (Royal Institute of British Architects, London)*

b *Scott's "Byzantine" design for the Government Offices, 1860; perspective view of Foreign Office from St James's Park showing Soane's State Paper Office (Royal Institute of British Architects, London)*

c *The approved Classical design for the Government Offices, 1861; perspective view from St James's Park showing Foreign and India Offices (Royal Institute of British Architects, London)*

d *The Ambassadors' staircase in the Foreign Office in 1975 (National Monuments Record, Crown copyright)*

e *J. O. Scott's unexecuted design for completing the corner towers on the Parliament Street front of the Home and Colonial Offices, 1896 (Royal Institute of British Architects, London)*

Some interiors survive unaltered with their original painted decoration. The best are in the Foreign Office in the north-west corner where there are the Foreign Secretary's rooms and a magnificent ceremonial staircase.

Palmerston died in 1865 and never saw the building completed.

The verdict of his successor, Gladstone, was that "about twenty years before the Foreign Office was rebuilt, the British Government, in want of a Gothic building, gave the work to one who had earned a noble reputation in the practice of Classical architecture; desiring a classical Foreign Office, the British Government employed the best known Gothic architect of the day to erect it".

Map 2 E3

30
Shops and Workshops
91–101 WORSHIP STREET, SHOREDITCH, EC2

1861–2
Philip Webb

This terrace of shops and workshops—with a drinking fountain at one end—was built by Major (later Lieut Col) William J. Gillum, on a site owned by the Gillum family since the 18th century. He chose as architect the then unknown Philip Webb (1831–1915), which was an odd choice but Gillum knew several of the Pre-Raphaelites.

William Gillum (1827–1910) was a philanthropist and soldier, who had lost a leg in the Crimean War. In 1860 he took an interest in the Boys' Home in the Euston Road and paid for the Boys' Farm Home at East Barnet where destitute boys could learn a trade. At the same time he was an amateur painter and a founder member of the Hogarth Club, and he became acquainted with the circle of Ford Madox Brown and William Morris and thus with Webb.

Webb had left G. E. Street's office in 1859 to design the Red House for William Morris at Bexley Heath. In all his early work the Gothic influence is literally evident; later it would manifest itself more subtly: in his approach to design and to the use of materials. There is a simplicity in the design of the Worship Street shops appropriate for their purpose and which allowed that structural honesty insisted upon by Gothic Revivalists. The brickwork is broken by the relieving arches over the pairs of first floor windows; the shops are iron-framed and the high-pitched roofs support dormers with prominent overhangs which John Brandon-Jones suggests reflect the journeys made to northern France with Morris.

An illustration of these shops appeared in the *Builder* in 1863—the first and last time Webb allowed his work to be published—and the comment of that journal is of interest in that it notes the consequence of that Gothicism or puritanism which Webb never shook off and with which William Morris could not live for long at the Red House. "One merit of the work consists in the use of sound materials: an objection is the degree of rudeness in the finishings, internally, which may militate against the speedy occupation of the houses and shops by persons able to pay the amount of rent which would be required."

At this time Webb was designing the monstrous Brobdingnagian furniture for Morris's firm and indulging in exposed brickwork in his domestic interiors. All of which adds force to that most perceptive remark of Webb's admirer, Edwin Lutyens, which he made in 1905: "Had Webb started his career under the influence of Alfred Stevens rather than of Edmund Street, had he come into touch with those who could have bent his constructive genius to the grand manner of architecture, there would have been produced a man of astounding mark in the authentic line of Western architecture". But where would Lutyens have been without that sense of mass and materials which came from the Arts and Crafts movement and ultimately from Gothicists like Street?

Maps 2 H1

Workshops in Worship Street, Shoreditch; woodcut published in the Builder, *1863 (Royal Institute of British Architects, London)*

31
Prince Consort National Memorial (Albert Memorial)

KENSINGTON GORE,
SW7

DESIGNED 1862
George Gilbert Scott
BUILT 1864–75

The Albert Memorial; steel engraving published in James Dafforne, The Albert Memorial, Hyde Park, *1879*

In the days when Victorian architecture was regarded by the educated as being so hideous as to be beneath criticism, the Albert Memorial, along with Keble College, were probably the chief symbols of all that was laughable and ludicrous in the 19th century; Lytton Strachey cleverly dismissed Scott's Memorial by observing that "it was rightly supposed that the simple word 'Albert', cast on the base [of the bronze figure] would be a sufficient means of identification".

At the time of its building, the Albert Memorial was much attacked (probably by those opposed to Gothic) and Scott wrote that "if this work is worthy of their contempt, I am myself equally deserving of it, for it is the result of my highest and most enthusiastic efforts". The Memorial is, indeed, the supreme expression of the stylistic, architectural and symbolic aspirations of Scott and his contemporaries and therefore is worthy of considerable attention.

Queen Victoria's beloved Consort, Albert of Saxe-Coburg-Gotha, died in 1861. In addition to several memorials promoted by his distraught widow, it was decided that a National Memorial should be erected. The site chosen was that of the 1851 Great Exhibition, with which Albert had been much involved. The first idea considered was for a huge monolithic granite obelisk; this was rejected and a panel of eminent architects, including Scott, were asked for their advice. In 1862 a limited competition was held; Pennethorne, Donaldson, P. C. Hardwick, Matthew Digby Wyatt, C. and E. M. Barry and Scott were asked to enter and Scott's design was eventually selected by the Queen.

His was the only Gothic design and, as such, had its critics, especially Henry Cole, Secretary of the South Kensington Museum, who was interested in determining that Scott would not design the contiguous Albert Hall.

Scott remembered "how long and painful was the effort before I struck out an idea which satisfied my mind"; it has been suggested that relief came when he saw Thomas Worthington's published design for the Albert Memorial in Manchester. What Scott proposed was "the realization in an actual edifice, of the architectural design furnished by the metal-work shrines of the middle ages. Those exquisite productions of the goldsmith and the jeweller profess in nearly every instance to be models of architectural structures, yet no such structures exist . . . my notion, whether good or bad, was for one to realize this jeweller's architecture in a structure of full size and this has furnished the key-note of my design and of its execution".

This conception was assisted by Scott's enthusiasm for the use of different materials and for craftsmanship—the great concern of Gothic Revivalists in the tradition of Pugin. So in the Memorial is to be found gilt and enamelled metal, mosaic, "polished gem-like stones"; enamel as well as several varieties of granite, marble, limestone and sandstone, all giving rich textural diversity and polychromy.

The basic scheme is "a colossal statue of the Prince, placed beneath a vast and magnificent shrine or tabernacle, and surrounded by works of sculpture illustrating those arts and sciences which he fostered, and the great undertakings which he originated". The didactic and symbolic messages of buildings, whether of the 19th or 13th centuries, are seldom bothered with today, but for the Victorians, the iconography or allegory of symbolic decoration was of immense interest and importance; buildings, like paintings, could tell a story. The meaning of sculpture can be ignored in many Victorian buildings and need not affect aesthetic appreciation; but, at the Albert Memorial, it is too dominant to dismiss.

Projecting from the Memorial are pedestals on which figure the industrial arts: Agriculture (by W. Calder Marshall), Manufacture (by Henry Weekes), Commerce (by Thomas Thornycroft) and Engineering (by John Lawlor—note the representation of Robert Stephenson's Brittania Bridge). The Memorial is at the centre of the four quarters of the globe, "and their production: thus referring indirectly to the International Exhibition of 1851": Europe (by Patrick Macdowell), Asia (by J. H. Foley); Africa (by William Theed) and America (by John Bell).

Perhaps the most impressive, and accessible, are the 169 portrait figures carved in bas-relief on the frieze and the podium, depicting "those men who have excelled in the arts of Poetry and Music, Painting, Architecture and Sculpture". The Poet, Musicians and Painter were by H. H. Armstead, the rest by J. B. Philip. The selection is interesting and indicates much about mid-Victorian taste; however, the roll-call of architects is catholic and not inhibited by Gothic Revival prejudice—even Vanbrugh and Palladio are there; and between Cockerell and Pugin (with his back to all the others) is discreetly placed Scott.

But this is not all; there are bronze statues (by Armstead and Philip) at the angles of the structure, representing the "greater sciences" and, in the niches of the spire there are Faith, Hope, Charity and Humility and, at the angles of these niches, Fortitude, Prudence, Justice and Temperance. All these, of bronze gilt, were by J. Redfern; the bronze angels above by J. B. Philip. There is also much heraldry. The glass mosaics—by Messrs Salviati & Co of Murano, Venice, from designs by Clayton and Bell—depict further improving thoughts about the Fine Arts. All the metalwork in the Memorial was carried out by Messrs Skidmore & Co of Coventry, the exceptional firm whom Scott often employed. The architectural carving was largely executed by Farmer & Brindley.

In short, with the number of artists and craftsmen involved in the realisation of the design, the Memorial is really an Arts and Crafts work in everything except style, and it emphasises how the Arts and Crafts movement had its roots in the Gothic Revival and that its real founder was not Morris but Pugin.

The Memorial was criticised even by Gothicists—Scott was fair game after all—on purist grounds. The piers do not look strong enough to carry the weight of the spire and the supports of the flèche are invisible; this was because the weight is taken by a structure of steel girders, firmly anchored to the concrete foundation. This deceit need scarcely worry us now. Scott admitted that the flèche might be a little too high; he heightened it from the original design.

The foundations were laid in 1864, the structure opened in 1872—in which year Scott was knighted at Osborne—but the gun-metal effigy of Albert by J. H. Foley, originally gilded, was not put in place until 1875.

Map 2 A3

32
National Provincial Bank, now National Westminster Bank

15 BISHOPSGATE, EC2

1863–5
John Gibson

The National Provincial Bank in Threadneedle Street; early-20th century photograph published in A. E. Richardson, Monumental Classic Architecture, *1914*

This magnificent building shows the continuing vitality of the Classical tradition surviving in the world of commerce in the years of the High Gothic Revival. It was recently threatened with demolition, but instead Col Seifert's tallest tower rises behind, and the building has been restored and continues to dominate the junction of Bishopsgate and Threadneedle Street.

John Gibson (1814–92) was articled to J. A. Hansom, architect of Birmingham Town Hall and inventor of the Patent Safety Cab. From 1835 to 44 he was assistant to Sir Charles Barry, and from Barry he learned to build in the Renaissance manner competently and grandly. In 1862 he became architect to the National Provincial Bank and was to build about forty of their branch banks as well as the head office.

For its head office on the site of the Flower Pot Inn, the bank decided upon conspicuous grandeur and dispensed with lettable office accommodation. Gibson could thus employ a single Corinthian order, rather than the usual layer-cake architecture of mid-Victorian commercial building, giving the building great monumentality like the old screen wall of Soane's Bank of England. The straight Bishopsgate front is given six bays, between paired columns at the ends. To deal with the curved end, where the entrance is placed, Gibson continues the order and the pairs of columns, but breaks back the entablature in between. The result has stylish freedom but retains the Classical logic.

The Classical manner is mid-Victorian rather than early Victorian, that is, richly sculptured and with round arches. For the entrance Gibson kept the level of the round arches of the windows, but made it contain a circular window above the arched door.

Also typically mid-Victorian is the descriptive sculpture, executed by Messrs Colley. A splendid carved frieze below the entablature—modelled by John Hancock—illustrating the arts, commerce, science, manufac-ture, agriculture and navigation, and above on the parapet, are figures representing the towns which the bank served, such as London, Birmingham, Dover and Manchester. This last was "represented by a female figure,—and having as 'supporters' seated, a negro with raw cotton, and a workman with a bale of goods".

The interior contains a fine banking hall, lit from three domes supported on marble columns.

The architect was highly praised by the architectural press, for so successfully dealing with the site and employing a Classical style well adapted to the atmosphere of London.

Map 2 H2

33
Offices
59–61 MARK LANE, EC3

1864
George Aitchison

The first example of the application of Ruskin's ideas to a London street building was the Crown Life Assurance Office in New Bridge Street by Deane and Woodward (architects of the Oxford Museum) in 1855–7, which was very rapidly swept away by the London, Chatham and Dover Railway cutting towards Ludgate Hill.

This building in Mark Lane is in the same tradition, but with greater sophistication. It was built for the Innes brothers, James & John, property speculators who, in 1864, founded what is now the City of London Real Property Company. It was a type of structure new to the mid-19th century—a block of lettable offices; a type which demanded a dignified and fashionable façade and a flexible interior. The interior here is of cast iron supporting wrought-iron beams, with fireproof brick-arched floors. Hitchcock commented on a significant aspect of the building: "except that the masonry screen is self-supporting, it is . . . technically not unlike a skyscraper façade. There is no wall as such and although the exterior masonry skeleton is arcaded, it expresses rather clearly the interior skeleton of metal".

As with an early skyscraper, the exterior elevation could have been extended upwards indefinitely. The ground floor was the characteristic Victorian segmental headed windows; above there are six bays of arcaded windows on three floors. As Ruskin demanded of the "wall-veil" he admired in Venice, there is no integration, in the Renaissance Classical manner, between each storey.

The style is Ruskinian: Venetian Byzantine arches on little columns (Summerson suggests the influence of de Vogüe's Syrian researches) which are in front of the plane of the windows. There is a little elaboration of the cornices; otherwise the decoration is incised into the Portland stone, and sometimes filled with mastic. Ruskin appreciated the great effect in the Mediterranean sun of the flatness and austerity of this style but it scarcely tells in the dark, dirty London streets, and it is no wonder that the richly modelled and sculptured palazzo façades of the Renaissance were usually adopted for commercial build-

ings. No 103 Cannon Street (1866 by Frederick Jameson) is a more attractive example of a Venetian façade.

George Aitchison the younger (1825–1910) was one of those well-connected architects outside the Gothic Revival tradition who is perhaps less well known today than his church-building contemporaries. He had a distinguished career, however, and came to be President of the RIBA in 1896–9. His father had been an architect-engineer of the old school and architect of the London-Birmingham Railway. His son was articled to him, also attended the Royal Academy Schools and travelled abroad. In 1861 he succeeded his father as architect to the St Katharine's Dock Company; and he executed several office buildings in the City. However, his later years were increasingly occupied by an interest in the decorative aspect of architecture—furniture and decorative schemes—as well as archaeology. Shortly after building this remarkable office block, he designed the exotic house of Frederick Leighton in Kensington (47).

Map 2 H2

Office block in Mark Lane; perspective possibly by D. Varry, 1864 (Royal Institute of British Architects, London)

34
St Mark

ST MARK'S RISE, DALSTON, E8

1864–6
Chester Cheston, Junior

1877–80
Edward Lushington Blackburne

This building is a good example of a mid-Victorian Evangelical (rather than Broad or High Anglican) church and typically exploits the style and motifs used by *avant garde* Gothic Revivalists, but vulgarised and exaggerated so creating a structure which is of a conspicuously different type.

The architect of St Mark is obscure and he would seem to have been young and inexperienced, which contributed to the delay between finishing and consecrating the church (1870), as there were endless wrangles over debts. Chester Cheston was the son of the solicitor to the Lord of the Manor, William Amhurst T. Amhurst.

The Evangelicals had no use for an ecclesiologically "correct" Gothic church with a deep chancel. They needed a large space to contain a large congregation within earshot of the pulpit. They were, however, prepared to use the Gothic style and even those mannerisms employed by architects such as Butterfield and Street. The exterior is of stock brick with stone dressings in a pedestrian Early English style, but typical of a low-church building are the prominent transverse gables forming the clerestory over the aisles. In the interior these obtrude into the varnished oak roof which is groined to allow for them. The interior is very wide and the chancel short, neither of which would have pleased the *Ecclesiologist* had they deigned to notice the building. Nor would they have approved of the fact that the arcades are supported on iron columns, which are thin with exaggerated capitals. The detail inside is vigorous, if bare, and there is unbridled use of brick notching and polychromy. To quote a description of 1870, "the ten pillars supporting the edifice are painted a dull chocolate colour, picked out with gold, and the bricks are painted (sic) blue, red, white and black, giving a very elegant and pleasing effect. All the windows are stained" (these were by Lavers and Barraud). The chancel is richly decorated and has a mosaic

reredos (1881) but this seems less important than the huge organ in the north transept, with its elaborately painted and gilded pipes.

The unsatisfactory nature of Cheston's services is suggested by the fact that when, in 1877, sufficient funds were available to complete the tower, a new design was secured from Edward Lushington Blackburne (1803–88), a friend of J. F. Bentley who helped him in his declining years. Blackburne, although older than most Gothicists, was capable of a vigorous design in his favourite French Gothic and here he provided a powerful and individual composition very similar to that of his (destroyed) Smithfield Martyrs church. The tower was finished in 1880, in which year the chancel roof was raised and new windows inserted. These included the strange but effective glazing of the groin above the transepts, which has figures of angels in pale blue and gold.

The interior of the church is remarkable for the completeness and unspoilt quality of its furnishings: the sea of varnished oak pews, with doors, and all the decorations and even the vintage electric lighting are intact. As Canon Clarke observed, "the church is difficult to describe; it needs to be seen"—and heard, for the largely black choir still wear Eton collars and pinstripe trousers.

Map 1 G1

St Mark, Dalston, in 1960 (National Monuments Record, Crown copyright)

35
Whitehall Club
47 PARLIAMENT STREET, SW1

1865–6
Charles Octavius Parnell

This former club-house stands on the south side of the junction of Parliament Street with Derby Gate. It is one of the most distinguished mid-Victorian palazzi in London; described at the time it was built as "florid Italian", it is a creditable essay in a Classic style which might be described as "Mannerist". There is the heavy rich cornice beloved by both 16th-century Italians and the early Victorians. Below this is a row of *oeil-de-boeuf* windows separated by luscious swags; indeed, the architect managed to make the windows on each floor interesting and different. The building is, in fact, closely modelled on Sansovino's St Mark's Library in Venice, but is none the worst for that.

In the handling of the orders, Parnell showed he was fully aware both of Classic grammar and its purely expressive and decorative potential. The building is essentially a rusticated stone cube with a very heavy cornice.

On the Parliament Street front, the arched ground floor windows are incorporated into an Ionic order where thick entablature runs right around the building. The Corinthian order above is differently treated, its entablature only appearing in places; the rusticated wall of the third storey above is left plain.

The building, therefore, gets less heavy as it rises, and this most satisfactory architectural treatment is subtly different on the longer Derby Gate façade, where there is a prominent entrance, complex in form with rich sculpture, by Tolmie. Altogether, the design merits study in its expressive and interesting handling of Italian Classicism, as does Sansovino's original prototype.

The Whitehall Club cost £25,000 to build. Originally, "although it includes a number of civil engineers, contractors and others, having occasional business in the Committee rooms of the Houses of Parliament . . . is not restricted to any special class, and is non-political". For many years the building has been used for government offices.

The architect, Charles Octavius Parnell, died in 1865 and the building was completed by his son C. Jocelyn Parnell. Parnell, Senior designed two other excellent Classic buildings in London, both of which have been demolished: the Army and Navy Club in Pall Mall and the Westminster Bank in Lombard Street. This Club was also to be swept away in the totalitarian schemes for making Whitehall a bureaucrat's paradise prepared by Sir Leslie Martin, et al. In the latest scheme for new Parliamentary offices by Sir Hugh Casson, this, with the other good buildings in Parliament Street, was to be spared but, fortunately, this project has been cancelled.

Map 2 E3

The Whitehall Clubhouse; woodcut published in the Builder, *1866 (Royal Institute of British Architects, London)*

36
St Pancras Station and Hotel

EUSTON ROAD, NW1

Train shed
1865–7
William Henry Barlow & R. M. Ordish

Midland Hotel
DESIGNED 1865
George Gilbert Scott
BUILT 1868–77

a *The Midland Grand Hotel and St Pancras Station; photograph taken soon after completion before the construction of the adjacent Midland Railway Somers Town goods depot (National Monuments Record, Crown copyright)*
b *Interior of the train shed of St Pancras Station; late 19th-century photograph*

"Railway termini and hotels are to the nineteenth century what monasteries and cathedrals were to the thirteenth century. They are truly the only real representative buildings we possess. . . . Our metropolitan termini have been leaders of the art spirit, of our time", remarked the *Building News* in 1875. In the following year, the hotel at St Pancras Station was almost complete. It is the most spectacular of all the great Victorian stations, yet its architect took his inspiration from the Gothic of the 13th century. In the days when it was fashionable to admire the functional simplicity of King's Cross, jokes like "c'est magnifique, main ce n'est pas la gare" were made about St Pancras. But not only is St Pancras visually marvellous and one of the great landmarks of London, it also works.

The heart of the wealthy Midland Railway was Derby. When the company secured permission in 1865 to build their own train line to London, they were determined that their new terminus would outshine both King's Cross next door and Euston down the road.

The line from Bedford and St Albans came in under Haverstock Hill, over the Regent's Canal and through old St Pancras churchyard (Thomas Hardy, working for A. W. Blomfield in his brief and unsuccessful career as an architect, had the unpleasant job of supervising the exhumation of the bodies). The railway arrived on the Euston Road, replacing the slums of Agar Town, high above the street level, whereas King's Cross is low down as the Great Northern went *under* the canal.

The first spectacular aspect of the station is the train shed, designed by the engineer of the line, William Henry Barlow (1812–1902) in conjunction with R. M. Ordish. So as to achieve the maximum flexibility, a shed was designed without any intervening columns: a height of 100 feet and a clear span of 243 feet which was the largest in the world for many years. It was, in fact, the ultimate expression of that desire for size and space which railway station builders pursued for no real functional or economic reason. The great trusses, made by the Butterley Iron Co, disappear through the floor, to be linked by tie-beams at ground level, in order to

c Design for the restaurant in the Midland Grand Hotel; perspective probably drawn by T. G. Jackson (Royal Institute of British Architects, London)

create a basement whose internal columns (supporting the tracks and platform) were spaced in a multiple of the size of barrels of Burton beer.

The station was opened in 1868. A competition for the station hotel was held in 1865, after Barlow had designed his shed. "As if by anticipation its section was a pointed arch", (for reason of wind resistance), remarked the winner, George Gilbert Scott (1811–78) who "was persuaded (after more than once declining) by my excellent friend Mr. Joseph Lewis, a leading director of (the) Company". One wonders how he was persuaded, for he defeated Owen Jones, George Somers Clarke and E. M. Barry in the limited competition, despite exceeding the brief in the number of storeys and having an estimate more than £50,000 over that of the next competitor (a storey was omitted in the executed building). No doubt the Midland Railway directors were content to have secured the services of the most famous Gothic Revival architect of the day. Work began in earnest on the Midland Hotel in 1868; it was opened in 1873 but not finally completed until 1877.

An old *canard* is that Scott simply re-used his rejected Gothic design for the Foreign Office (29). Comparison of the two designs is enough to disprove this: the 1856 design was symmetrical about a central tower with an axial plan; the Midland Hotel is supremely picturesque, with a clock tower and spire at one end, and the other bending round to meet the street. Scott himself admitted that "having been disappointed, through Lord Palmerston, of my ardent hope of carrying out my style in the Government offices . . . I was glad to be able to erect one building in that style in London".

That style was one which Scott evolved to show that Gothic was not just a style for churches, but a rational way of building for all purposes, a fundamental principle of the Revival after Pugin, which was the theme of Scott's book *Secular and Domestic Architecture* of 1857. Scott recalled that for the Government Offices he "designed windows suited to all positions, and of all varieties of size, form and grouping; doorways, cornices, parapets, and imaginary combinations of all these, carefully studying to make them all thoroughly practical. . . . I did not aim at making my style 'Italian Gothic'; my ideas ran much more upon the French . . . I did, however, aim at gathering a few hints from Italy [and] . . . I also aimed at another thing which people consider Italian—I mean a certain squareness and horizontality of outline. This I consider pre-eminently suited to the street front of a public building. I combined this, however, with gables, high pitched roofs, and dormers".

All this also applies to the Midland Grand Hotel, which is like no mediaeval building. Scott gave the maximum richness and visual interest to the vast bulk, and made each storey different in treatment. Indeed, perhaps Scott made it too rich for a mere railway hotel, and he thought "it is possibly *too good* for its purpose". This was an opinion endorsed by one hostile critic. Writing in 1872, J.T. Emmett thought that "there is here a complete travesty of noble associations, and not the slightest care to save these from sordid contact. An elaboration that might be suitable for a chapter-house of a Cathedral choir, is used as an advertising medium for bagmen's bedrooms and the costly discomforts of a terminus hotel". Such was the Victorian principle of "propriety": there was a scale of degree of ornament thought desirable for the level of importance of a building, from a humble cottage to a cathedral. Pugin, like Emmett, would have placed a railway hotel lower in the hierarchy than the status suggested by Scott's architectural treatment.

The materials are throughout magnificent: Gripper bricks from Nottingham, Ketton stone and terra cotta; Leicestershire slates, iron work by Skidmore of Coventry—this, like the careful carving of the capitals, shows Scott's great interest in all the arts and crafts connected with building.

Most of the interior has been spoiled, but the Grand Staircase survives untouched, with four flights rising under the vault of the western tower, and cantilevered out into space on girders, moulded and pierced for decoration. These show Scott's affection for "architecturalizing cast-iron beams" and that he, as a Victorian Gothicist, was not at all ashamed of being seen to be using iron, as so often is claimed, but thought that "iron constructions are, if anything, *more* suited to Gothic than classic architecture", although "it is not, perhaps, suited to every class of building."

It must be stressed that Scott's plan at St Pancras is very practical. The space left between the hotel (sensibly placed to conceal the great arch of the train shed and separated from it so as to limit the noise and smoke) and the Euston Road contains a ramp to attain the two arches piercing the hotel, that in the west going through to the booking hall, conveniently placed at the corner of the concourse (and which still retains its original ticket office although the timber roof was destroyed in 1938), and that on the east for the exit of arriving passengers.

When built, with its hydraulic lifts and electric bells, the Midland Hotel was the height of luxury. Curiously Sir Gilbert Scott's eldest son, a brilliant architect, whose career had been ruined by drink and bouts of insanity, was staying there in 1897 when he died. By 1935, the hotel had become shabby and it was closed by the London, Midland and Scottish Railway and has been used ever since as offices.

The LMS has been criticised for this action, but the building still stands when it might well have been demolished as a "hideous Victorian" white elephant. In

d *Photograph of the Booking Hall in 1876 by Bedford Lemere showing Scott's original roof and ticket office (Public Record Office)*

the 1930s St Pancras was condemned by architects and men of taste while Classic Euston was appreciated. The Chairman of the LMS, Sir Josiah Stamp, complained at the RIBA Annual Dinner in 1933 that "vain are my struggles to invent any plan for a new Euston which will not involve the destruction of that Hall! With the sight of Carlton House Terrace and the Adelphi in front of me in the papers daily I can hear the cries of those whose responsibility to sentiment and the aesthetic is greater than it is to my shareholders".

Such may seem depressingly familiar from a businessman, but Stamp, who confessed that "I am the last remaining man, with the mid-Victorian spirit, who is sufficiently philistine and bourgeois and altogether out of the running, to be an unashamed admirer of the Albert Memorial", felt differently about the work of Sir Gilbert Scott "whose methods and ideals I, personally, still revere". He put it to the architects that, "Here I am responsible in less than sixty years, for a building which is completely obsolete and hopeless as an hotel, and even worse than useless as offices; will it be vandalism of the worst order to destroy it? . . . We can either keep it for a revival of appreciation, with a dead economic loss for the site it occupies and the use to which it is put, or we can pull it down and impose on the site something that can be equally condemned in its turn in 60 years' time".

Fortunately Stamp did not listen to the advice of experts and his intended destruction of old Euston was prevented by the outbreak of war. That station's sad eventual fate awaited the advent of the nationalised railway industry which also made strenuous efforts in the 1960s to do the same to King's Cross and St Pancras. At the time of writing British Rail are cleaning and repairing the Midland Hotel while the future of the original St Pancras booking hall remains in doubt.

Map 2 E1

37
Holly Village

SWAIN'S LANE AND CHESTER ROAD, HIGHGATE,
N6

1865
Henry Darbishire

This curious group of cottages was built by the great Victorian lady philanthropist Baroness Burdett-Coutts. She was described by Charles Dickens as "that Lady Bountiful, at once wise gentle and charitable". Lady Burdett-Coutts was England's most eligible heiress. She thought that the only suitable man for her to marry was the Duke of Wellington; in later life, she fell matrimonial victim to a young American adventurer. She lived in some splendour in Regency Holly Lodge (demolished in 1922) and erected nearby this fantasy village to house her most trusted servants. Like other benefactors, the Baroness lived up on the northern heights of London but she worked all her life to improve the lot of the poor in the more squalid easterly parts of the metropolis, as well as being the sole benefactress of St Stephen, Rochester Row. She had a favourite architect, H. A. Darbishire who devised the prototype block of dwellings for the Peabody Trust. Darbishire's best work was the great towered Columbia Market (99) in Bethnal Green which stood at the centre of the Baroness's dwellings for the poor, Columbia Square. At Holly Village, Darbishire placed eight cottages ornés around a green. The symmetrical gatehouse gives a foretaste of the elaborate Gothic style timber ornament. The archway bears the inscription, "Holly Village erected by A. G. B. Coutts A.D. 1865", between two saintly figures. The little houses all vary slightly from each other in their irregularity and quaintness and the two that face across the lawns at right angles to the gatehouse have handsome, if architecturally odd, timbered towers. The materials are simple, stock brick, slates and unpainted timber detailing. It is the timber that is particularly delightful, especially some of the more artfully contrived bargeboards on the gables. The whole ensemble is the apotheosis of Victorian rustic fretwork. One cannot be certain why Darbishire and his rich patroness chose to build such a wilfully rustic conception. They must have had one eye on Nash's Blaise Hamlet and the other on his Park Villages, but the result is a very late flowering of the picturesque. Today the tiny village has a more eccentric air than it would have possessed when it was a part of the entire Coutts estate. The cottages no longer house devoted domestics and the Baroness's benevolence has been replaced by burglar alarms and the sprouting of aerials for colour television sets. But the atmosphere of a secret Gothic world beside Highgate cemetery is still very powerful. Densely planted holly, ivy and a pair of appropriate Araucarias perfect the prickly illusion.

Map 1 E1
Holly Village, Highgate (Country Life)

38
Abbey Mills Pumping Station

ABBEY LANE, WEST HAM, E15

1865–8
J. Bazalgette & E. Cooper

This building is, perhaps, more of a curiosity than an example of distinguished architecture. It is, however, very typical of many mid-Victorian public and utilitarian buildings in the cheerful, vulgar and practical eclecticism of its style.

The pumping station lies next to the embankment of the northern outfall sewer, the level of which its pumps raise. Although a utilitarian building, it is far from utilitarian in appearance, and in its details and finish is given all the quality and solidity the Victorians gave to their public utilities. The pumping station, like the railways, was built to last. The building is cruciform in plan and its Byzantine, almost Russian appearance is accentuated by the central dome. The style is a sort of Italian mediaeval, with the round arch and pointed extrados of a Ruskinian flavour favoured by architects like Aitchison and Deane and Woodward in the City. The interior, however, is all iron, a vast galleried space

Abbey Mills Pumping Station in 1968 (Greater London Council)

designed to contain the big beam engines which once stood here (replaced by electric motors in 1933). The cast-iron columns are in a mediaeval style with rich capitals; these support iron arches and railings embellished with typical High Victorian motifs including decorative infills of the spiky forms associated with designers like Christopher Dresser.

Cooper was the architect and Bazalgette the engineer to the whole London main drainage system. The Metropolitan Board of Works, created in 1855, set about dealing with the obnoxious problem of London's sewage after 1859. Since the abolition of cesspools in 1847, the Thames had been an open sewer, the smell of which in hot weather occasionally obliged Parliament to adjourn.

Bazalgette planned a series of east-west main sewers to connect with the many which flowed into the Thames. The most difficult to construct was the one which ran by the river, and which was facilitated by the construction of London's greatest mid-19th-century improvement—the Victoria Embankment. This, with its massive granite walls and cast-iron dolphin lamps, was designed by Bazalgette to contain the low level sewer in 1862 and built, from Westminster to Blackfriars, in 1864–8. It was then immediately dug up again to build the Metropolitan District Railway and was opened in 1870. The Albert Embankment (opposite Westminster) and the Chelsea Embankment followed in the next decade.

As part of this system Bazalgette planned other pumping stations. The Western Pumping Station, on the Embankment at Chelsea by the Grosvenor Railway Bridge, SW1 was built in 1873 to the design of Bazalgette and T. Lovick in a utilitarian French Renaissance style with a full pavilion roof. That at Deptford Creek was built in 1862 in an Italianate style. Bazalgette was knighted in 1874.

Map 1 H2

39
St Saviour

ABERDEEN PARK, HIGHBURY, N5

1865–6
William White

This church was paid for by Canon Morrice of Salisbury and the site was given by F. T. Mackreth of Canonbury Park so as to provide a place of worship with a daily service and an Anglo-Catholic ritual in the very Protestant parish of Islington. The resulting church was exotic in style, materials and religion.

The architect was William White (1825–1900), an architect approved of by the *Ecclesiologist* since the 1840s and associated in his work with Butterfield and Street. In the 1850s he became as obsessed as Butterfield with brick polychromy and his architecture was inventive in plan and detail. St Saviour was one of his finest churches (perhaps the best is at Lyndhurst, Hants, of 1859), constructed almost entirely of brick, including the piers and shafts, and the vaulting of the sanctuary. The nature of the material determined the sometimes strange profiles of the arches and, in different parts of the structure, different patterns of the polychromatic combination of red, white and black bricks are evident. Furthermore, in places such as the chancel arch, conventionalised floral decoration is thinly painted over the brick, " as a kind of see-through lace".

Unusually for a mid-Victorian church, there is a central tower, about which the nave, chancel and transepts are grouped. The nave is higher than the chancel, and great play is made with the different heights of arches internally. The rather Continental flavour of the brick Gothic is increased by the low octagonal tower with its short spire; internally the transition from the square to octagon is made by brick squinch arches which are also reminiscent of Islamic architecture.

Throughout there is evidence of an original mind at work. The chancel is particularly strange: most of it has a wooden roof except for the easternmost bay which has the side walls canted in towards the 14th-century style window, creating a complex shape which is vaulted in brick.

William White is not to be confused with two other architects of the same name. He was also an inventor and a man of many enthusiasms, including Swedish gymnastics and mountaineering, and the author of *The Tourist's Knapsack and its Contents* and *Domestic Plumbing*. Mark Girouard notes that he "spent much of his life balanced on the boundary between crankiness and brilliance; in the end he fell off on the wrong side . . ." He designed several other churches in London, notably All Saints, Talbot Road, Notting Hill, W11 (1852–5), of stone, whose colossal west tower has never received its spire, and several churches in Battersea, SW11: St Mark, Battersea Rise (1873–4); St Peter, Plough Road (1875–6); St Mary-le-Park, Albert Bridge Road (1881, unfinished) and St Stephen, Battersea Park Road (1886–7), all comparatively cheap but interesting brick churches.

Map 1 F1

St Saviour, Aberdeen Park; perspective by Cory, 1865 (National Monuments Record, Crown copyright)

40
St Martin
VICAR'S ROAD, NW5

1865–6
Edward Buckton Lamb

Edward Buckton Lamb (1806–69) was one of those Victorian architects characterised as a "rogue" by Goodhart-Rendel, as he was a man who did not fit nicely into any tradition but who was conspicuous for his eccentricity. This, his principal church, has been illuminatingly compared by Summerson with St James-the-Less (23) of a few years before. It differs from Street's Tractarian essay in the Vigorous style in almost every way: in its type of Gothic, in its plan, its materials and its patronage.

It was built for John Derby Allcroft, an Evangelical glove manufacturer (who also paid for St Jude, Collingham Gardens (1870–1)) by Godwin and who built Stokesay Court, Salop for himself in 1889 (it was designed by Thomas "Victorian" Harris). Most of Lamb's churches were Low Church and he had no interest in a "correct" ecclesiological or Tractarian plan. Instead, his churches experimented with centralised plans in the tradition of Wren. At St Martin the plan is cruciform with the roof over a large central space supported on four columns; Goodhart-Rendel thought this was "a completely original and, I think, almost perfect solution of what a large auditorium for protestant services should be".

The *Ecclesiologist* had long given up noticing Lamb's churches, and when it had done before its comments had been unflattering: Christ Church, West Hartlepool (1854–5) was described as "one of those uncouth and grotesque combinations of incongruous architectural *tours-de-force* which it requires the inartistic and withal presumptuous mind of Mr. Lamb to conceive". They did not like his plans, or his style, as Lamb was quite untouched by the orthodoxy which demanded Decorated or Middle Pointed Gothic for reproduction. Instead he used the despised Perpendicular or Third Pointed style which Ruskin and others thought "debased".

Lamb handled this style in an utterly idiosyncratic manner. The exterior of St Martin—in rubble stone, not brick as Street or Butterfield were using in London—had odd Perpendicular windows, odd buttresses and odd pinnacles. Lamb's recurrent motif was his manner of both cutting back and building up wall surfaces by means of repeated 45° chamfers and then corbelling out. This is due to the asymmetrical placed tower which, when it had its full complement of pinnacles, must have been even more strange.

The interior is simply extraordinary. The rough stone is exposed on the inside as well as outside and the central space is covered by a massive and self-consciously complex timber roof whose supporting columns demonstrate all of Lamb's chamfering mannerisms in their height.

Lamb was fully aware that he was unorthodox. He even dared to admire Georgian architecture, including Gower Street which symbolised all that was most depressing for Ruskin and Scott, and stated that "few have dared to traverse the paths of original thought—few have dared to shake off the fetters and enter the broad field of invention . . . the efforts at original thought, and where a disposition is evinced to shake off the trammels of precedent, are met with doubt and ridicule". Whether Lamb's designs are aesthetically successful, of course, is quite another matter.

One explanation for Lamb's eccentricity is that he was much older than all the Tractarian Gothic Revivalists. He had been educated in the purely picturesque school of Gothic and had worked for J. C. Loudon on his *Encyclopaedia*. His Gothic style and approach were formed

a *St Martin, Gospel Oak; woodcut of the exterior published in the* Builder, *1866*

85

b *Interior of St Martin in 1966 (National Monuments Record, Crown copyright)*

before Pugin and the Cambridge Camden Society laid down their doctrinaire principles.

Lamb designed St Mary Magdalen, Addiscombe, in 1868 and was Disraeli's architect when Hughenden was transmogrified in 1862. He died, bankrupt, in 1869. His obituarist in the *Builder* noted that "he was by no means an architect of the pattern book school, but constantly endeavoured, even at the expense of beauty, to exhibit originality".

Map 1 E1

41
St Peter
LONDON DOCKS, WAPPING LANE, E1

1865–6
Frederick Hyde Pownall

1884–94
Maurice Bingham Adams

The story of this church is really the story of its great founding priest Father Charles Lowder. It stands now, lonely among the deserted docks of Wapping. The entrance is under an arch into a little courtyard where the church and the rather solemn clergy house meet. Father Lowder, as he was always known to his parishioners, came to East London from a curacy at St Barnabas, Pimlico (9), the scene, in 1851, of riots and disturbances sparked off by resentful and ignorant Puritans. Lowder survived these "No Popery" mobs promoted by Lord John Russell but was to face more controversy in his next post, when he moved to Hawksmoor's church of St George-in-the-East in 1856 to take charge of the Mission which was to be the scene of even more appalling riots in 1859–60 and to become the seed from which St Peter, London Docks would grow. Father Lowder was thirty-six when he moved in to the Mission House in Calvert Street; for twenty-four years, he laboured in the vice-ridden, diseased and poverty-stricken streets of East London. It was not until St Peter's Day, 1865 that the first stone of a permanent new church in Old Gravel Lane was laid. Because of the swampy nature of the site, exceptional foundations were needed—the clergy house is in fact built on piles—and accordingly the cost was high. Building started to the designs of F. H. Pownall.

The most straightforward description of the church is that given by Father Lowder himself in the year of the church's consecration, 1866: it is "in the style of the later First Pointed Gothic, being faced externally with yellow stock bricks, relieved with stone dressings, and internally with red bricks, having bands and patterns of black bricks. The columns of the main arches are of blue Pennant stone. The plan consists of a lofty nave, sixty-eight feet by twenty-seven, with clerestory lights. It is at present four bays in length; the three western have north and south aisles ten feet wide. The west walls are tempor-

St Peter, London Docks; interior in 1950 (National Monuments Record, Crown copyright)

ary, with provision for an extension, and for a north-west tower and slated spire. Eastward of the nave are transepts north and south, connected with it by lofty arches piercing the clerestory. The chancel is thirty-five feet long by twenty-two feet wide, with two trefoiled windows in the east end, surmounted by a shafted wheel window about seventeen feet in diameter. On the south side of the chancel is a chapel much beloved by the people, called after the iron church, the Chapel of the Good Shepherd."

When Lowder died in 1880, further works at the west end were proposed as his memorial. Frederick Hyde Pownall (born 1825) was no longer the architect: very possibly he had gone over to Rome in the meantime. In 1881 the new clergy house by the street was commenced; the church is now approached through the tile-lined passage behind its Gothic entrance arch. Its architect was an obscure and mediocre figure, Bowes A. Paice, who retired owing to ill-health in 1882 and died the following year. Paice was succeeded by the much more interesting Maurice B. Adams (1849–1933), the prolific draughtsman and editor of the *Building News*, who prepared elaborate designs for a baptistery, mortuary chapel and a new west front and tower for the church. Work on these was begun in about 1884 and the mortuary chapel finished the following year but the designs for the west end of the

church were greatly altered and cheapened before being finished in 1894. Adams's redbrick new front only rose to half its intended height, leaving Pownall's old stock brick gable above and behind. Adams's best work is the baptistery on the south side of the new front; this is vaulted in brick and has a font-cover suspended from a charming Queen Anne style bracket.

In 1939 it was decided to complete the building and finally to abandon the projected tower and spire. The idea of a west organ gallery was also then abandoned which means that the staircase in Adams's baptistery goes nowhere. As soon as the new work was completed it was seriously damaged in 1940 by a bomb which virtually destroyed the clergy house. Both were repaired in 1948–9, the clergy house losing a floor.

The interior of St Peter is filled with pictures and pious relics of its founders. There is a pulpit from the Margaret Street Chapel and another one from A. W. Blomfield's St Barnabas, Jericho, Oxford. The organ remains in a temporary position and the capitals of the columns are as yet uncarved, but none of this diminishes the almost brutal integrity of the brick architecture. St Peter may not be of the highest architectural distinction but it is well worth visiting the neglected and now rather desolate streets of Wapping to see a noble social experiment as well as a powerful example of the Vigorous style.

Map 1 G3

42
Royal Albert Hall of Arts and Sciences

KENSINGTON GORE, SW7

DESIGNED 1866
Francis Fowke and Henry Young Darracott Scott

BUILT 1867–71

Indisputably, the Victorians were obsessed with style, but that did not prevent the production of a genuinely original and characteristic architecture of their own. Although very much the creation of committees of artists and experts, the Albert Hall is an extraordinary structure quite without precedent but perhaps it is loved less for its style and decoration than for the place it has occupied in the cultural life of London.

The building is now the most conspicuous example of the "South Kensington Style", the product of the curious circumstance that the Government turned, not to architects, but to Royal Engineers for the design of the cultural buildings in Kensington—just as happened with the public buildings of the Indian Empire. The first designs were prepared by Captain Francis Fowke, RE (1823–65) architect of the South Kensington Museum (26) and the buildings for the 1862 International Exhibition on the adjacent site. After Fowke's death, the artistic dictator of South Kensington, Henry Cole, determined that no outside architect should be brought in but that the Albert Hall should be designed by Fowke's colleague in the Science and Art Department, Lieutenant Colonel Henry Young Darracott Scott (no relation), RE (1822–83). It was always very much Cole's policy at the South Kensington Museum to keep work in the hands of those he could influence rather than employ outside and more talented professionals. Lord Derby, Prime Minister when the Hall was begun, described Cole as "one of the most generally unpopular men I know".

From the beginning the problem with the Albert Hall was its indeterminate function; Cole envisaged it as both a giant music and choral hall and also as a conference centre. The idea may have originated with the Prince Consort back in 1853; when he died in 1861 his former secretary, General Charles Gray, actively promoted the idea of a memorial hall as a cultural project close to Albert's heart. The following year the architects invited to submit designs for the Albert Memorial (31) naturally also considered the Hall; possibly Matthew Digby Wyatt's scheme was its real prototype. Gilbert Scott's project of 1863 was a domed "hall of science" based on Santa Sophia.

Cole, a virulent critic of the winning design for the Albert Memorial, could scarcely ignore Gilbert Scott's claim for consideration. In 1863, he proposed a compromise, that Scott should do the exterior—a masking block of chambers in the Gothic style facing the Memorial—while his own man Fowke should do the interior. In 1864, realising that all the Memorial funds available would be consumed by Gilbert Scott's Gothic shrine, Cole became impatient and wrote to Grey that "I have come to the conclusion that the only way to the get the Memorial Hall done is to *do* it!" He appealed for subscribers—with the Queen's approval—to buy seats and boxes in the Hall and in the event it was built entirely without recourse to public funds. In the 19th century, private enterprise got things done.

By 1865 Gilbert Scott's name and masking block had been quietly dropped and Fowke prepared a scheme for an oval hall based on the idea of a Roman Amphitheatre. The general interior configuration was largely settled by the time of Fowke's untimely death; H. Y. D. Scott, firmly in possession by 1866, had to deal chiefly with the exterior. Scott's design of 1866—on which construction began the following year after the foundation stone had been laid by the Queen—was further simplified before the building was completed. Perhaps it should be said that the plan is very simple—if not crude and naive—compared with the contemporary Opéra in Paris. It is simply an oval surrounded by corridors, with no great public spaces.

One remarkable feature, the great wide "promenade" behind a continuous arcade which circles the interior high above the seats, was Fowke's. Perhaps Scott's chief contribution was the roof over the vast internal space, 185 by 219 feet. This is a triumph of Victorian engineering: a construction of great trussed girders which, on the exterior, supports a glazed flat oval dome. Scott was here assisted by J. W. Grover and R. M. Ordish—the latter, shortly before, had been connected with the train shed at St Pancras Station (36). Another triumph of construction was the great organ which dominates the interior; this, designed by Henry Willis, was, naturally, the largest in the world at the time.

The exterior of the Hall is characteristic of South Kensington: a round arched, North Italian style in modern materials: red brick and terra cotta. This was certainly the style favoured by Prince Albert thanks to his architectural mentor, Gottfried Semper, who was exiled in England from 1849–53, and, indeed, Scott's design of 1866

a *Exterior of Albert Hall (National Monuments Record, Crown copyright)*

was redolent of Semper's first Dresden opera house of 1837–41. Scott later dispensed with the buttresses to the dome and added a continuous balcony. Above this last is the conspicuous "Art" on the exterior: the continuous

b *The interior of the Albert Hall at its opening in 1871 (Illustrated London News)*

frieze designed, in sections, by Stacy Marks, Pickersgill, Yeames, Poynter, Armitage, Armstead and Horsley.

Their drawings were enlarged by photography and handed to the South Kensington Museum Ladies' Mosaic Class, who produced the black, chocolate and buff ceramic mosaic with the help of Mintons. Other terracotta decoration in the building was designed by two artists attached to the South Kensington Museum: James Gamble and Reuben Townroe.

Queen Victoria opened the "Royal Albert Hall of Arts

and Sciences" in 1871; she recorded that "I had never been at so big a function since beloved Albert's time, and it was naturally trying and 'émotionnant' for me". The public were suitably impressed by a modern building which could hold up to 10,000 people. Some were more critical; Sidney Colvin, Slade Professor at Cambridge, thought it "more of an engineer's than an architect's building and is far from faultless" and Lady Eastlake considered "the Hall looks ill at a distance, being low and formless in ouline; but, seen near, it . . . is both sumptuous and elegant. Much depends in its keeping its agreeable colour", a first judgement which surely still holds.

Then came the usual controversy about who really designed it, ie Scott or Fowke, after Cole quarrelled with Henry Scott. Scott, after all, was not an architect and had little experience of such work; he depended much on his draughtsmen: Gilbert Redgrave and Thomas Verity, the latter detailed the interior. Scott was also advised by professionals, notably Richard Redgrave and Digby Wyatt, who took a close interest in the project. There was also that interesting and ubiquitous figure in South Kensington, J. W. Wild, hovering in the background. All things considered, the resulting architectural treatment is remarkably coherent and successful.

The Albert Hall was bedevilled by financial difficulties in the early days. The Hall always suffered from two great problems: first its comparative inaccessibility from central London—the short underground passage opened in 1885 from South Kensington Station was the optimistic beginning of a tram and pedestrian tunnel; and second, the famous echo. This was finally cured in 1968–9 by the suspended mushroom "diffusers" which are rather less attractive than the original calico "velarium" suspended from the ceiling and decorated by Townroe.

Behind the Albert Hall are two more characteristic monuments of South Kensington: the Memorial to the 1851 Exibition (1858), rightly surmounted by a statue of Prince Albert, and the Royal College of Organists (1875), an incredibly Germanic little building with *sgraffito* decoration, designed by another Royal Engineer, H. H. Cole.

Map 2 A4

43
London University Buildings, now the Museum of Mankind
BURLINGTON GARDENS, W1

1866–9
James Pennethorne

The Classical tradition may have become enfeebled during the heady years of the High Gothic Revival, but it never died, and one of its ablest exponents was Sir James Pennethorne (1801–71). He trained in the office of John Nash, to whom, and to whose important client, the Prince of Wales, he is sometimes supposed to have had a rather unorthodox family connection. Certainly Pennethorne's career enjoyed Establishment patronage: he became a joint architect to the Commissioners of Woods and Forests in 1838 (sole architect in 1845) and as such continued Nash's type of work. He laid out New Oxford Street (1845–7) to connect Oxford Street with High Holborn, Kensington Palace Gardens (1843) and several parks, including those at Kennington, Victoria Park (Hackney) and Battersea. He was always the Government's choice for an important commission and it was Pennethorne's appointment in 1855 to design the new Government Offices which provoked the pressure to hold a competition.

Pennethorne's executed buidings show that he was perfectly competent to carry out such commisions, particularly as he was not at all doctrinaire about style and respected London's building traditions.

Pennethorne's building in Burlington Gardens is a more distinguished Classical work than the buildings by Banks and Barry rising at the Piccadilly end of the Burlington House site at the same time. Employing a giant Corinthian order, with lower wings, on a rusticated basement, the design is well adapted to being seen obliquely, as it always must be: the building has a projecting portico; there are twin square towers, the cornice breaks forward repeatedly and the skyline is enlivened with sculptured figures. These are typical choices: scientists and philosophers, ancient and modern. Those above the portico were carved by J. Durham; those in the niches by P. MacDowell and W. Theed; those on the balustrade by

Former London University building in Burlington Gardens; woodcut published in the Builder, *1867 (Royal Institute of British Architects, London)*

E. W. Wyon, J. S. Westmacott, W. F. Woodington and M. Noble.

Although Pennethorne's wings are well scaled to his tall central block, and their order is carried through consistently behind the giant Corinthian order, supporting arches, this building exemplifies well the contrast between the early and mid-19th-century approaches to Classicism. The neo-Greek phase of the beginning of the century continued the 18th-century concern with organised pure form and the logic of the orders. After the 1830s, however, there was a reaction against the austerity, or boredom, of the Greek; and Victorian Classical buildings are conspicuous for their sculptural richness and greater concern for picturesque variety than for Classical purity.

This may be seen on another of Pennethorne's buildings, the west façade to Somerset House along the approach to Waterloo Bridge. This was a work of 1852–6 which was admired by Pennethorne's contemporaries for its tact and skill in making a grand, monumental composition. Pennethorne commendably continued Chambers's orders and general scheme of articulation, but there are significant differences, notably the profusion of sculpture on the skyline and the fact that the architect was never content to carry through a cornice height consistently. The level of the attic cornice changes, and the central pediment springs from a higher level than the attic storey of the wings. Instead of Chambers's academical reticence there is picturesque movement and a greater impression of sculptural richness, which is not to say that it is not a good work of its sort.

Pennethorne was also adept at Gothic. Indeed the first designs for London University were Gothic but were changed to Classic owing to a change of government in 1866 (Tory to Liberal), similar to the change which so upset Scott's scheme for the Government Offices. Pennethorne's flat brick Gothic may still be seen in the narrow passage which separates the building from the back of the Royal Academy (and A. E. Richardson thought the vertical emphasis of the Burlington Gardens façade was due to its originally being concieved in Gothic terms). Another Gothic work by Pennethorne was the Public Record Office, Fetter Lane, WC2 (1850–1), where a late Gothic style is most rationally adapted to a module determined by the fireproof iron and brick construction and the galleried depository cells. The interior boasts much rational construction and the exterior, with its "horrid crumbly rubble surfaces" (Pennethorne wanted red brick), does not do the design justice. The Chancery Lane end continued Pennethorne's scheme but was built in 1891–6 by Sir John Taylor.

London University moved from Burlington Gardens to Charles Holden's new building in Bloomsbury in the 1930s. Albert Richardson—a stylish and logical Classicist himself—thought this building was Pennethorne's "masterpiece" and wrote (in 1914) that "vulgarity and bad taste were as foreign to Pennethorne as to Cockerell. He occasionally lapsed into megalithic heaviness, such as his two churches evidence [eg Christ Church, Albany Street], but these errors he more than atoned for by the elegance and refinement which distinguish his later works. Pennethorne knew the value of continuing a sound tradition, and while his works reveal his grasp of antique classic architecture, their character is always unmistakably English".

Map 2 D3

44
Dulwich College
COLLEGE ROAD, SE21

1866–70
Charles Barry, Junior

The 19th-century story of Dulwich is that of many public schools: a small, inefficient charity institution being transformed into a large school, modelled on Rugby, destined to turn out the officers and officials the Empire would need. The instrument of change was the Master, the Rev Canon Carver, and the means the fortune made from the south London railway lines which crossed the College's Estate (and which were made to erect ornamental railway bridges cast with the College's arms).

Large new buildings were laid out half a mile south of the old College and Soane's Gallery, just below Sydenham Hill, now surmounted by the re-erected Crystal Palace. The architect chosen was the younger Charles Barry (1823–1900) (Sir Charles had designed the old Grammar School of 1842 on the corner of Gallery Road and Burbage Road). From 1847–72 he was in partnership with R. R. Banks, with whom he designed St Stephen's church, further up College Road (1868–75) and the new Piccadilly front to Burlington House (1869–73). Barry later designed parts of the Great Eastern Hotel, Liverpool Street, and was President of the RIBA (following Sir Gilbert Scott) in 1876–9.

In his Dulwich College buildings, Barry seems to have tried to resolve several of the architectural issues of the day, notably the "Battle of the Styles" and the use of new materials, but it cannot be claimed that he was wholly successful.

In style, the buildings attempt to combine the round-arched Italianate with the picturesqueness and colour achieved by Gothic Revivalists but without the use of the pointed arch. The axial formality of the three big blocks, connected by "cloisters" is broken by picturesque accents: the tower on the south block, the belvedere on the north and the gables and "wedding cake" on the centre block. The skyline was even more romantic before the removal of the chimneys.

So as to achieve sculptural richness, with portrait medallions of Ancient Worthies, the Renaissance style was used, with segment headed windows, as on several office buildings in the City, but in the central block the round-arched tracery of the big windows lighting the hall does not sit at all well under the triangular gables.

The basic material is red brick, but relieved by bands of white brick set at an angle to produce a notched effect comparable with the polychromatic restlessness achieved by some of the "rogues". However, the buildings are remarkable in being the first experiment in the use of terra cotta on a large scale. Barry remarked in 1868, "I have endeavoured to produce a building almost wholly in terra cotta, of varied colours, and striven to embody these in something of the stateliness, and, at the same time, the elegance and fancy in details of old specimens". The porches, window shafts, cornices, parapets and other ornaments are all of terra cotta.

Eclecticism was a perfectly reasonable answer to the limitations of the Renaissance Classical tradition (which was thought boring) and the rigidity of Gothic, but Barry would seem to have combined indifferent aspects of various styles into a fusion which has no consistency. Eclecticism had to wait for the stylishness of Shaw and the Queen Anne before achieving a successful alternative to Gothic. One can only agree with the *Building News* who considered in 1869 that "neither the stateliness nor the eleg-

Dulwich College; woodcut published in the Builder, *1868*

ance [Barry] desired are wanting in the building. As regards the limitation in cost, we cannot think there is evidence of his having suffered much in this respect at the hands of his employers, and cannot bestow much pity on him on that score. We wish he had taken advantage of their liberality in the choice of a style, and adopted a purer and better type".

Ruskin, who lived not far away at Denmark Hill, did not record his views on the new building, but they were unlikely to have been favourable. In 1876 he did comment, however, that "the ghastly squalor of the once lovely fields of Dulwich trampled into mud, and strewn with rags and paper by the filthy London population, bred in cigar smoke, which is attracted by the Crystal Palace, would alone neutralise all possible gentlemanly education in the district". The school library, by the Dulwich Common entrance, was designed by E. T. Hall and built in 1902 and 1909.

Map 1 F5

British and Foreign Bible Society; perspective drawing by I'Anson (Royal Institute of British Architects, London)

45
British and Foreign Bible Society
146 QUEEN VICTORIA STREET, EC4

1866–7
Edward I'Anson

This big Portland stone palazzo is a very fine example of a fusion between Classical proportion and more Gothic styles of decoration achieved by some architects in the mid-19th century.

The basic organisation of the building is Classical: four storeys of diminishing height and a basement; seven regular bays along the newly laid-out Queen Victoria Street and an interesting 1:3:1 rhythm on the side elevation, which was that employed by Barry on the garden side of the Travellers' Club. The palazzo quality is emphasised by the heavy dentil cornice and the battered profile and blunt profiles of the granite basement.

In detail, however, the Classicism is not at all correct: the pilasters are not like proper pilasters, nor are they pilaster strips. They vary in width—those at the corners are made much wider—and between each storey, they become squat flat columns with stiff-leaf capitals of the Italian mediaeval variety liked by Ruskin. The very squashed pilasters of the top storey have sunken ornamental panels with typically High Victorian decoration.

The overall impression, however, is of Italianate dignity, and the windows—both round and square headed, are logically incorporated into the Classical discipline. The large doorway, surmounted by a balcony, is particularly fine as it rises from the pavement through the basement and ground floor. Below the balcony is carved an open book and "The Word of the Lord Endureth for Ever". The incised lettering above the third floor is interesting and good. The interior of the building was designed half as offices and half as a warehouse. The British and Foreign Bible Society had been founded in 1804; in 1865 the Society issued two and a half million Bibles. The President was Lord Shaftesbury.

Edward I'Anson the younger (1812–88) died during his term as President of the RIBA. He was the son of a prosperous surveyor and commercial architect of the same name (1775–1853). According to Alfred Waterhouse, he was "a man of extraordinary industry . . . simple and unostentatious tastes who habitually rose at 5 a.m. and designed buildings in the Italian style remarkable for their breadth and refinement of treatment". He paid particular attention to the design of modern commercial premises and, in 1864, delivered a paper to the Institute on "Office Building in the City" and he was one of the first to use white glazed bricks for City courtyard walls. In 1857 he designed an office block in Fenchurch Street which had more glass than wall in the façade (destroyed). His Corn Exchange Chambers in Seething Lane, EC3 (1859) survive: a redbrick palazzo with Lombardic tracery in the round-arched windows which gives the building the character of Munich. The Corn Exchange itself, designed by I'Anson, has been destroyed. His 65 Cornhill (64) was much more eclectic in style, but his School of Medicine for St Bartholomew's Hospital in Giltspur Street, EC1 (1883) has a seven-bay façade of the utmost Classic gravity and rectitude. Comparatively little-known architects, like I'Anson, John Gibson and James Williams, the Post Office's architect, carried on the best aspects of the Classical tradition, not without skill and originality, much longer than is usually realised and right through and beyond the years of the Gothic Revival.

Map 2 G2

General Credit Company building in Lothbury; perspective, 1866 (Royal Institute of British Architects, London)

46
General Credit Company, now offices
7 LOTHBURY, EC2

1866
George Somers Clarke, Senior

Gothic never really displaced the Classical tradition for commercial patronage. This building is one of the few, and certainly the best of the Gothic buildings in the City.

The General Credit Company, incorporated in 1863, was one of several joint-stock discount companies with limited liability promoted after the mid-1850s. Gothic was, no doubt, considered more fashionable and striking for the new company than the Classical buildings around, but the Gothic chosen, Venetian, was no longer current in advanced architectural circles. No matter; the architect, George Somers Clarke (1829–82), (not to be confused with his son who, in partnership with J. T. Micklethwaite, was a late Victorian church architect) had had a Classical training with Sir Charles Barry and was not at all doctrinaire about style. His Merchant Seamen's Asylum at Wanstead (93) is the most splendid of Venetian Gothic buildings.

Certainly, this building is very literally derived from the *Stones of Venice* and the tall, narrow Lothbury façade could be overlooking a canal. Here is everything Ruskin liked: much carved detail, a sculptured frieze. a balcony, and each storey is treated differently as far as possible. But the elevation—particularly the long one to Tokenhouse Yard—is very logically organised and has little of the asymmetrical whimsy indulged in by the hard Goths. The areas of architectural detail are balanced against areas of bare wall and are framed by the liberal use of the billet moulding. Indeed, the area of bare wall stretching the full height of the building can almost be read as pilasters like those in Edwardian stripped Classic work which organise several floors of a commercial building in a logical system. The top floor, with banks of small windows placed next to each other, can almost be read as a big cornice.

The building has been altered by a door opening on the Lothbury front.

Map 2 G2

47
Leighton House
12 HOLLAND PARK ROAD, W14

1865–79
George Aitchison & Frederick Leighton

This house, and Val Prinsep's house next door, were the first to be built in what became an artists' quarter. They were not, however, for the first artists to arrive. In 1850 George Frederick Watts had arrived at Little Holland House, occupied by the nabob Henry Thoby Prinsep and his artistic wife, the sister of the photographer Julia Margaret Cameron. Watts "had come to stay for three days and remained for thirty years"; here he was to meet and marry the young Ellen Terry—a short and disastrous liaison which ended with Ellen running off with E. W.

Godwin and fathering Edward Gordon Craig.

Frederick, Lord Leighton (1830–1896) was beginning to enjoy the fruits of his highly successful career. His *Cimabue's Madonna* had been exhibited at the Royal Academy in 1855 and bought by the Queen; in 1864, the year he took the lease for his new house, he was elected an associate of the RA (he was to be President from 1878 until his death). That Leighton should build his own, lavish house with its large studio was evidence of the increased social status and expressiveness of Victorian artists; the studio, with its large north-facing window, was necessary for painting the very large canvases of historical and naturalistic scenes achieved with the help of models, and the house itself was a vital element as an aspiring Academician held "open house" on Varnishing Day.

Leighton's architect was his "old friend" George Aitchison (1825–1910), who, although a highly competent industrial architect who designed the contemporary office building in Mark Lane in the City (**33**), turned

a *Leighton House, Kensington; perspective view of the Arab Hall drawn by Maurice B. Adams for* Artists' Homes, *1883*

ARTISTS' HOMES Nº7.
STUDIO·AND·RESIDENCE AT HOLLAND PARK
KENSINGTON W
SIR FREDᵏ LEIGHTON PRA GEORGE AITCHISON BᵀA. ARCHITECT

increasingly to the decorative and archaeological side of his art.

The first parts built, completed in 1866, were the three right-hand bays of the façade, an unremarkable neo-Georgian design in redbrick. E. W. Godwin criticised it and observed that "Mr. Webb's work, in Mr. Val Prinsep's house next door, comes into close comparison with it , and is chiefly admirable for the very things in which its neighbour is so utterly deficient—viz., in beauty of skyline and pleasing arrangement of gabled mass". The symmetry of this façade was destroyed in 1877–9 when two lower bays and the Arab Hall were added. Meanwhile the studio had been extended to the east in 1869–70.

The interior of the house, although not furnished and hung as Leighton left it, is a remarkably complete survival of an early Aesthetic interior of the 1860s and 70s, with the added exotic glory of the Arab Hall. The ebonised doors and frames, with their gilded incised decoration, and the odd forms of the lintels being supported by squat columns, are typical of that advanced interior and furniture style of the late 1860s often associated with C. L. Eastlake, author of *Hints on Household Taste* (1869).

The Arab Hall is more archaeological and rich; it was designed by Aitchison, and based upon the Palace of La Zisa in Palermo. Many of the tiles are real Islamic pieces, looted from Persia and Turkey by Leighton (who was an enthusiastic traveller and had been to the East) and his friends Sir Richard Burton and Sir C. Purdon Clarke. The most colourful tiles, however, are those in characteristic Peacock blue by William de Morgan, which also appear lining the staircase walls.

The dome of the Arab Hall, originally gilded, is developed from a square and then an octagon in the usual Islamic manner of squinches. Above the mosaic frieze, designed by Walter Crane, is the lattice screen of a Damascus *zenana* looking down from the painting room on the first floor. The gilded capitals of the column were modelled by Edgar Boehm after Aitchison's design but with the birds designed by Randolph Caldecott, the illustrator. Burke & Co carried out the mosaic; Messrs George P. White the marble work and Marsland and Fisher the painted decoration.

This comparatively small, if tall, room, with its fountain quietly playing in the pool of black marble, succeeds in being both domestic and yet an exotic fantasy, and unites in splendour the best decorative work of the 1870s with the intricacy of Islamic art.

The Great Studio upstairs has a large north-facing window overlooking the garden. There are casts of part of the Parthenon frieze and of Michelangelo's tondo in Burlington House.

Since 1969 Leighton House has housed a fine collection of mid-Victorian paintings, including several by Leighton, whose own collection had been sold at his death. The building adjoining Leighton's winter studio, on the right, is the Perrin Gallery, an unfortunate and very late design by Halsey Ricardo, the architect of the masterpiece of ceramic architecture at 8 Addison Road, nearby.

Map 1 C3

b *Sections through the Arab Hall from the same source*

48
St George's Church, now St George's Theatre

TUFNELL PARK ROAD, N7

1866–8
George Truefitt

St George, Tufnell Park; perspective of 1865 showing original design for top of the tower (National Monuments Record, Crown copyright)

George Truefitt (1824–1902) was surveyor to the Tufnell Park Estate in Holloway, for whose new population he had to provide a temporary church in 1858. His solution was novel: a circular wooden structure with a roof span of 64 feet. Those firm upholders of ecclesiological rectitude and correct church planning, the editors of the *Ecclesiologist*, naturally disliked it and thought that it "would be thoroughly suitable for Cushing's American Circus".

The centralised plan was maintained in the permanent structure. The building is basically circular, with an inner arcade supporting a clerestory. At one end of this auditorium is a projecting apsed chancel; at the other, a detached bell-tower. Even the *Ecclesiologist* had to admit "that a plan of this shape will accommodate a very large number of people with an almost uninterrupted view of pulpit, chancel and altar. . . . It is impossible to deny the credit of much invention and ingenuity to this very abnormal design".

Truefitt was one of those rather noisy young men who were founders of the Architectural Association in 1847 and who were determined to move beyond a tame adherence to precedent in the direction of an original modern architecture. This he thought could be achieved in the Gothic style, in accordance indeed, with Pugin's ideas and the *Ecclesiologist's* doctrine of "development"; however, he was not to be tied by the Tractarian architectural establishment's orthodoxies about church design.

Truefitt thus qualifies to be one of Goodhart-Rendel's "rogues", like E. B. Lamb. In his attempt to be original, his architecture clearly reflects the Vigorous style of Butterfield and Street: there is a strong concentration on basic geometrical forms, no projections forward of the rubble-stone wall, pierced by simple tracery, and the octagonal form of the tower (damaged in a fire) reflects the mannered design Truefitt published in his *Design for Country Churches* of 1850.

However, Tuefitt, like Lamb, tended to be low church and rejected orthodox Tractarian plans in favour of cen-tralised designs; hence the criticisms of the *Ecclesiologist*. The interior, with its awkward arches on ungainly brick columns, can never have been attractive but now with little alteration performs superbly as an Elizabethan theatre in the round.

Map 1 E1

49
House for George Howard
1 PALACE GREEN, KENSINGTON PALACE GARDENS, W8

1868–70
Philip Webb

This house was built by the Hon George Howard, later 9th Earl of Carlisle, an important patron of the arts whose *avant–garde* tastes were shown by his choice of Philip Webb as architect. Webb, in 1867, was comparatively unknown but prominent in the Pre-Raphaelite circle of William Morris, Burne-Jones and Rossetti, in which Howard, an amateur artist, moved.

Howard, despite his wealth and heirdom to Castle Howard, did not get his town house without considerable difficulty; indeed the controversy over Webb's design provides one of the paradigms of battles against conservation on which the ideological history of *avant–garde* art is based.

Because his lease was from the Crown, Howard submitted Webb's original design of 1867 for a house of red brick to the Commissioners of Woods and Forests to see if there was any objection in principle; there was. The Commissioners' architect, James Pennethorne, did not like it and thought the house would be "far inferior to anyone on the Estate—it would look most commonplace—and in my opinion be perfectly hideous". He objected to the materials: "So far as I understand the drawings there would scarcely be any stone visible in the fronts of the house , the whole of the surfaces would be masses of red brickwork without relief from stone or from any important strings or cornices".

Anthony Salvin and T. H. Wyatt were brought in as referees, and rather agreed with Pennethorne who, although an old-fashioned Classicist, had built in Gothic and probably would not have minded if Webb's design was pure Gothic. But it was not, and Webb's attitude to precedent is well expressed by his retort "that Messrs Salvin and Wyatt are 'unable to discover what actual style or period of architecture' I have used, I take to be a sincere compliment".

Some of Webb's details were Gothic, like the porches on the executed design, but, unlike so many 19th-

century architects, he did not rely on pattern books of styles; he thought in Gothic. Here Webb was apparently trying aggressively to be modern; the elements he used in his architecture, like those employed by the early Queen Anne architects, he chose from precedent as appropriate to town houses in England and were an answer to the problem of the Gothic Revival being too churchy. He wrote to Pennethorne: "I must also beg to differ from your opinion that the materials used would not give the proper relief; a well chosen full coloured red brick, with pure bright red gauged brick mouldings, arches, string courses etc. with the addition of white Portland stone, white sash frames, lead and grey slates are in my opinion the very best and most harmoniously coloured materials to be used in London, more especially in a neighbourhood full of green foliage . . . I must express my great surprise that you should consider it worth your while to hinder the erection of a building which—whatever may be its demerits—possesses some character and originality, tempered most certainly with reverential attention to the work of acknowledged masters of the art of architecture, and as certainly framed with the wish to avoid adding another insult to this irreparably injured neighbourhood."

1 Palace Green, Kensington, in 1959 (National Monuments Record, Crown copyright)

But Pennethorne remained adamant. Howard approached Butterfield, who declined to get involved and Webb prepared new designs in 1868 with rather more stone in the elevations. Pennethorne was prepared to accept these, if an 18 inch stone cornice was included. Webb refused to comply and T. H. Wyatt agreed that Webb's brick cornice was quite acceptable. The building was finished and occupied by Howard in 1870.

Many elements in the design—the rubbed brick detail, the white painted sash-frames, the brick lesenes, on pilaster strips, etc—were employed by Queen Anne architects like Shaw, Nesfield and Stevenson. But this is not a Queen Anne house. Number 1 Palace Green exhibits all the high seriousness which Webb originally absorbed from his master G. E. Street; the elevations are composed theoretically according to Pugin's principles of rationality and not with that romantic artistic eye which gave Shaw's houses such style. Webb, indeed, could refer to the "dilettante picturesque of the so-called Queen Anne style". So many of Webb's buildings have a certain awkwardness which was proof of his Gothic Revival and puritanical conscience—Webb was the man who "had to refrain from a lovely fruit pie and strawberries with cream set out to tempt me from the path of wisdom", even though he worked almost exclusively for the rich and grand—and this house is no exception. What compels admiration is the catholic inspiration from varied precedents and the skill with which they are integrated and adapted.

Webb's panelled interiors were once lavishly decorated by Morris & Co, but most were destroyed when the interior was altered in 1957; canvas panels painted by Burne-Jones and Walter Crane are now in the Birmingham City Art Gallery.

Number 1 Palace Green was Philip Webb's principal London house. The house for Val Prinsep, 14 Holland Park Road, of 1864–6, is much more in the redbrick Gothic parsonage manner which Webb first used for William Morris's Red House (1859) while 35 Glebe Place, Chelsea of 1868–9, built for another painter, George Price Boyce, may well indicate how Webb's first design in brick for Palace Green would have looked.

Next door, 2 Palace Green is often thought of as being the prototype Queen Anne house, as its creator, William Makepiece Thackeray, is thought to have given it the character of the 18th century in which many of his novels were set. Built in 1860–2, the rather dreary house was not, in fact, ever noticed by his journals as anything special, although Pennethorne advised Thackeray's dim architect, Frederick Hering, to copy details from Marlborough House.

Map 1 D3

50
St Mary Magdalene
ROWINGTON CLOSE, W2

1867–78
George Edmund Street

This church was founded by the Rev Richard Temple West, curate of All Saints, Margaret Street, whose Paddington members of that Tractarian congregation wanted a more local place of worship. A site was found in 1865 next to the Grand Junction Canal. Building was begun in 1867 and almost completed in 1872 when a fire destroyed the roof. The tower and spire were raised in 1873 and the church was finally consecrated in 1878.

The architect did not mind the time taken over building; indeed Street wrote to West, "happy is the architect who is allowed to build in this way. Most of our churches in these days are built in a hurry, just as if what ought to last for centuries would do appreciably less work if it were, itself, more than a twelve-month coming into full existence. If clergy would do as you do, begin on a large scheme, and build bit by bit, we should have more fine churches, and architects would not complain that nothing grand or noble is possible".

Unfortunately, the logic of the clever plan and form of St Mary Magdalene is rendered immediately unintelligible by the redevelopment of the surrounding area. Originally the church was fitted onto a tight tongue of land where the curve of Clarendon Crescent, following the canal, met Woodchester Street. The spire and apse fitted the apex while the curving wall of the north aisle followed the street line.

Inside, Street cleverly concealed the irregularity of the site of which he was obliged to take full advantage. On the south side there is a full aisle and a transept, but on the north side there is an irregular and almost useless space just beyond the nave arcade. The north and south arcades cleverly balance, but that on the north side is filled in with intervening columns and solid spandrels so as to conceal the irregular space behind.

The stone carving here and the figures on the nave walls and the reredos were the work of Street's favourite carver, Thomas Earp. The reredos dominates a particularly lavish chancel, lined with marble and mosaic, and raised high above the nave, as was the Anglo-Catholic fashion of the 1870s. The superb stained glass was designed by the Pre-Raphaelite painter and illustrator, Henry Holiday, in association with Street. The rather obscure painting of the wooden ceiling was carried out by D. Bell.

In style, St Mary Magdalene marks the change in Street's work from the squat, aggressive toughness of St James-the-Less (23) towards that almost classically assured 13th-century English Gothic he employed at the Law Courts. This church is certainly still High Victorian, with its red brick, banded with stone, both inside and out, its apse and its strange and wonderful spire. It is much more vertical than St James, but still reflects Street's enthusiasm for Italy—*Brick and Marble Architecture in Italy* had been published in 1855— particularly in the tight red and white banding of the tower. In this building, every element shows the mature genius of the architect.

There is a crypt—necessitated because of the dampness of the adjacent canal—vaulted with Dennett's patent concrete. The south aisle of this was transformed, beginning in 1895 by the young J. N. Comper, into a neo-mediaeval fantasy from a late Gothic painting: the blue vaults with stars of mirror glass, extravagant gilt reredos, painted wooden organ and pale glass with figures copied from Memling.

The Lady Altar in the south transept (1922–3) is a good and characteristic work in his Baroque style by Martin Travers.

Map 1 D2

a *St Mary Magdalene, Paddington; photograph taken in Woodchester Street in 1874 (National Monuments Record, Crown copyright)*
b *The church from the east in c1900 with Clarendon Crescent on the right (Courtesy of Paul Joyce)*

51
St Luke

OSENEY CRESCENT, KENTISH TOWN, NW5

1867–9
Basil Champneys

This church was built after the newly erected St Luke, King's Cross, was demolished by the Midland Railway coming into St Pancras. The old church was designed by J. Johnson, who naturally hoped to get the job of another church but, instead, the commission was given to the young Basil Champneys (1842–1935), son of the vicar of St Pancras, who was later Dean of Lichfield.

The result was a powerful essay in the extreme Vigorous style, that is, the no-nonsense reduction of Gothic form to the simple, geometrical forms. In this case the materials are red brick with stone dressings.

The plan is interesting. As at Butterfield's St Matthias, Stoke Newington, the tower is placed over the chancel, a position which eschews the picturesque asymmetry of the north-west or south-west towers favoured by less "hard" Goths, and which gives a church a satisfactorily powerful outline from all angles. Here the sanctuary beyond is apsed and vaulted in brick, and the lean-to aisles are carried either side of the tower, giving an effect which Eastlake called "quasi-cruciform". The windows are either simple lancets (Bumpus calls the style "simple Early Pointed . . . of rather a severe French cast") or, in the apse, Geometrical, with heavy plate tracery. At the west end there is a wheel window.

The most powerful part of the design is the dominating tower, with a bold triangular gable on each face containing a wheel window of plate tracery. This form, which has all the Geometrical simplicity desired by Vigorous style architects, has precedent in the tall brick church towers of north Germany, such as Hanover.

Inside, there is an iron screen, and some Pre-Raphaelite glass; that in the apse was designed by Henry Holiday and made by Heaton, Butler & Bayne, and four windows in the clerestory were by Morris & Co.

This is very much a young man's church. For his first job, Champneys employed the extreme Continental style of the 1860s *avant garde,* but he soon became a master and leader in the next fashionable style—the Queen Anne—and the character of his architecture changed from deliberate coarseness to the most subtle prettiness in such works as Newnham College, Cambridge, begun in 1874.

Champneys became best known for his work for schools and universities. Unlike most of his architect contemporaries, he was an educated man, a Cambridge MA (like George Gilbert Scott, Junior) and the author of several literary works: *A Quiet Corner of England* (1875) and *The Memoirs and Correspondence of Coventry Patmore* (1900).

St Luke's vicarage, described by Eastlake as of "mixed character" with Gothic and Queen Anne elements, was destroyed in the Second World War.

Map 1 E1

St Luke's church and vicarage, Kentish Town; perspective drawn by T. D. Nisbet and published in the Builder, *1870*

52
City Offices Company Building
39–40 LOMBARD STREET, EC3

1868

Frederick John Francis and Horace Francis

Sadly little remains of Victorian Lombard Street, the very epicentre of the world of banking—"by far the greatest combination of economical power and economical delicacy the world has ever seen," Walter Bagehot wrote in 1873—which was the product of a lavish and rapid rebuilding in the 1850s and 1860s. This rebuilding was a result both of mid-Victorian commercial prosperity and the depopulation of the City of London effected by commuter railway lines to the new suburbs.

The process of turning the brick Georgian City into a concentration of stone palazzi of commerce began earlier in the century. It really began in Lombard Street in 1857 when the Royal Insurance Office made a deliberate show with a new building designed by the City architect, John Belcher. In 1863 the same company built again, with a new edifice by the Belchers, father and son (J. & J. Belcher were the architects of the prominent Gothic Mansion House Buildings, opposite the Bank at the very end of the new Queen Victoria Street, happily still extant).

Other new buildings in Lombard Street included the excellent London & County Bank by C. O. Parnell, the architect of the Whitehall Club (35). The premises of the Clydesdale Bank (1865) were remarkable, for its architect Alfred Waterhouse, a young Goth from Manchester, could not bear to design in degenerate Italian Classic and chose a better but appropriate style—Romanesque—which was still round-arched and (vaguely) Italian.

The great boom of the 60s ended dramatically in 1866—and in Lombard Street—when the house of Overend and Gurney suspended payments and closed its doors. "Black Friday" (11 May 1866) produced a panic with political effects; the following economic depression helped cause the riots in Hyde Park (when the railings were uprooted) and, eventually, another measure of Reform.

The City Offices Company building comes right at the end of the Lombard Street rebuilding, both chronologically and physically, as it is right on the corner of Gracechurch Street. Ironically, it survives when all the other palaces have gone—but only recent pressure from the Victorian Society prevented its demolition and now its façade is being restored while the interior is, as always, being gutted and rebuilt.

The brothers Francis provided an epitome of what was required in the City in the 60s—a splendid show in stone, with as much surface richness as possible. All the possibilities of the style are exploited: a ground floor with rustication and big arched windows; columns on the first floor, urns on the second; paired arched windows on the third floor and above that the obligatory thick modillion cornice. Above that, a balustraded parapet, mansard roof and dormers and, finally, a cast-iron decorative railing against the sky. Parnell's building was better (as is the very different type of building by Gibson in Bishopsgate (32)), but this is a fine example of the City tradition, a tradition which received its most sophisticated expression later in the century, when the younger Belcher designed in 1888 the highly influential Institute of Chartered Accountants in Great Swan Alley, off Moorgate.

Frederick John Francis (1818–96) and Horace Francis (1821–94) would do anything: Italianate, as here; Gothic, in several dull churches, such as Christ Church, Lancaster Gate; or in that formless commercial eclectic style of the 70s and 80s, such as the (former) Grand Hotel, Charing Cross (1878–80), on the corner of Trafalgar Square and Northumberland Avenue (now so stupidly shaved of all its mouldings).

Map 2 H2

City Offices Company Building, Lombard Street; woodcut from the Illustrated London News, *1868 (*Illustrated London News*)*

53
Vinegar Warehouse
33–35 EASTCHEAP, EC3

1868
Robert Lewis Roumieu

The architect of this vinegar warehouse and office building was Robert Lewis Roumieu (1814–77) who was a pupil of Benjamin Wyatt and a partner of A. D. Gough from 1836–48. Most of his earlier work was middle-class housing in areas like Islington and Hackney. This building in Eastcheap is one of the reasons why he was identified by H. S. Goodhart-Rendel as a "rogue-architect". Milner Square in Islington (1841–3) is an early example of his talent for strangeness and distortion. The cramped scale, stretched pilasters and horizontal bands of this square produce a design that has been absurdly described, "as near to expressing evil as design can be". Was Roumieu a high Victorian original ahead of his time or just a simple architect with a taste for the picturesque who had not discovered the works of Pugin? There can be no doubt that today we look upon the Eastcheap façade as a very original commercial building. It has always divided the critics. Nikolaus Pevsner described it as "utterly undisciplined and crazy", while Ian Nairn saw it in a more serious light, as a "truly demoniac" building—"the scream you wake on at the end of a nightmare". It certainly is a violent break with its contemporary commercial neighbours in the city—the high gables broke through the standard cornice line and the confident canopies gave tremendous vigour to the façade.

How does the building fit in to the architectural thinking of its day? It has all the qualities of the High Victorianism of the 1850s with the additional elements of the picturesque tacked on for emphasis. The walls are thick, the colouring is strong and the whole composition is redolent of the Italian Gothic of G. E. Street and Ruskin. Roumieu had sniffed the wind and caught Venice in the air—he transferred it to Eastcheap in a manner that manages to be both inspired and naive.

The *Builder* thought it "picturesque and original . . . if a little overdone". In fact, this aggressively striking Gothic was rather old-fashioned by 1868; certainly it was not particularly appropriate for a vinegar warehouse, "in

the Gothic of the South of France, with a Venetian impress". It was built for Messrs Hill, Evans & Co, on the site of the old Boar's Head Tavern, and cost £8170.

Map 2 H2

Vinegar warehouse in Eastcheap; woodcut published in the Builder, *1868 (Royal Institute of British Architects, London)*

54
Offices
19 LINCOLN'S INN FIELDS, WC2

1868–70
Philip Webb

This building was almost exactly contemporary with George Howard's house in Palace Green and it shows the same attitude to precedent and to urban architecture being applied to office premises with a tall narrow frontage.

Number 19 Lincoln's Inn Fields was designed for L. R. Valpy of Valpy & Leadsam, Solicitors. The contract drawings are dated 1868 and the offices were built in 1869–70. The narrow façade is given a distinctive character by the use of brick and stone, the use of stone clearly and logically articulating the central projecting bay. With comparatively simple means, Webb managed to give the frontage as much variety as possible: the windows are given different pediments on different floors; on the fourth floor there is a balcony and the façade is finished off by a gable with a large segment-headed window.

Typical of Webb is the beautiful handling of the materials—brick and stone—and the stylised interpretation of a wide variety of traditions. The acutely pointed pediments to the first floor windows have a primitive Byzantine character which would permeate Webb's later works, while the octagonal piers—which frame the projecting bay and support the balcony—are possibly Tudor in inspiration. They rise boldly through four storeys, but are relieved by the projection of the regular horizontal string courses.

The offices originally had a top lit central stairway, but this has been replaced by a lift and the chimneys have gone.

Webb's design makes a most interesting comparison with 17–18 next door, especially as the asymmetrical porches of both buildings are contiguous. This building was designed by Alfred Waterhouse and is actually later in date (1871–2) than Webb's design. Both Waterhouse and Webb were essentially rational Gothic men, but Waterhouse kept to a heavy 13th-century Gothic built entirely of stone. His building is very much High Victorian, which cannot be said of Webb's clever and elegant façade, the very narrowness of which perhaps prevented

its architect from exercising his usual puritanical awkwardness.

Further west, of course, is Sir John Soane's house (12–14); it must be said that neither Webb nor Waterhouse much respected the Georgian character of Lincoln's Inn Fields.

Map 2 E2

19 Lincoln's Inn Fields; drawn by W. Curtis Green and published in the Builder, *1897 (Royal Institute of British Architects, London)*

55
Sunnydene
108 WESTWOOD HILL, SYDENHAM, SE26

1868–70
John Francis Bentley

What at first sight seems to be an ordinary mid-Victorian middle-class suburban villa reveals sophistications in its design which show it to be more than the work of an estate builder. The house was designed by the young John Francis Bentley (1839–1902) for the millionaire carrier entrepreneur, W. R. Sutton, for whom Bentley later designed a carrier's warehouse in Golden Lane. The plan was drawn out by Bentley's friend, the organ builder, T. C. Lewis who was Sutton's brother-in-law. Their friend J. H. Metcalfe made some of the drawings.

The house was sufficiently interesting to be noted by Eastlake in his list of buildings at the back of his *History of the Gothic Revival*: "Tudor and Jacobean, a well-appointed residence, designed with great care, the garden etc., being laid out in a style corresponding with the date of the house. House of red brick with stone dressings . . .". The stone lintels to the windows seem like many ordinary sub-Gothic villas of the 1860s, but Bentley gave this type the sophistication of the new tendencies in domestic architecture which were blossoming into the Queen Anne. Some windows have the brick relieving arches which characterise the simple parsonage work of Butterfield and Street, a tradition of decent building in brick which runs through the best later Victorian domestic architecture. Other features have the vigour of the 1860s: the bay window supported on a solid brick pier, embellished with a sunburst and "Ave" carved in stone, the asymmetrical porch cut into the brick, the hipped gables. The tall rubbed brick chimneys and the bands of brick and stone hint at a knowledge of what Nesfield was doing while details like the flat buttresses on the rear elevation and the parapet of diagonal brickwork are Bentley's own invention.

The stables and coach-houses added to the west in 1869 have been replaced by a modern house; beyond that, on the corner of Sydenham Hill, is Ellerslie, built in 1870 for Sutton. The first tenant was John Pike, a hop merchant. This house has been much altered and spoiled, but the bay window at the back still sports a most interesting

parapet carved with a sun-flower motif. Sunnydene itself has been altered internally and divided into flats; the stained glass and decorative work described by Mrs de l'Hôpital has all gone.

This is the saddest part of Victorian London. In front of Bentley's house, until 1936, Brunel's water tower and the great glittering mass of the Crystal Palace once towered. Now the wealthy houses, which clustered all around Sydenham Hill after the Palace was re-erected there in 1854, have almost all been demolished. The house built by J. L. Pearson for himself nearby in Westwood Hill has gone, the remaining redbrick villas climbing up from Dulwich have slowly given way to bijou town houses and maisonettes. What is still the finest site in London, the top of Sydenham Hill, is desolate. On the east side of Crystal Palace Parade stood the Palace, on the west the site of the old High Level Station, built in the 1860s to handle the vast traffic generated by the Palace and its garden. There survives only the tile-lined First Class passage under the Parade which connected the station with the Palace. Bentley's house is one of the few sad survivors of the visible symbol of mid-Victorian confidence and enterprise which was Sydenham. The only other objects of interest are Pearson's St John's church (1875–87), Sylvan Hill, SE19, on the Upper Norwood

Sunnydene, Sydenham, in 1978 (Architectural Press)

side of the hill, where, in Auckland Road and Belvedere Road, some good mid-Victorian houses are left, and, strangest of all, prowling by the Boating Lake at the bottom of the Palace Park, off Thicket Road, full-sized prehistoric monsters which were erected as one of the attractions of the Palace in 1854. There can be found the iguanodon, the plesiosauris and pterodactyl; their creator Professor Owen (qv the Natural History Museum, **66**) was entertained at dinner by the Palace directors, inside the hollow belly of the iguanodon. Afterwards he delivered an addressed from the monster's skull. The survival of these creatures should be a salutary reminder of the fragility of our civilisation. The Victorians thought the world could be made better and better by the benefits of reason, of free trade, of education, of culture and, of course, by British Parliamentary democracy. Fire destroyed the Palace, war the rest of the area, and recent events give us no cause to feel confident in the continuing benefits of the 19th-century ideal of Progress. The savagery of the jungle is never far away; here, at Sydenham, primaeval life almost alone remains.

Map 1 F5

a *St Columba, Haggerston; Brooks's perspective drawing showing the completed scheme of church, clergy house and schools (Royal Institute of British Architects, London)*

56
St Columba
KINGSLAND ROAD, N1

1868–73
James Brooks

57
St Chad
DUNLOE STREET, E2

1868–9
James Brooks

"There are districts and suburbs in London in which if a new building is raised it stands no more chance of being visited by people of taste than if it had been erected in Kamschatka. What amateur or *dilettante* would ever think of exploring such neighbourhoods as Shoreditch, Hoxton, and Plaistow in search of architectural beauty? Yet those oulying regions in the far east of London contain some of the largest and most remarkable churches which have been built during the Revival."

Thus Charles Eastlake on James Brooks in his *History of the Gothic Revival* of 1872. Unfortunately, Brooks's works in the East End have rather suffered: St Saviour, Hoxton, was bombed; St Michael, Mark Street, Shoreditch, and St Andrew, way out on the Barking Road, E13, are both redundant. Even the future of St Columba is uncertain, but it is included here because it is so close to St Chad, which is still in use, and is the most magnificent of Brooks's slum churches.

The two churches were among those built as part of the Haggerston Parish Extension scheme, an attempt to bring religion to the slums by building impressive new churches which would tower above the surrounding mean houses—a neo-mediaeval vision which was the inspiration behind the urban Anglo-Catholic Masterpieces by Butterfield, Street, Pearson and Bodley.

In Haggerston, there was little money to spend on trimmings: the intention was to produce a structure impressive through its size and proportions. In this Brooks was extremely successful: he adhered to that early French phase of Gothic fashionable after the Lille Cathedral Competition of 1855 and which, in the hands of Street, became the Vigorous style, a style of the sublime, of massive walls and heavy geometrical forms. Brooks clearly revelled in the gaunt simplicity of red brick; beyond the simple shape of the building, interest is given only by the addition of solid buttresses and the windows which seem to have been punched through the wall. There is no elaborate tracery; St Chad sports extreme examples of the plate tracery; which is a sim-

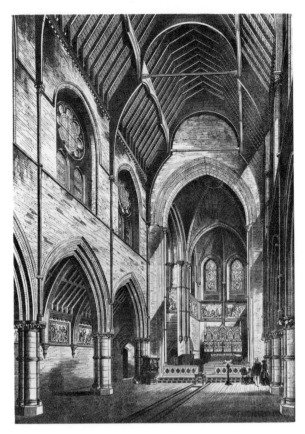

plification of those forms of French 13th-century windows admired by Ruskin and Viollet-le-Duc.

St Columba's church forms a group with vicarage (1873), clergy house and school, arranged around a courtyard. The severe exterior elevations demonstrate a characteristic Vigorous-style concern with the integrity of the wall plane, and the architect clearly enjoyed the mannerisms this discipline allowed in treating buildings with different functions next to each other. The tall interior of St Columba has been spoiled by whitewash and is now in a sorry state. The pyramidal roof of the crossing was an optimistic temporary alternative to a tower and spire. The mortuary chapel and cloister were added later by the Rev Ernest Geldart.

The interior of St Chad is comparatively unaltered (though tampered with by good taste, and there is a recent interior addition at the west end) and is a good example of the mission church style: a clear, tall space terminated by an apse—a favourite of the Vigorous-style architects, later eschewed by Bodley and others in favour of the English square east end.

St Chad once stood in the corner of the pretty Gothic houses of Nichols Square, since gratuitously swept away by the LCC. All that is left is Brooks's Vicarage (1873).

Francis Bumpus remarked that "though a practitioner of the Gothic Revival period and a builder of Gothic churches, Brooks had a robust contempt for precedents when they interfered with his independence as a designer".

Other impressive cheap churches by James Brooks (1825–1901) include the Ascension, Lavender Hill, SW11 (77); the Transfiguration, Algernon Road, Lewisham (now converted into a club); Holy Innocents, Padderswick Road, Hammersmith, SW6, (1877). St

b *Interior of St Columba; woodcut published in the* Builder, *1869 (Royal Institute of British Architects, London)*
c *and* d *St Chad, Haggerston; photographs taken in 1944 from the west and south-west before the houses in Nichols Square were demolished (National Monuments Record, Crown copyright)*

John the Baptist, Holland Road, W14, is an interesting design in stone by Brooks of 1872 but the west end was added by W. S. Atkins in 1909 and the tower never built. Brooks's last church, All Hallows, Savernake Road, Gospel Oak, NW3 (1891) was never finished and was continued by Giles Scott in 1913: it is particularly interesting and magnificent.

Other churches in London in this simple brick Gothic mission church style include St Peter, Vauxhall, SE11 by Pearson (28)—perhaps the prototype—and St Mary, Bourne Street, SW1 (68).

St Columba: Map 1 F2
St Chad: Map 1 G2

St Stephen, Rosslyn Hill; woodcut published in Eastlake's Gothic Revival, 1872

58
St Stephen
THE GREEN, ROSSLYN HILL, HAMPSTEAD, NW3

1869–76
Samuel Sanders Teulon

This is one of the most impressive 19th-century churches, an expensive example of High Victorian architecture which, although rooted in Gothic precedent, was deliberately and conspicuously modern. St Stephen demonstrates many of the qualities characteristic of that original movement, the Vigorous style, a powerful impression of weight, of the combination of simple geometrical forms, of architecture as pure sculpture.

The basic style is that favourite of the late 1850s and 60s, a muscular French 13th-century Gothic, but, as Bumpus observed, the unusual square-headed aisle windows are of a Kentish type. The massive tower with capped roof, placed over the chancel, is a superb composition of Continental flavour, and yet utterly mid-Victorian; it looks particularly impressive from the east when its tough, complex shapes rise from above the heavy, polygonal apse which takes advantage of the steeply sloping site. Nothing could be deliberately less picturesque than the building materials—Luton brick, originally "ranging in colour from pale grey to India red" but now looking dark purple, with granite and stone dressings.

The interior is a full expression of Victorian originality: elaborately notched brickwork, rather Moorish pointed arches resting on squat columns with boldly carved capitals, an apse richly decorated with mosaic and alabaster, a dominating timber roof almost aggressively exhibiting its strong structure (the stalls and other fittings of 1905–13 are of a rather different character).

Bumpus wrote in 1907 that "St. Stephen's exhibits evidence of Teulon's ingenuity and vigour of design side by side with those eccentricities of form, either structural or decorative, which distinguished nearly every building he erected. How far these eccentricities resulted from individual caprice, whether they were the consequences of some peculiarity in early studies, of whether they arose from an endeavour to escape from conventionalities in design, it is impossible to say". Certainly Samuel Sanders Teulon (1812–73), who lived nearby, designed some of the most aggressively original of all High Victorian buildings and his architecture often combines an extreme form of Ruskinian polychromy and rich naturalistic sculpture with a highly mannered and expressive experimentation with the massive geometrical possibilities of 13th-century Gothic. This is very evident in his wildly eccentric country houses: Bestwood Lodge, Shadwell Park and Elvethan, and also in his churches. Unfortunately, many of his interesting London churches have been destroyed, only St Mark, Silvertown, E16 (1859), now redundant, and his "restoration" (ie complete transformation) of Ealing parish church, St Mary's Road, W5 (1866–73) survive. Indeed, St Stephen may not survive long, as the building of the hospital down the hill in Pond Street has, apparently, caused structural damage, but it would be a tragedy if Teulon's extraordinary masterpiece were lost.

At the end of his *History of the Gothic Revival* (1872), Eastlake selected St Stephen as an example of one of the two dominant tendencies in modern Gothic design. This was an expression of Continental influence (although "in many respects it retains a national character, while certain details—as, for instance, the ornamental brickwork of the interior—can scarcely be referred to any precedent but that of modern fashion"), in contrast to a pure English design, of which type Eastlake selected Bodley and Garner's St John, Tue Brook, Liverpool (1869). He concluded that "there seems no reason for supposing that the present struggle for pre-eminence between French and English types of Gothic in the country will terminate for some time to come". He was wrong; after *c.* 1870 a strong reaction against the extremes of tough High Victorian Gothic emerged, and the future lay with Bodley's refined style.

Opposite St Stephen, on the other side of Rosslyn Hill, is another church whose future is currently in some doubt: the Congregational Church of 1883–4, designed by another Hampstead resident, Alfred Waterhouse (who, unlike so many of the mid-Victorian Goths, was not High Anglican). Typical of a non-conformist church is its centralised hexagonal and galleried plan; typical of Waterhouse are the hard, imperishable materials, purple brick and terra cotta.

Map 1 D1

59
St Mary Abbot
KENSINGTON HIGH STREET, W8

1869–79
George Gilbert Scott

The mediaeval parish church of the village of Kensington had been rebuilt in 1697. In the 1860s this structure was not only deeply unfashionable in style and date, but falling down. Bishop Blomfield thought it the ugliest church in his diocese. For a new church, suitable for what was now an important suburb of London, the vicar of Kensington, Archdeacon John Sinclair, naturally turned to the most fashionable established architect of the day, George Gilbert Scott, R.A. "Mr. Scott's European reputation renders it altogether unnecessary on the part of the Committee to enter on any justification of their choice." The old church was taken down in 1869; the new consecrated in 1872 and the spire completed in 1879.

The modern observer too often admires only conspicuous originality in Victorian architecture, and often this was as much the result of economy and a remote site as of artistic intention. On a prominent site in West Kensington, for a wealthy parish, something sober and dignified was required, and the quality of the work lies not in any rejection of precedent but in the scholarly interpretation and composition of historical styles. The church is well built, solid and well proportioned but, it must be admitted, although Scott built a very large number of churches, his secular buildings are usually the more interesting of his works. Here, as Francis Bumpus wrote (1907), "through the whole of St. Mary's we perceive that spirit of academicism, that fearfulness of overstepping the limits of conventionalism, from which the architect could never free himself. Kensington Church must, however, be pronounced a truly majestic edifice, worthy in every way of the Old Court suburb".

Brick would not do; the church is faced in the Kentish ragstone always favoured by the orthodox ecclesiologists. The interior is of Corsham stone with shafts of Irish marble. The plan is orthodox, except for the double transept which projects from the east end of both nave aisles. Typical also of 1840s ecclesiology is that the impressive tower and spire are placed asymmetrically, at the north east. The style is one that Scott liked: Transitional, between Early English and Decorated. The architect would seem to have been rather taken with the severity of Scottish Gothic at this time; the east and west ends recall Dublane Cathedral and the nave Paisley Abbey. The nave is groined in wood similarly to St Mary's Cathedral, Edinburgh, which Scott won in competition in 1873.

St Mary Abbot, Kensington; designs drawn by Maurice B. Adams and published in the Building News, *1881*

With the exception of tablets and the pulpit, all the furnishings are by Scott. The tracery, altar and reredos were executed by Clayton and Bell who did most of the glass (which has, unfortunately, been tampered with). The south chancel aisle was made into a war memorial chapel in 1921, with a new east window, by Scott's grandson, Giles Gilbert Scott (1880–1960). The vaulted cloister from the street to the south porch was added by J. O. Scott in 1889–93.

Map 1 D3

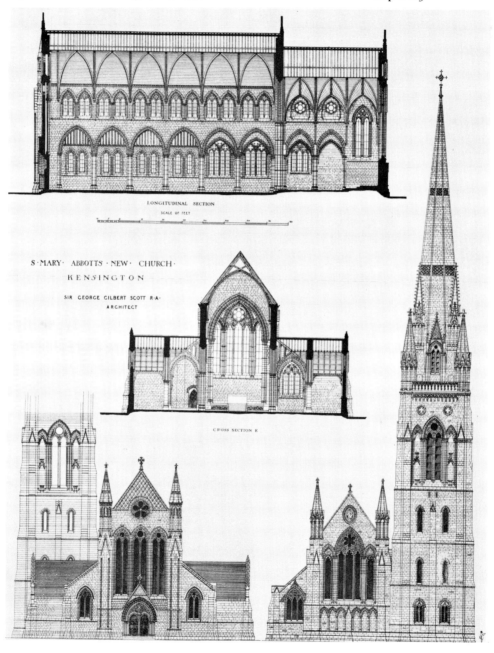

LONGITUDINAL SECTION
SCALE OF FEET

S·MARY· ABBOTTS ·NEW· CHURCH·
KENSINGTON

SIR GEORGE GILBERT SCOTT R·A·
ARCHITECT

CROSS SECTION E

60
Royal Courts of Justice
THE STRAND, WC2

DESIGNED 1870
George Edmund Street
BUILT 1874–82

The old Law Courts at Westminster, by Kent and Soane, had been spared in the conflagration of 1834. They stood on the west side of Westminster Hall. Stylistically incongruous with the new Palace of Westminster and, apparently, too small and inefficient, it was soon planned to remove them to a new site. A competition was announced in 1866, one which was conducted in the usual absurd and arbitrary manner of Victorian architectural competitions and which resulted in the erection of the last great Gothic public building, a building which became unfashionable long before it was completed and which was described as "the grave of modern Gothic". George Edmund Street (1824–81), perhaps the greatest architect of the High Gothic Revival, was enabled to design his one big public building, but the strain of getting it built killed him, and he and his building, rather unfairly, bore the brunt of the reaction against the earnest attempt of the mid-Victorian years to make 13th-century Gothic a modern and universal style.

The 1860s were the high-tide of Gothic; despite the defeat in the Battle of the Styles over the Government Offices, it was assumed that the new Law Courts would be Gothic even though style was not specified in the competition brief. Many architects felt that only the freedom of Gothic, that functional flexibility of the style insisted on by Pugin and Scott, could meet the complexity of the lawyers' requirements. These were for a minimum of twenty-four courts arranged with separate circulation systems for lawyers and spectators, all to be fitted onto a site on the north side of the Strand. A central hall was not specifically required, but it seemed to answer best the requirements of circulation.

Most of the great Goths of the day entered the fray, and even those who were more classically or eclectically minded were alive to the importance of submitting a Gothic design: E. M. Barry, Raphael Brandon, William Burges, T. N. Deane, H. B. Garling, H. F. Lockwood, J. P. Seddon, George Gilbert Scott, G. E. Street, Alfred

Waterhouse and H. R. Abrahams (this last had prepared a pilot scheme in 1864 and his idea of a plan with concentric rectangles influenced the other competitors).

The designs were exhibited in 1867. Burges's and Seddon's, in particular, produced huge and wildly romantic schemes in which their neo-mediaeval picturesqueness and scholarship produced designs which bordered on the fantastic and all the architects poured out their considerable talents onto the paper, and, of course, provided colossal towers. Designs quite like these would never be seen again. The condition that the cost should be not more than £700,000 could not be met by any competitor, and only Waterhouse's estimate—at £1,339,328— was found to be realistic by an independent surveyor. The professional architect judges put Barry first and Scott second; the lawyers put Scott first and Waterhouse second. The absurd result was announced that Street and Barry were recommended as joint architects. Scott, who had much more right to angle for the commission than with the Government Offices competition, resigned noisily, but to no avail. Barry did well because of his plan, but his late Gothic elevations and wretched dome were not liked, while Street's severe 13th-century elevations had been admired but his plan not highly considered.

In 1868 Street was made sole architect; Barry was fobbed off with the proposed National Gallery rebuilding, which never got done, and Waterhouse, whose plan, as always, was also admired, took the Natural History Museum. Street's victory, indeed, was curious, but he was an architect whose colossal reputation among his brother architects justified his ability to deal with the commission.

Then A. H. Layard, the First Commissioner of Works, decided to change the site to one by the new Embankment; new drawings were prepared in 1869 and then the

a *Bird's-eye perspective view of Burges's unexecuted competition design for the Law Courts, 1866 (National Monuments Record, Crown copyright)*

b *Street's unexecuted design for the Record Tower on the Law Courts; perspective drawings published in the* Building News, *1882*

project was taken back to the Strand. Street had to begin again. The cruel demands of the First Commissioner of Works, A. S. Ayrton, who believed it was his duty to pare down the public money spent on architecture to a minimum, ensured that a much reduced design was built. Street's original estimate was £1½m; the contract was signed in 1874 for £826,000 with Messrs Joseph Bull. Street had to abandon his splendid Record Tower and had to fight hard to keep the Great Hall; he adopted a new plan in 1870 based on Waterhouse's competition entry and his final designs were worked out in 1870–1.

His new design was savagely attacked the moment it was published; public mistrust of architects then, as now, was growing and his Gothic was seen as doctrinaire, gloomy and too ecclesiastical in character. James Fergusson used the Law Courts as an attack on the whole Revival. This criticism, together with the difficulties

presented by his clients and the sheer labour of producing the detailed drawings, wore Street out. Street could never delegate. In his concern with all the details of a design, with wood and metalwork, stone carving and glass-painting, Street, like Pugin, was one of the true founders of the Arts and Crafts movement, and it is not surprising that William Morris, Philip Webb and J. D. Sedding were all in his office. But he would not let them design anything. Another famous pupil, Norman Shaw, remembered that "when a new work appeared, his custom was to draw it out in pencil in his own room—plans, elevations, and sections, even putting in the margin lines and places where he wished the title to go; nothing was sketched in, it was *drawn*, and exactly as he wished it to be, so that really there was little to do, except to ink in his drawings, and tint and complete them. The rapidity and precision with which he drew were marvellous. . . . He was the *beau idéal* of a perfect enthusiast. He believed in his own work, and in what he was doing at the time, absolutely; and the charm of his work is that when you are looking at it you may be certain that it is entirely his own, and this applies to the smallest detail as well as to the general conception. I am certain that during the whole time I was with him I never designed one single moulding". For all the carving in the Law Courts, all the woodwork, the metalwork, the mosaic and tile floor, thousands of drawings were necessary. The details of the building—as always with Street, especially the iron-work—are full of interest.

And so is the general conception. The acoustics of the courts were reported not to be all that was desired, but the plan was well handled and Street obviously loved the complexity of corridors and spiral staircases which the Gothic style and approach allowed. In the centre of the building lies the Great Hall insisted upon by the lawyers, who had become accustomed to using Westminster Hall, as the old Law Courts were then adjacent. This impressive vaulted space—230 feet long, 48 feet wide and 82 feet high—is an utterly authoritative essay in 13th-century English Gothic. Although ecclesiastical in character, it is not based on any one source, but is an assured, almost Classical, composition in a style which, to Street, had become an unthinking tradition.

Street's elevations are a vindication of the theoretical Gothic approach to composition, although Summerson has said they "represent the pathetic collapse of an over-strained imagination". There is no forced symmetry—it was for this that the Renaissance styles were condemned—and the functions of the interior are clearly read on the exterior. It is, though, probably true to say that architects like Street deliberately put their staircases by the street so as to give an excuse for varied composition. All the façades, and the Strand front in particular, are ingenious compositions of different types of elevation.

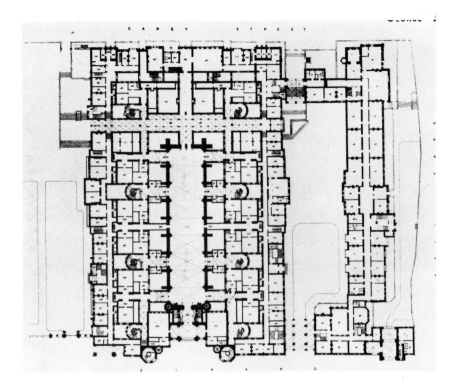

c *The ground floor plan (at the Strand entrance level) and the
first, court floor plan (at the Carey Street entrance level) of the
Law Courts as executed (The Royal Institute of British
Architects, London)*

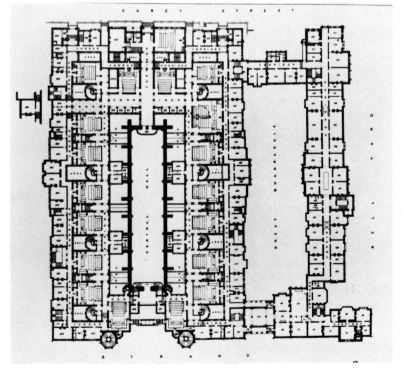

d *The Great Hall of the Law Courts in 1945 (National Monuments Record, Crown copyright)*

Along the Strand the elevations are grouped either side of the main entrance which leads, quite clearly, into the Hall. The elevations either side look symmetrical, but are not. There are changes when required, arcades keep the street line constant when necessary and there is a tower at the east end. But the whole elevation looks logical and, from any position, the composition looks satisfactory as it employs repeating elements and symmetrical arrangements which overlap. What Street did was design his elevation for a narrow street, in which the whole composition can never be appreciated in total. His success in this may be contrasted with the conspicuous failure of Aston Webb's symmetrical façade to the Victoria and Albert in very similar conditions.

Street never abandoned his faith in 13th-century Gothic. In the Portland stone of the Law Courts, beyond the necessity of making original statements in his vigorous style, Street handled his Gothic almost as a Classicist. It is a pure, learned and intellectual essay in an austere, bold style. It does, however, seem cold compared with the richness of texture of the Perpendicular Gothic of the Palace of Westminster, undeniably a much more lovable building and contemporaries tired of the "correct" style when the possibilities of Queen Anne were being demonstrated by Shaw and those of Jacobean by T. G. Jackson. But, as "James Kinnaird" has said, "the Courts did not deserve the insults of the time; they remain a great work of uninviting architecture, but within is one of the glories of English architecture, the Hall, the perfect embodiment in stone of the majesty of the law".

Street died in 1881, just before the removal of the scaffolding from the Hall. He had been worn out, first by the constant demands for economy made by the rebarbative Ayrton until Gladstone replaced him in 1873, and then by the worries caused by considerable difficulties with the builder (who eventually went bankrupt). He was further undermined by the death of his second wife in 1876. There is a fine monument to him, by Armstead, placed against the east side of the Hall in 1886 which depicts all the ideal architectural skills, such as metal-working and stone-carving.

Map 2 F2

e *The Street Memorial in the Great Hall of the Law Courts, designed by Maurice B. Adams, published in the* Building News, *1886*

61
St Augustine

QUEEN'S GATE, SW7

1870–91
William Butterfield

⚓⚓

One of Butterfield's most uncompromisingly independent works, contemporary with Keble College, this church was for Francis Bumpus, "perhaps the most original work he ever designed". That aggressive originality always evident in his architecture is present here, but must not be exaggerated. The hard polychromatic façade, placed at an angle to the street, was not necessarily a deliberate affront to the dull smug stucco terraces of Kensington—they arrived shortly afterwards.

This church should be compared with Butterfield's All Saints, Margaret Street (11), designed some twenty years

before. Both churches are conspicuous for the use, inside and out, of permanent colour, but in St Augustine the architect moved much further from orthodox precedent. The plan and Middle Pointed style of All Saints was what the ecclesiological orthodoxy demanded, but by 1870 it was realised that a 19th-century church needed a wide nave and Butterfield provided narrow aisles which are little more than passages. Unlike Street, he always kept to the traditional English east end, but for the strange façade he was inspired by a recondite exotic building, the west front of the church at Chorin in Germany.

All Saints gives an impression of great height; St Augustine of breadth. The arcades, on their stumpy round columns, are low and above these is a tall clerestory, as was sensible in a city. The interior is conspicuous for the typical awkwardness of its forms: the large quatrefoil spandrels of the arcades, the chancel arch—serving only a liturgical function as the roofline is unbroken from west to east—pierced by a traceried window, the simple shapes of the roofs. The same materials were used inside and out: red and yellow bricks, bands of stone and Pether's patent bricks, moulded with a fleur-de-lys pat-

Butterfield's working drawings for St Augustine, Queen's Gate; sheet showing sections through the nave looking east and west (Victoria and Albert Museum, Crown copyright)

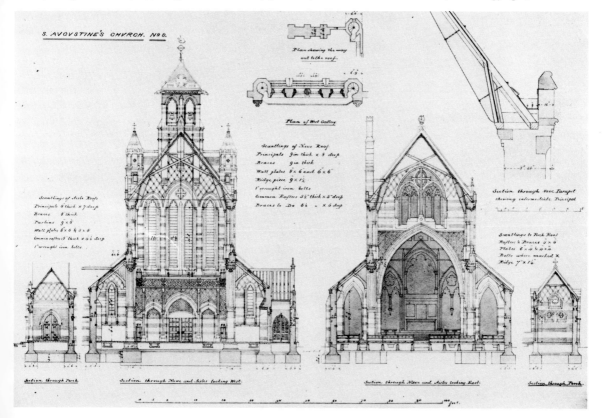

tern. That Butterfield's colour scheme was not strident and crude but subtle and distinctive is shown by the grey and mauve marble lining the sanctuary.

The nave was completed in 1871, the chancel in 1876. Butterfield remained untouched by late Victorian changes in style and fashion. When in 1890 he added to the church by decorating the walls of the aisles and the spandrels of the nave arcades, he used ceramic murals and tile mosaic by Gibbs, as he did at All Saints. Bumpus thought these "puerile in the extreme".

The remainder of Butterfield's surviving furniture—the inlaid marble font with painted wooden cover, the marble and alabaster pulpit and the wrought-iron lectern—are characteristic and fine. The stalls and benches were made to Butterfield's design.

Taste changes, and in the early 20th century Butterfield's polychromy could not have been more unfashionable. In 1925 the interior was whitened with lime wash, obliterating both Butterfield's colour and his murals. At the same time the incumbent, the Rev Carrick Deakin, made the interior a model of the "Anglo-Catholic Congress Baroque" with the Counter-Reformation style fittings fashionable with High Church Anglicans at the period. Carrick's architect was Martin Travers (1886–1948) (who did *not* whiten the interior—he left the brick when he installed his gold Baroque reredos at St Mary, Bourne Street (**68**), and St Savior, Hoxton). Travers designed the War Memorial (1926), the Stations of the Cross (1928), the sounding board above the pulpit, the north aisle Lady Chapel (1928) and the great reredos and frontal, and the communion rails and screens in the sanctuary. The reredos, of 1928, is one of his masterpieces; carefully gilded and lacquered, its Baroque is not literal but touched by a contemporary stylisation which makes it unmistakably a work of the 20s and explains why the church became known as the Essoldo, Queen's Gate. To install his reredos, with its solid wooden frontal, Travers blocked the lower half of the east window.

Taste moves on, and has turned full circle. Under the direction of Sampson Lloyd, of Green, Lloyd and Adams, the interior was restored in 1974–5. Unfortunately, it was apparently not possible to remove the whitewash from the brick walls or stone piers; instead the garish polychromy of Butterfield has been achieved by painting over the whitened surfaces but, most commendably, while the marble in the sanctuary has been exposed, Travers's fittings, just as worthy of preservation in their own right, have been retained.

Map 2 A4

62
St Augustine
KILBURN PARK ROAD, NW6

1871–98
John Loughborough Pearson

This magnificent church of cathedral scale is one of the most intellectually satisfying as well as moving buildings in London. It is its architect's masterpiece. St Augustine was a product of the mid-Victorian feud between the Tractarian "ritualists" and Protestants within the Church of England (which was responsible for the appalling riots at St Barnabas, Pimlico, and St George-in-the-East). When a provocative and low church vicar arrived at St Mary, Kilburn, in 1867, the Tractarian curate, the Rev Richard Carr Kirkpatrick left, with most of the congregation, to found a new church.

The foundation stone was laid in 1871, the chancel was ready in 1872 and the nave and aisles in 1877. St Augustine was consecrated in 1880 and the huge tower and spire (254 feet high) built in 1897–8. Kirkpatrick remained vicar until 1907 and died in 1916.

After St Peter, Vauxhall (1860–5) (**28**), this is John Loughborough Pearson's masterpiece and the prototype of all his best late churches—St John the Divine, Sylvan Road, Upper Norwood, SE19 (1875–87); St Michael, Poplar Walk, Croydon (1876–85) and St Agnes, Sefton Park, Liverpool (1882–3)—which are variations on the

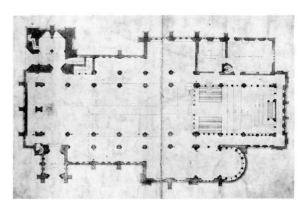

a *Plan of St Augustine, Kilburn, 1871, used in set of contract drawings (Royal Institute of British Architects, London)*

b *Interior of St Augustine; perspective view in south transept showing St Michael's chapel, exhibited at the Royal Academy in 1874 (Royal Institute of British Architects, London)*

theme set here, a theme of magnificent space and consistent vaulting achieved by a solid 13th-century Gothic, in brick.

The church is in the lancet style, a rather French 13th-century Gothic to which Pearson remained loyal. He was untouched by the important developments in late Victorian ecclesiastical design, by, that is, the new appreciation of later English Gothic Styles, as exemplified by Bodley and G. G. Scott, Junior, and by the more sympathetic and catholic attitude to old buildings, inspired largely by Ruskin and Morris's Society for the Protection of Ancient Buildings (1877)—Pearson's "restoration" of the north transept front of Westminster Abbey in 1888 was peculiarly ruthless—but in one respect St Augustine manifests a late Victorian characteristic, the emphasis on space rather than on wall surface

and mass such as in the work of Street and Butterfield.

The space is complex. The thick brick buttresses necessary to support the principal vault (the nave is 28ft wide and 58ft high) are *inside* the building, that is, the intervening walls are pushed to the ouside, as at Albi (an idea adopted by Bodley at the contemporary St Augustine, Pendlebury, Lancs). The weight of these buttresses is dispersed onto a double aisle at ground level, while at a higher gallery level each is pierced by a passage. This gallery was right round the building as arched bridges run across the transepts, so that the grandeur of the central vaulted space runs uninterrupted from east to west. The transepts themselves only project as far as the outer aisle walls (as at G. G. Scott, Junior's contemporary St Agnes, Kensington, now destroyed). Several of these features, notably the bridges across the transepts and the double aisles were used by Bentley in Westminster Cathedral, begun in 1892, a very similar structure in essence. Every one of the complex and tight spaces formed by Pearson's clever plan is beautifully and logically vaulted.

Most of the structure has a gaunt nobility in stock brick, though the wall paintings by Clayton and Bell contribute little to the effect. The stained glass is also by Clayton and Bell. Only the sanctuary is more elaborate, where the galleries are of stone and embellished with a scheme of statuary carved by Nichols. The line of these galleries is continued by the stone screen—the visual and liturgical division between nave and sanctuary—which emphasises the clarity of the space, a space which should be experienced by walking right around the church, on both ground and gallery level.

The stone reredos of the High Altar is also by Pearson and carved by Nicholls. It was much enhanced by Sir Giles Scott (1880–1960) in 1922, who added the subtly coloured background and the tabernacle. Scott made several sensitive additions to St Augustine: the Lady Chapel reredos in 1934 (north transept), the Shrine of our Lady and Stations of the Cross (1939, carved by Walter Gilbert), the War Memorial by the west door and the panelling in Pearson's extravagantly decorated St Michael's chapel (south transept). The rather unsatisfactory green wall of the south transept marks where several remarkable Italian paintings once hung, which were some of the several splendid benefactions to the church. St Augustine still maintains a powerful tradition, and the splendour of the building is a testimonial to the selfless generosity and love of the 19th-century Anglo-Catholic congregation.

Map 1 D2

63
Criterion Theatre

PICCADILLY CIRCUS, W1

1870–4 and 1884
Thomas Verity

Very few truly Victorian theatres survive in London; most were built in the boom years around the turn of the century, from about 1888 until the Great War, when literally dozens of new theatres were designed principally by Frank Matcham and his two pupils, W. G. R. Sprague and Bertie Crewe. The Garrick, in Charing Cross Road, designed by C. J. Phipps and Walter Emden (1888–9) and the Palace Theatre in Cambridge Circus, by T. E. Colcutt, (1889–90) both fall outside the chronological limits of this guide. Theatre buildings in the 19th century tended to have comparatively short lives, owing to changing fashions, rebuildings and, not least, fires. Of the large number of music halls which were so popular in the mid-Victorian decades, hardly any are left—the most interesting survivor is the Hoxton Hall, off Hoxton Street (c. 1863–7), a simple but effective little theatre.

The theatre was originally part of the Criterion Restaurant, a "monster" eating house with many different rooms, some for entertainments, whose size, quality and respectability were novel in Victorian London. It was built in 1870–3 by the catering firm of Spiers and Pond on the site of the old White Bear Inn to the east of Piccadilly Circus. Before it was completed, the proprietors sought permission to convert the basement concert hall into a theatre, which was opened in 1874.

The architect was Thomas Verity (1837–91), who gave the building a rich and ornate façade in a Victorian Renaissance manner which is best characterised as French. It is, however, a well-organised composition, with the decoration, statues in niches, etc subservient to the basic scheme of pedimented bays framing a large arched entrance. Verity would seem to have been trained in Paris during the Second Empire; certainly he was remarkable in Victorian England for his French style, although that was a style more favoured for structures designed for entertainment than for other building types. His francophilia was passed on to his son, Frank Verity (1864–1937), who trained in Paris and who brought Parisian *chic* to Edwardian London. At the end of his life

Thomas Verity was in parnership with his son, earlier he had been with G. H. Hunt; he was consulting architect to the Lord Chamberlain and, in London, also designed the Comedy Theatre, off Haymarket (1881).

Verity's real skill is most evident in the interior of the Criterion, where he made the best use of the limited space. The foyer, staircases, bars, etc are enlivened and enlarged by mirrors, painted ceilings and coloured tiles. The Criterion was one of the first buildings to use ornamental tilework for interior decoration, a manner very popular at the end of the century until spoiled by association with underground stations and Turkish baths. The Criterion was also remarkable because the theatre was so cleverly tucked into the basement. Owing to official concern with fire risk, it was rebuilt in 1884 by Verity, who exploited modern services such as mechanical ventilation and lifts. The auditorium seats 660 in stalls, dress circle and upper circle.

The façade was extended to the east in 1884. It soon after became much more prominent as the creation of Shaftesbury Avenue swept away the block of buildings between the circus and Titchborne Street in 1885, leaving Piccadilly Circus the unhappy triangular shape it still is today. Opposite the Criterion, on the other side of the new triangle, the London Pavilion rose in 1885, designed

The Criterion Theatre, Piccadilly; photograph of c1874–84 taken before the construction of Shaftesbury Avenue removed the "island" of buildings in front. Nash's original Piccadilly Circus buildings are on the right (National Monuments Record, Crown copyright)

by Worley & Saunders in a charming but illiterate Palladian manner, very strange for the 1880s. The Criterion now stands between Reginald Blomfield's rebuilding of Regent Street in the 1920s and a good Edwardian block above the underground station (1905) on the corner of Haymarket. Behind Verity's façade, Spiers and Pond's once fashionable dining rooms have long disappeared but the subterranean theatre remains a remarkable survival from the 1880s.

Map 2 D3

64
Offices
65 CORNHILL, EC3

1871
Edward I'Anson

I'Anson's principal surviving building in the City is the British and Foreign Bible Society's premises in Queen Victoria Street (45). In this tall office building on a narrow site, which used to be typical of the City and which, when street lines were respected, gave it its character, the architect moved on from the usual Italian style to experimenting with (for the City) new fashions. The style is a sort of Ruskinian Italian mediaeval, that is, the voussoirs are Gothic in profile but the windows themselves are still round. The organisation of the fenestration is essentially Classical, with three storeys of three bays, almost identical, but then the fourth floor has a group of six windows and, above, there is a pedimented wide wooden dormer. I'Anson was modern in the materials he used: brick and terra cotta for the richly moulded decoration beneath each cornice. The ground floor, originally a shop, has been characteristically and fatuously mutilated with a modern doorless fascia of granite.

Map 2 H2

65 Cornhill; woodcut published in the Builder, *1871*

65
St John the Divine
VASSALL ROAD, KENNINGTON, SW9

1871–4, 1887–8
George Edmund Street

This was Street's last London church and it exhibits that tendency towards a scholarly, almost Classical interpretation of Gothic evident in his later work. The church is, however, far from being archaeological and is remarkable, particularly in its plan.

A church in this part of Kennington was originally proposed in 1870 and its architect was to be C. A. Gould, a local man. However, on the advice of the rich new curate, Charles Edward Brooke (who contributed £10,000 to build the nave and aisles), Street was appointed instead. His design was made in 1871, the chancel and vestries completed in 1873, the nave, aisles, porch and baptistery in 1874. His son, A. E. Street, loyally completed the magnificent and dominating tower and spire to his father's design in 1877–8.

The interior is interesting because it has no clerestory. At the time Street was building the nave of Bristol Cathedral, a hall-church with nave and aisles of equal height which may have induced him to try the plan in Kennington. The clustered shafts of the arcade have capitals carved by Earp.

Another feature characteristic of Street is that the easternmost bays of the arcades are canted in to meet the chancel arch. Street fitted a wider nave onto a narrow chancel in several of his churches: a strict "ecclesiological" plan was found less convenient than a wide nave, with narrow aisles, for a large congregation, while the architectural and liturgical effect of a wide chancel was unfortunate.

In 1890–2 Street's interior was modified in accordance with late Victorian refined taste by G. F. Bodley, but his large reredos and decorations were destroyed in the bomb damage of 1940–1. The church was magnificently restored by H. S. Goodhart-Rendel with H. Lewis Curtis in 1955–8. Goodhart-Rendel carefully employed Street's special thin red bricks (which gave a building greater apparent scale), refrained from whitewashing the interior and reinstated Street's original painted wooden reredos, since, most regrettably, banished to the crypt store. The

Blessed Sacrament chapel had been earlier added by Sir Charles Nicholson. The neo-Victorian Gothic clergy house was also designed by Goodhart-Rendel.

Map 1 F4

Interior of St John the Divine, Kennington; early 20th-century photograph

66
Natural History Museum
CROMWELL ROAD, SW7

FIRST DESIGN 1868, FINAL DESIGN 1872
Alfred Waterhouse
BUILT 1873–80

The Natural History Museum is part of the British Museum. It was first proposed in 1858 to transfer the zoological, botanical, geological and mineral collections from Bloomsbury to a new building. The prime mover in this project was Professor Sir Richard Owen, who became the first Superintendent of the Natural History Museum. From the beginning he wanted top-lit galleries (with the light coming from the junction of wall and roof) and symbolic decoration; the specimen plan prepared in 1862 under his influence formed the basis of all subsequent designs.

An attempt to use the redundant building for the 1862 Exhibition was thwarted, but the Cromwell Road site was acquired for the Museum. In 1864 a competition was held. Of the thirty-three entries, only two were Gothic and two Greek (one of which was Alexander Thompson's), which suggests that most architects suspected that a building in the *Rundbogenstil* of South Kensington was required. They would have been right: first came Captain Francis Fowke, who had been persuaded to enter by Henry Cole; second: Robert Kerr; third: Cuthbert Brodrick. One of the judges, James Fergusson, expressed "surprise" when the authorship of the winning design was revealed.

Fowke's design was in a busy round-arched Classical "Bramantesque", and was conspicuous for its use of terra cotta. However, before work began, Fowke inconveniently died in 1865. His successor was not, as usual, General H. Scott; in 1866 the First Commissioner of Works Lord Cowper appointed Alfred Waterhouse architect, an odd choice, but presumably a consolation prize for his involvement in the Law Courts competition of that year.

At first Waterhouse was to execute Fowke's design—an unlikely task—but by 1868 he had prepared his own. These were in a surprising Romanesque style. There is a functional reason for this: Owen wanted "objects of natural history" to be used as ornament and

the Romanesque allowed the integration of much naturalistic sculpture better than Fowke's Classical round-arched style. Waterhouse called it "the round arched style common in Southern Germany as late as the 12th-century" which would "afford both the grandeur and simplicity which should characterise a building of this description". There were clear similarities to Fowke's style in such details as the coupled round-arched windows, but Romanesque was much more acceptable to a Gothic man than Renaissance, and it was a style approved by Ruskin who said in the *Stones of Venice* (1854) that "its highest glory is, that it has no corruption. It perishes in giving birth to another architecture as noble as itself" (ie Gothic). Naturally this 1868 design, with a dome in the centre, did not meet with the approval of the stylistic dictator of South Kensington and opponent of Gothic, Henry Cole, who called it "a manufacturing sort of thing Byzantine".

Then the Government changed its mind and thought of putting the Museum by the Thames Embankment. In 1870 it was back in South Kensington, but the hateful Liberal, A. S. Ayrton, now First Commissioner of Works, was demanding his usual tough economies. In 1872, despite attacks from Cole and Fergusson, a new design by Waterhouse was approved and, after further economies (brick instead of terra cotta in the internal courts, plaster ceilings instead of wooden), work began in 1873. In 1876 Disraeli's Conservative Government was willing to restore Waterhouse's twin towers and in 1878 the centre was redesigned. The building was completed in 1880 but the last galleries were not opened until 1886. The Lodge, by Queen's Gate, was built in 1883.

The style of the building is Romanesque, inspired by French and German sources, but never literally copied; it is, as Goodhart-Rendel described it, "a development of Romanesque". The coupled round-arch is the ruling motif of the design, and this duality appears right in the centre, in the double entrance door in the centre of the huge recessed arched portal. There is no artificial picturesque asymmetry in the design; the big regularly articulated wings reflect the long galleries behind. Visual interest is given by the complex geometry of the very Germanic roofs of the end pavilions and by the towers (the big southern towers contain offices and fire cisterns, the northern pair are chimneys for the heating apparatus). Further interest is given by the elaborate scheme of naturalistic decoration, for the façade is crawling with animals, modelled by M. Du Jardin of Farmer and Brindley and executed in terra cotta. As Owen wished, they symbolise the functions of the different parts of the building; on the west side (zoology), there are representations of living organisms, on the right (geology and palaeontology), there are extinct specimens. In the centre, on the gable, was a nice touch, showing the

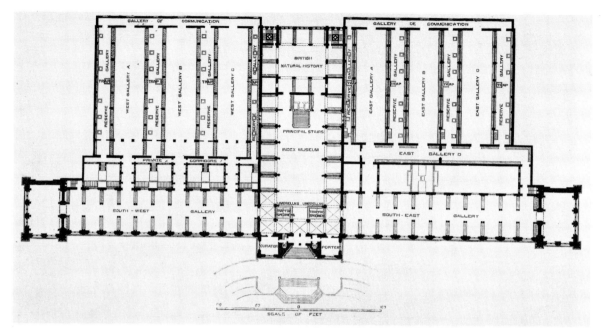

a *and* b *Natural History Museum; plan and perspective of exterior almost as executed, published in the* Builder, *1873*

influence of contemporary Darwinism: at the suggestion of Professor T. H. Huxley, "Man: the greatest beast of all" was placed there (since removed!). This degree of elaboration together with the use of different forms of shaft, continue in the interior.

Al! is finished in terra cotta, of a most subtle combination of buff and blue-grey. The virtues of terra cotta, for durability, washability and colour, were being explored in the 1860s but as the architect claimed, "the Museum is the largest, if not, indeed, the only modern building in which terra cotta has been extensively used for external façades and interior wall surfaces, including all the varied decoration which this involves". It was made by Gibbs and Canning of Tamworth, who had trouble in supplying enough. The contractor, Baker and Sons, also had trouble and failed in 1879.

The interior was carried on a steel frame, mostly encased in terra cotta . From the entrance, long galleries on three floors stretch east and west, and further, lateral galleries, three on each side, run towards the north; all are of the most straightforward and honest construction, well

c *Interior of the Museum looking from the entrance towards the principal stairs; perspective by Waterhouse, 1878 (Royal Institute of British Architects, London)*

proportioned and lit, and yet delicately decorated. The most impressive area is the Central Hall, 170 feet long, 97 feet wide and 72 feet high, crossed by a bridge carrying a staircase. Originally, as Owen planned, this contained an "Index or Typical Museum": "of specimens selected to show the type and character of the principal group of Organised Beings. It would form an Epitome of Natural History, and would convey to the eye, in the easiest way, an elementary knowledge of living nature". Behind the principal stairs were placed specimens of British natural history. All of this, and the building itself, reflected the extraordinary contemporary interest in and enthusiasm for the study of the natural world: botany, geology and zoology, of which the controversy over the origin of species of the 1860s was but one product. Geology and botany obsessed architects, particularly the Goths, who wished to use natural forms for their ornament and have their walls like geological strata

(ie Butterfield's and Street's polychromy). One expression of this was Deane and Woodward's Oxford Museum, which was so closely inspired by Ruskin. Waterhouse's building is another, with the only missing symbolic element, geology, the use of different stones and marbles being rendered impossible by the overall use of terra cotta.

The terra cotta is far from repetitive, however, for there is constant invention in pattern-making and in appropriate subject matter. The terra cotta finish is nevertheless subsidiary to Waterhouse's rational plan, with the steel roof structure of the long lateral galleries clearly comprehensible and a clever and unselfconscious fusion of masonry, decoration and iron everywhere evident, particularly in the Central Hall. Waterhouse was never ashamed of his ironwork, nor did he have a conscience about using industrial methods to achieve decorative richness.

Alfred Waterhouse (1830–1905) is usually associated with the Gothic Revival, with such buildings as the Manchester Assize Courts (1859) and the Manchester Town Hall (1868–76). But he was never associated with the High Church, ecclesiological wing of the movement and, inspired as he was by Pointed architecture and by Ruskin, there was always a hard, no-nonsense rationalism, if not bloody-mindedness, in his work which has often made it hard to stomach. This may be a reflection of his training with the Beaux Arts trained Manchester architect, Richard Lane. Waterhouse was very content to use new materials, like iron and terra cotta. With terra cotta he appreciated its durability and suitability for repetition of motifs (something a real Ruskinian, believing in the value of the sculptor's handiwork, would have disapproved of).

Indeed, Waterhouse is the one architect who justifies the belief of the Gothic Revival theorists in the universality and practicality of the Gothic as a way of building. Waterhouse—a practical, commercial and prolific architect—carried on in his own rational, hard, imperishable Gothic style for years after the apparent decease of secular Gothic in Street's Law Courts. He was brilliant as a planner, particularly on awkward, irregular sites, where his façades were satisfactorily resolved with the freedom of his Gothic style and detail. A good example is the Prudential Assurance Building in High Holborn, EC1, in its strident red terra cotta chiefly of 1899–1906.

At the Natural History Museum, he had no conscience about using a direct, axial Beaux Arts type plan, any more than he minded using a style which was not in the mainstream of fashion (though he had used a form of Romanesque for the Clydesdale Bank in Lombard Street (demolished) and for the Strangeways Prison in Manchester). It was a style, however, which had definite affinities with work abroad, particularly with that of the American H. H. Richardson (1838–86) who was using his own form of massive Romanesque from the early 1870s onwards (and whose influential and extraordinary house for the painter Herkomer; Lululaund at Melbourne Road, Bushey (1886) is, alas, demolished but for the porch). Waterhouse's building, in its style and with its Gothic emphasis on the integrity of the wall-plane, was admired by the Dutch architect H. P. Berlage (1856–1934) whose own work has definite affinities with the High Gothic Revival. Indigestible as his style often is, Waterhouse must be respected as one of the most significant of English Victorian architects: his work was always irreproachably and conspicuously *modern*. He was also a magnificent watercolourist.

Map 2 A4

67
Lowther Lodge, now the Royal Geographical Society
KENSINGTON GORE, SW7

DESIGNED 1872
R. Norman Shaw
BUILT 1873–5

This large mansion was in the tradition of the aristocratic town houses of earlier times, but in a strange style and on a strange site. William Lowther, MP, a rich ex-diplomat, asked the rising star in domestic architecture, Norman Shaw, (1831–1912), to design him a house on the one big freehold site available in the Albert Hall area. The stucco Italianate terraces were still creeping westwards, but this was not central London so that a Classic palazzo would not have been appropriate, even had Lowther wanted such an old-fashioned style. On the other hand, Kensington was no longer the country either. As Andrew Saint remarks, "What the Lowthers wanted was the country house come to town; it is this which makes their building so difficult to place. There were other early Queen Anne houses on open sites, notably on the Holland Estate, but nothing with quite the ambition of Lowther Lodge or with its reticent but distinct arrogance of mood".

The style is that vernacular Queen Anne which Shaw and his associate Nesfield had been evolving for the previous decade: a brick manner with tall chimneys, brick cornices and gables, leaded-light windows; a mixture of English vernacular, 17th-century urbanity and a touch of Aestheticism (particularly evident here with the sun-flowers carved into the brickwork). Perhaps there is more of Nesfield here—the coved cornices, tall rubbed brick chimney and brick pilasters of the Kew Lodge (91)—as Shaw seems still to have been searching for a more formal, urban style for building. This he soon found on the Chelsea Embankment; here he indulged in all the artful asymmetries met with in his Old English country houses.

The Kensington Gore front would be symmetrical if the entrance were not in the west wing, and the east wing did not sport a colossal chimney and have a subsidiary stable wing beyond it. The garden front is quite asymmetrical: two great bay windows below gables and then

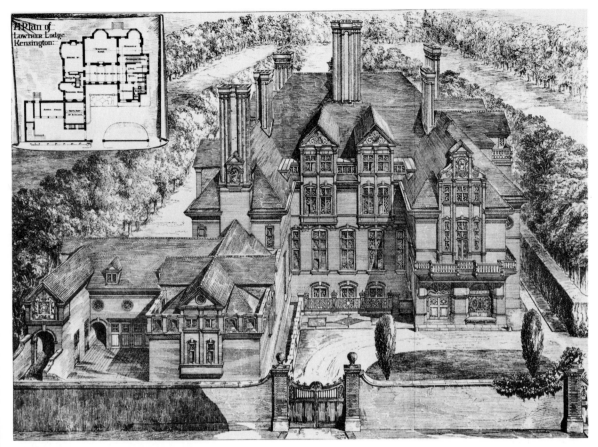

Inset: A Plan of Lowther Lodge Kensington

a Lowther Lodge, Kensington; perspective drawing by Shaw published in the Building News *1875 (Royal Institute of British Architects, London)*

another tall chimney stack at one end. The details of the exterior are excellent, all executed in the special thin 2 inch bricks; cornices, pediments, gables, pilasters are all made of gauged and cut brick. No stone dressings are used at all: the contractor, Lascelles, used a special brick-cutting machine. This revelling in the cheerful beauty of red brick extends to strange features, such as the fascinating (but pointless) arcading above the eaves on the east side of the courtyard. For complex asymmetries, movement and good brickwork, there is nothing else quite like Lowther Lodge in London.

The house did not have a great double-height hall, as in his country houses, but a large saloon on the ground floor, with wide Classical arches and a flat walnut ceiling. Alice Lowther had much to do with the interior and painted the tiles in the saloon fireplace. In 1912, after Lowther's death, the house was bought by the Royal Geographical Society who added a lecture hall on the site of the stables on the corner of Kensington Gore and Exhibition Road. This, designed by Kennedy and Night-

ingale and built in 1928–30, is seen clearly as a later addition yet is discreet and harmonises with the Shaw work by being in brick. The statue of Shackleton is by C. Sargeant Jagger (1932).

A further puzzle with Lowther Lodge is what Lowther thought would happen to the area. He had bought from the Commissioners after the 1851 Exhibition a strip of land on the west side of Exhibition Road. At first Lowther's Garden overlooked those of the Royal Horticultural Society, but already at the bottom end of this the Natural History Museum was rising and Lowther could not have expected it to remain open for long. Indeed Lowther himself built Lowther Gardens in 1877–8 on the corner of Exhibition Road and what would become Prince Consort Road (designed not by Shaw but by J. J. Stevenson) and he must have expected the site between his house and the Albert Hall to be developed. He may not have expected so huge a building, which overlooked his garden and dwarfed Lowther Lodge itself; yet he made no claim for compensation.

The irony is that the architect for Albert Hall Mansions was none other than Shaw himself. The project for a block of (very un-English) "mansions" or flats, began in 1876. Shaw was then consultant architect to the Com-

b *Albert Hall Mansions; perspective drawing by W. R. Lethaby published in the* Building News, *1881 (Royal Institute of British Architects, London)*

missioners, but the builder, Thomas Hussey, had an architect, C. H. Driver. By 1879 when construction began, Shaw was sole architect. He produced a highly ingenious and complex internal plan for the high-class flats, the result of his study of Paris flats. But there was nothing Parisian about the exterior. Shaw articulated the giant block (100 feet high) by three huge gables and brick arcades over some of the balconies. With its red brick-work, variety of fenestration and picturesque skyline, Shaw's Albert Hall Mansions was the prototype for the many turn-of-the-century blocks of flats which still provide civilised urban living in so many parts of London.

Map 2 A4

✠
68
St Mary
BOURNE STREET, SW1

1873–4
Robert Jewell Withers

1926–34
Harry Stuart Goodhart-Rendel

✠

Although not a Victorian architectural masterpiece, this famous church is included here, first, because it is a good and accessible example of James Brooks's honest brick style now that so many of Brooks's own churches have gone; and, secondly, because part of the building is the first and most distinguished example of neo-Victorian.

This was originally a chapel of ease to St Barnabas, Pimlico, built right on top of the Metropolitan District Railway by Robert Jewell Withers (1823–94), a little-known architect but who designed the interesting premises of Lavers and Barraud, stained glass makers, in Endell Street, WC2 (1859) in an austere polychromatic brick Gothic and who built "a good cheap type of brick church". This one is very much in the manner in which James Brooks built in the East End, and, with its straight-forward redbrick walls, apse and lancet windows, is reminiscent of the destroyed St Saviour, Hoxton. Least visually satisfactory is the manner in which the architect carried his arcade around the apse with three awkward arches. These were later filled with rather bad murals, and the spandrels in the nave with rather good ones.

After the turn of the century the church built up a rather grand High Church tradition and became known as St Mary, "Grah'm Street", (its proper appelation used to be Graham rather than Bourne Street). As Betjeman wrote,

> Those were the days when that divine baroque
> Transformed our English altars and our ways.
> Fiddle-back chasuble in mid-Lent pink
> Scandalised Rome and Protestants alike . . .

Martin Travers (1886–1948) carried out some fine work here in the fashionable Anglo-Catholic Baroque style in about 1919 (High Altar, wall tablets, figure of Our Lady,

a *St Mary, Bourne Street; perspective drawing of the exterior seen from Graham Terrace, published in A. Capes,* Old and New Churches of London, *1880*

b *Interior of St Mary in 1979 looking from Goodhart-Rendel's Seven Sorrows Chapel towards the High Altar (Architectural Press)*

etc) but, when the Parish Church Council expressed doubts about his ability to design actual architecture and consulted another architect for an extension, Travers resigned in a huff.

The architect consulted was the highly cultivated composer and Guardsman, H. S. Goodhart-Rendel (1887–1959), the real pioneer in the re-evaluation of Victorian architecture and whose writings about it are devoid of cynicism or smug superiority and as valuable as they ever were. His architecture was also of considerable, if idiosyncratic interest. For St Mary in 1924 he designed a new north aisle and entrance porch, which are both neo-Victorian and yet modern, as is his later work at St Wilfrid, Brighton (1933). His aisle continued Wither's brick Gothic but, with its subtle interesting mouldings and brick window details, has the flavour of contemporary Continental Expressionism. The entrance porch, brilliantly disguising a change of axis, is a modern, subtle re-interpretation of Brooks's work at St Columba, Haggerston. The additions were begun in 1926.

Goodhart-Rendel's witty appropriateness continued in his furnishings. The confessional and reredos in the Seven Sorrows chapel are tributes to Burges's heavy castellated style (the reredos was painted by Eric Gill's brother Macdonald Gill); at the same time, Goodhart-Rendel could handle Baroque as well as Travers. The gold High Altar, which, standing out against the red brick, dominates the church, has a turn-of-the-century core by S. Gambier-Parry, Baroque embellishments by Travers but its final form (1934) is due to Goodhart-Rendel. Goodhart-Rendel also turned the corner pub, the Pineapple, into a presbytery by heightening it with a strange slate-hung Gothick pitched roof.

The font (1953) is by J. Harold Gibbons and the centenary panelling (1974) in the sanctuary by Roderick Gradidge.

Map 2 C4

69
Greek Orthodox Cathedral of Aghia Sophia

MOSCOW ROAD, BAYSWATER, W2

DESIGNED 1874
John Oldrid Scott
BUILT 1877–82

Greek Orthodox Cathedral, Bayswater; woodcut of the interior published in the Builder, *1882 (Royal Institute of British Architects, London)*

It is strange to find Sir Gilbert Scott's second son, John Oldrid Scott (1841–1913), designing one of the first British buildings in that important stylistic movement of the late 19th-century the Byzantine Revival.

This style was used here for obvious reasons. The Greek community in London had arrived chiefly because of the early 19th-century war of independence. Their first church was in London Wall, in the City. In 1874 a site in Bayswater was purchased and a committee, chaired by Mr Mavrogordato, formed to raise money to build a church. It is not clear why Scott was chosen as architect. His first designs were prepared in 1874, the structure was built in 1877–9 and the church consecrated in 1882.

The Byzantine was a style of which British architects had no immediate experience, and Scott's is a most creditable essay in the style. Ruskin had admired the Byzantine, in the form of St Mark's, Venice, and had praised the style in the *Stones of Venice.*

J. W. Wild's Christ Church, Streatham, of 1841 (3), was possibly partly Byzantine in inspiration and Byzantine influences appear in the later designs of Philip Webb. The great builder and patron of the arts, the 3rd Marquess of Bute, admired the Byzantine and commissioned his architect Robert Rowand Anderson to build a church in the style at Troon in Ayrshire in 1882 and at Galston, Ayrshire, in 1884. With its coarse detail, in hard dark red brick this last is much inferior to Scott's Bayswater church.

The real vogue for the Byzantine was in the 1890s and the style was taken up in particular by Arts and Crafts architects. The style appealed to architects tired of the Gothic Revival, as it had the merit of being Christian (like Gothic), the qualities of structural honesty and constructive vigour, vitality in sculpture and decoration and, above all, because the style represented a departure from the orthodoxy of Roman Classicism. The Orders were still forbidden for their stiff formality, but the consciences of Gothicists were at rest with the Byzantine. In 1887–8 Robert Weir Schultz and Sidney Barnsley travelled in Greece studying Byzantine churches; in 1894 W. R. Lethaby and Harold Swainson's book on Haghia Sophia, Constantinople, was published, but the great monument to the Byzantine Revival is, of course, J. F. Bentley's Westminster Cathedral of 1894–1902.

J. O. Scott's church had an orthodox Byzantine plan: a Greek cross, with a central dome. The massing of the exterior, to buttress the dome (of 40 feet span, constructed of an outer and inner shell of brick and concrete, bonded together and secured with copper chain band) is satisfactory but the polychromatic brick and decoration, the frosted glass of the windows, and the early Christian rather than pure Byzantine style of some of the details gives the building a definite mid-Victorian appearance

(Scott would not, presumably, have known many Byzantine buildings at first hand).

The interior is most impressive, for its spaciousness and the richness of its furnishings. The lower parts of the walls are lined with rich coloured marbles, of a quality and disposed in a Byzantine style quite as good as work of the 90s. The elaborate stalls and the splendid iconostasis of contrasting coloured woods and inlaid mother of pearl were designed by Scott and made by Farmer and Brindley. The icon paintings on this screen were done in the proper style in 1880 by Professor Ludwig Thiersch of Munich (1825–1909). Thiersch specialised in this sort of work. A pupil of the distinguished romantic Schwantaler and J. S. von Carosfeld, he had been Professor at the German Academy in Athens in 1852–5 and later did work in the Greek churches in Paris and elsewhere.

Scott originally intended to put mosaic in the dome but the arches supporting the dome were to be left with the alternate red and white voussoirs which still appear around the edge of the vaults and on the windows. All the vaults and the dome were covered by mosaics which were completed in 1893. These are in a more convincing Byzantine style than might have been done earlier. The tesserae are individually disposed, so as to diffuse the light, and therefore not having that rather flat appearance which much mid-Victorian mosaic has (eg Salviati's). The scheme was designed by A. G. Walker, the sculptor and painter, and carried out by Mecenero. The critic of the *Builder* in 1893 considered this "one of the most important pieces of interior church decoration in London", and noted that "it is carried out in accordance with what the late Mr Burges, with much less reason, proposed to introduce into the interior of St Paul's".

Further down St Petersburgh Place (the street names commemorate the visit by the Allied Sovereign to London in 1814) is another very exotic and contemporary Victorian building, the Synagogue of 1877–9, designed by the Audesleys, known for their books on colour decoration. The Russian Orthodox Church now use another interesting Victorian church, the former All Saints, Ennismore Gardens, SW7, of 1846–9 by Vulliamy, with 1890s decorations by Heywood Sumner.

Map 1 D3

Messrs T. Goode & Co in South Audley Street; perspective drawing published in the Building News, *1876 (Royal Institute of British Architects, London)*

70
Messrs Goode
17–21 SOUTH AUDLEY STREET, W1

1875–91
Ernest George & Harold Peto

Goode's premises in Mayfair are remarkable both as a shop which has survived in all its Aesthetic Movement splendour and the first example of the Queen Anne style on the Grosvenor Estate. In the next few decades many more terraces of shops and flats, in red brick and terra cotta would be built in the surrounding area, designed by George and other architects, such as W. D. Caroë, A. T. Bolton, Col Robert Edis, etc.

The 1st Duke of Westminster (1825–99) did not rest content with his surveyors developing his London estate; he took a great interest in architecture. He employed Waterhouse for the massive rebuilding of Eaton Hall, Cheshire in 1870–3 and Bodley for the nearby church at Eccleston. Having been MP for Chester, Earl Grosvenor succeeded to the Marquisate in 1869 and in 1874 was elevated to a Dukedom, the last to be created; he was colossally rich. He was an enthusiast for the new style of brick and terra cotta and evidently did not want his estate to remain in drab stock brick and stucco. When Thomas Goode & Co wished to build their Artistic china and glass

shop, selling objects which were an integral part of the new Queen Anne style, the Duke recommended Mr Goode to visit a certain house in South Kensington—doubtless by Norman Shaw or J. J. Stevenson—to show him the style to use. But it was Goode who chose the architect, and allowed Ernest George (1839–1922) to build his first essay in the picturesque Queen Anne manner, in which he was highly successful.

The mellow picturesqueness was enhanced by the property being built in stages. Originally 18–19 were built as a pair of terrace houses with symmetrical gables in 1875 but 17—much lower—on the corner soon followed. Numbers 20–21 and the house in Chapel Place followed in 1889–91. George indulged in the full panoply of fashionable detail, with plenty of rubbed brick decorations in a 17th-century manner, railings with sunflowers and niches containing blue and white Nankin vases, of the sort with which, in a smaller form, the artistic could fill their sideboards and what-nots. In only one detail did George not get his way; he wanted to cut up the shop windows with plenty of white glazing bars to harmonise with the rest of the building, but commercial caution made the clients insist on more conventional plate-glass.

Sir Ernest George was the most frankly romantic and picturesque of the successful London architects of the later 19th century; he had never had the hard, moral Gothic training which Shaw, Stevenson, or E. W. Godwin had to shake off. He was in partnership with Harold Peto (1828–97). George was a superb architectural water-colourist and a competent etcher, and all his buildings reveal a principal concern with visual qualities—the antithesis to the moral approach of, say, Philip Webb.

As the peer rival of Norman Shaw in the domestic field after the 1870s, Ernest George has never been taken sufficiently seriously; the apocryphal legend that Shaw had cards printed saying that he was too busy to oblige Lord So-and-so and would cross out "Lord" and insert "Mr" where appropriate, and direct the disappointed client to E. George's office, is a reflection of this. Nevertheless, the list of those who were pupils or assistants in his office—Lutyens, Herbert Baker, Guy Dawber, J. J. Joass, R. Weir Schultz, Sidney Barnsley, Ernest Gimson—is at least as impressive as that for Shaw, and not without significance.

Map 2 C3

71
Board School

BONNER STREET AND GREEN STREET, BETHNAL GREEN, E2

1875
Edward Robert Robson & John James Stevenson

This school has been selected as a complete and unextended example of the many surviving Board Schools which were built from the creation of the London School Board until its absorption by the London County Council in 1904. These schools, towering above poor London streets, were conspicuous examples of the new Queen Anne style; Girouard has called them examples of the "Architecture of Light", a rare association between an *avant-garde* style and a progressive ideal: the ideal of state education for all.

The London School Board was set up as a result of W. E. Forster's Education Act of 1870. The immediate task was to build a large number of big, cheap schools in inner London. Edward Robert Robson (1835–1917) was the first Architect to the Board, from 1871 until 1889, but, in 1872, the first schools were designed in competition. Some were Gothic, for example those designed by T. Roger Smith. However, the one which was most influential was the Harwood Road School, Fulham, designed by Basil Champneys, the doyen of school builders and the architect of the sweet, redbrick Dutch-style buildings of Newnham College, Cambridge. Champneys' school was in brick, with dormer windows, Flemish gables and large windows with a lot of small (leaded) panes. This, the "Queen Anne", was the style adopted for the future schools of the Board under Robson's influence. Other architects also designed Board schools, such as Bodley and Garner, who were responsible for the Turin Street School, Bethnal Green, E2 of 1872–3.

There were practical reasons for adopting this style. Brick was cheap. The buildings had to be tall, often on confined sites, so the big gables and chimneys were appropriate as the schools were "henceforth to take rank as public buildings . . . planned and built in a manner befitting their new dignity", as Robson explained in his book, *School Architecture*, published in 1874. Here he explained why the new style was preferable to Gothic: "It

The Board School in Bonner Street, Bethnal Green; photograph taken soon after completion (Greater London Council)

is clear that a building in which the teaching of dogma is strictly forbidden can have no pretence for using with any point or meaning that symbolism which is so interwoven with every feature of church architecture as to be naturally regarded as its very life and soul. *In its aim and object it should strive to express civil rather than ecclesiastical character.* A continuation of the semi-ecclesiastical style which has hitherto been almost exclusively followed in England for National Schools would appear to be inappropriate and *lacking in anything to mark the great change which is coming over the education of the country"*.

From 1871–6 Robson was in partnership with another important domestic architect in the new style whom he had met when in Gilbert Scott's office, the Scot John James Stevenson (1832–1908). Robson and Stevenson's Board Schools, of which many were built, were of London stock brick with redbrick trimmings. Often the arched ground storey would be of redbrick with stone bands and voussoirs. Their school buildings relied for effect on their size and proportions: usually of three storeys of 14 feet high classrooms, the gables, dormers and occasional towers gave the prominent skyline a picturesque silhouette. White-painted tall sash windows lit the big classrooms. (Originally these were for sixty to eighty children with the sexes strictly segregated; in 1891 the class size was restricted to fifty). The only literal decoration would be ornamental panels—cartouches—of rubbed redbrick and stone on terra cotta, sometimes with sunflowers and always with the date of construction and the monogram of the LSB. A second tablet often gives the date of enlargement. Separate entrances for boys and girls are clearly labelled with stylised Roman capitals.

These buildings, still eminently serviceable if main-tained and modernised, are often ignorantly condemned as grim and oppressive. The ideal of their architects was the very reverse of this (always bearing in mind the tough circumstances of the 1870s—in Deptford the workmen building a school had needed police protection) and the Board Schools have a solidity and a truly urban character sadly lacking in most modern school buildings.

The effect these schools had on their contemporaries can still be experienced when travelling on the elevated railway lines of London, particularly those south of the Thames. On one of these Sherlock Holmes was travelling, while investigating the stolen Naval Treaty as Dr Watson recounted:

Holmes was sunk in profound thought, and hardly opened his mouth until we had passed Clapham Junction. "It's a very cheering thing to come into London by any of these lines which run high and allow you to look down on the houses like this."
I thought he was joking, for the view was sordid enough, but he soon explained himself.
"Look at those big, isolated clumps of buildings rising above the slates, like brick islands in a lead-coloured sea."
"The Board Schools."
"Lighthouses, my boy! Beacons of the future! Capsules, with hundreds of bright little seeds in each, out of which will spring the wiser, better England of the future."

Alas that such optimism should seem a period-piece. Robson's other public building in London is the People's Palace (now the nucleus of Queen Mary College) in the Mile End Road, E1, a brave attempt to bring civilised entertainment to the East End. It was built in 1885–90 in a stone Free Classic style.

Map 1 G2

72
Old Swan House

17 CHELSEA EMBANKMENT, SW3

1875–7
R. Norman Shaw

Swan House is, perhaps, the quintessential example of a Shaw town house: pretty, urbane Queen Anne, of red brick and white woodwork, and flagrantly "dishonest" by the high moral standards of Pugin or of the Modern Movement.

The construction of the Chelsea Embankment was completed in 1875 by the Metropolitan Board of Works, who thereupon let sites along the Embankment and in the newly created Tite Street. Of the many artistic houses which were raised in the next few years, several were designed by Shaw. All are variations on his Queen Anne style: a playful style for the town, derived chiefly from the brick architecture of the 17th century both in England and the Low Countries. Shaw's "Old English" style, with which he is much associated (tile-hung gables and half-timbering), was for the country.

Shaw's client for Swan House was Wickham Flower, a solicitor with artistic tastes, "a connoisseur who inclined to the Morris circle," who had Morris & Co. decorate his house when it was finished.

Shaw gave him a very special design, rather different from his other "elegantly fantastic Queen Anne houses at Chelsea", as Morris later described them. Instead of the usual artful asymmetry and picturesque disposition of gables and bay windows, Swan House is severely symmetrical—seven bays—with a straight cornice and only three dormers above. In this it points the way towards neo-Georgian, but not in its type of windows. On the first floor Shaw used three of his favourite oriel windows, gently bowed out, with an arched centre and leaded lights—a feature he derived from the 17th-century Sparrowe's House in Ipswich. Above this is a generous storey, articulated by strange tall and thin windows, alternately flat and in tiny bays proud of the wall. This last was a feature Shaw abandoned, but was taken up by Lutyens in his most eccentric phase in the late 1890s.

Shaw also played deceitful tricks with this façade, which he made project forward of the ground floor, as did old English houses. On the first floor, therefore, the three

The Swan House, Chelsea Embankment; photograph published in Hermann Muthesius, Die englische Baukunst der Gegenwart, *1900*

delicate oriels appear to be supporting the great mass of brick wall above. This is clearly impossible, and Shaw achieved the effect by the liberal use of double steel girders, twelve inches deep, bolted together. Shaw designed his own structural ironwork—rather than calling in an engineer—but the aesthetic effect was what interested him. Webb, on the other hand, not only eschewed concealed steelwork, but designed façades which, by the arrangement of the architectural elements, actually *look* as if they are doing the job they are performing.

What is curious about Swan House is that it was ever erected—not because the design was unstable, but because it flagrantly ignored the Metropolitan Building Act. London's fire regulations were framed with the experience of the Great Fire in mind: wood must not project in front of the brickwork, etc. Shaw had trouble with the regulations over several of his buildings, such as New Zealand Chambers in the City, and sometimes got around them by making his "woodwork" of white-painted concrete. At Swan house he kept a brick pier stretching from ground level flush with the face of the upper storeys: this doubtless represented the "real" face of the building, behind which plane are the wooden oriels. Nevertheless, the second floor windows project in front of the brickwork, yet Shaw had none of the trouble with the Board of Works such as plagued E. W. Godwin in Tite Street (79). Doubtless Shaw was more respectable and trustworthy in the view of his peers. (The interior of Swan House, now occupied by Messrs Securicor, is greatly altered.)

Shaw's other Chelsea houses are nearby. Next door is Cheyne House, No 18, which takes the corner round into Swan Walk (1875–7), then Farnley House, No 15, (1887–9) and Clock House, No 8, Chelsea Embankment (1878–80), built for Mrs Erskine Wemyss. This has all the prettiness and cleverness typical of Shaw, with its three gables, slight asymmetry and projecting clock. It is instructive to compare this house with No 7 next door, a pathetic and pedestrian attempt, exactly contemporary, by the academic and Beaux Arts trained R. Phené Spiers, to handle the new Queen Anne style.

Map 2 C5

St Thomas's Seminary, Hammersmith, in 1979 (photograph by Martin Charles)

73
St Thomas's Seminary, now the Convent of the Sacred Heart
HAMMERSMITH ROAD, W6

1876–88
John Francis Bentley

Behind the high wall which protects it from the bustle of Hammersmith Broadway is one of the most interesting and subtle examples of later Victorian domestic architecture.

The seminary for training Roman Catholic priests was planned by Cardinal Manning, Archbishop of Westminster, in 1868; in the event the building has changed functions several times—in 1893 it became a convent, with a school, and it is now a school.

Bentley's designs were made in 1875; the chapel (in the east wing abutting the street) was completed in 1884 and the infirmary, lodge and boundary wall in 1888. By the 1870s John Francis Bentley (1839–1902) had moved from his early taste for French 13th-century models and his admiration for the vigorous architecture of G. E. Street; in common with Bodley and Garner, J. D. Sedding and G. G. Scott Junior, he returned to English prototypes and the hitherto forbidden later styles.

For these buildings, which he felt should have collegi-

ate character, he chose a redbrick Tudor style, and the chapel has tracery in "debased" Perpendicular Gothic. Bentley displayed as much sophistication with his domestic as with his ecclesiastical designs. The detail is now literally Tudor and throughout there are subtleties, such as the shapes of the gables and the details of the domestic windows, which are characteristic of the architect. Particularly glorious are the ranges of brick chimneys, whose pointed arrises are continued down through the elevation below. Bentley, like other Gothic Revival architects from Street and Butterfield onwards, displayed a mastery in the handling of essentially ordinary brick domestic styles. The Redemptorist Monastery buildings behind St Mary in Clapham Park Road, SW4 (1891–3) are another fine example of Bentley's straightforward brick domestic manner.

The Hammersmith buildings best exemplify, in London, Bentley's sophisticated style of the 1880s. Several of his churches, such as that of Our Lady of the Holy Souls, Bosworth Road, Kensal Green, W10 (1881) have been mutilated and spoiled internally in accordance with current liturgical fashion. Of his majestic design for the church of Corpus Christi, Brixton Hill, SW2, only the chancel and transepts were built. The Church of St Mary in Cadogan Street, SW3 (1887) is in a more severe Early English style. His most characteristic and sumptuous work before building his masterpiece in the Byzantine style, Westminster Cathedral (1894–1902), was the Church of the Holy Rood, Watford (1879–1900). Bentley built comparatively little, but what he built was always sensitively and subtly conceived and executed.

Map 1 C3

River House, Chelsea Embankment, in 1979 (Architectural Press)

74
River House
3 CHELSEA EMBANKMENT, SW3

1876–9
George Frederick Bodley & Thomas Garner

George Frederick Bodley (1827–1907) and Thomas Garner (1839–1906), both of them pupils of Scott became partners in 1869, and are best known as church architects. Indeed, in later life, Bodley tended to disparage his early domestic work. However, in the late 1860s Bodley designed several houses which were conspicuous for their use of the new style of Dutch gables and rubbed brick classical detail. A conspicuous example is St Martin's vicarage at Scarborough of 1866–7.

An *avant-garde* style in church design was often paralleled by adherence to new fashions in domestic work, and in the early 1870s Bodley and Garner designed several of the new Board schools in the Queen Anne Style—that at Turin Street, Bethnal Green, survives—and they were entrusted with the first section of the now demolished Board School Offices on the Embankment, begun in 1873.

River House, designed in 1876 for the Honourable J. C. Dundas, and completed in 1879, competes with and compliments the range of fine brick Queen Anne houses by Norman Shaw and others in the Chelsea Embankment—Tite Street area developed by the Metropolitan Board of Works in the mid-1870s after this stretch of the Embankment had been completed in 1875. With its walls of stock brick and rubbed redbrick detail and large area of window (just like the Board Schools), the house is noticeably different in style from those by Shaw nearby. With its height and the roof topped by a cupola, the house sits well on the important river end of Tite Street.

Edward Warren remembered that Garner was usually more responsible for domestic design, although here both architects collaborated over the interior, and F. W. Simpson, another pupil, observed that the "design is based on Kew Palace, the front of which they had measured purposely, and the curious can trace the resemblance between the two buildings, although one is very far from being a copy of the other". The 17th-century brick Palace at Kew was, perhaps, the principal inspiration for most Queen Anne architecture.   Map 2 C5

75
Tower House
29 MELBURY ROAD, KENSINGTON, W14

1876–81
William Burges

When the Melbury Road area was developed after 1875 with artists' houses, there was one house which stood out conspicuously from the rest—Tower House—and which emphasised, in contrast to its exactly contemporary neighbour designed by Norman Shaw for the painter Luke Fildes, the change which had come over domestic architecture in the 1870s. It was built for himself by William Burges, a convinced Gothicist who was untouched by the new Queen Anne style.

William Burges (1827–81) was the son of a prosperous engineer and although his house must have been very expensive, he nevertheless left £40,000 when he died. Compared with Scott or Street he built comparatively little, but what he did design was large and expensive: a cathedral (Cork), estate churches (Studley Royal and Skelton, Yorks), a country house (Knightshayes, Devon) and, best of all, not one but two castles: Cardiff Castle and Castell Coch in south Wales. These were done for a client who was an architect's dream, the fabulously wealthy 3rd Marquess of Bute, who had a passion for building. Burges shared Bute's enthusiasm for the mediaeval world, for decorative and rich complexity, for scholarly and recondite symbolism; at Cardiff, Burges added massive new works with dramatic outlines and sumptuous interiors, at Castell Coch he "restored" a complete working castle from the ruins of the foundations.

Burges was the hero of young architects in the 1860s as his work seemed to exemplify the "muscular Gothic" of the Vigorous style. His win, with Henry Clutton, of the

a *Tower House built for Burges in Melbury Road, Kensington; drawn by Maurice B. Adams in 1880 and published in his* Artists' Homes, *1883*

competition for Lille Cathedral (1855) heralded the vogue for French 13th-century Gothic. While his interiors were far from simple, his exteriors are of powerful shapes with bold outlines and massive areas of plain masonry. This taste may have been due both to his knowledge and enthusiasm for the military architecture of the middle ages and also to the fact that he was very short sighted.

Unlike the other leading Revivalists, Billy Burges's love of Gothic did not have a religious inspiration: he just liked it. He seems to have been a jolly, romantic figure; with Bute, Lethaby thought "the idea of being a mediaeval jester must have occurred to his quick mind" and there is a limerick by Rossetti about him:

> There's a babyish party named Burges
> Who from infancy hardly emerges
> If you had not been told
> He's disgracefully old
> You would offer a bull's eye to Burges.

His Tower House sums up Burges in miniature. Although clearly a redbrick suburban house, it is massive, picturesquely composed, with a prominent tourelle, for the staircase and which is surmounted by a conical roofed turret. On a small scale it shows both Burges's love of castles and his knowledge of Viollet-le-Duc's work on domestic architecture—after all it was Burges who admitted "We all crib from Viollet-le-Duc".

However, in the interior of his house, which was unfinished at his death in 1881, Burges poured out for personal consumption a rich new mediaeval decoration, symbolism and humour. All the rooms tell a story. The dining room was meant to convey an idea of Chaucer's House of Fame; the library, with its birds painted by H. Stacy Marks, has an elaborate castellated stone chimney-piece illustrating the dispersal of the parts of speech with the famous joke of the H dropped below the frieze containing the other letters of the alphabet. A staircase window illustrates the "storming of the Castle of Love". Burges furnished his own bedroom so that he could imagine himself—when in an opiate haze—at the bottom of the sea: a wavy frieze containing fishes and eels, stars on the ceiling of tiny convex mirrors, and a splendid chimney-piece carved with a mermaid. Burges's bed (along with other examples of his Brobdingnagian furni-

b *House adjacent to Tower House, for Luke Fildes, from the same source*

c *Burges's own bedroom in the Tower House (Greater London Council)*

ture) is in the Victoria and Albert Museum. All these interiors, like those for Lord Bute, are overloaded with astrological symbols, signs of the Zodiac, real and mythical heroes and heroines; Lethaby called the house "massive, learned, glittering, amazing". All the carving was carried out by his favourite, Thomas Nicholls; the stained glass cartoons were prepared by H. W. Lonsdale.

Perhaps, in the 1960s, the originality of Burges as a High Victorian designer was overestimated; the heaviness and personal preferences displayed in his designs does not alter the fact that he relied heavily on his profound knowledge of the art and crafts of the middle ages. But Handley-Read was fair when he wrote that "for sheer power of intoxication on the borderline between romantic historicism and romantic fantasy, Burges seems to me to stand unrivalled in his period. It was a case of total immersion in a vision of the past, and Burges identified himself so wholeheartedly with his work that in

a sense the charge of sham becomes irrelevant".

From 1962–6 Tower House was unoccupied and vandalised, but since then, having been owned at one stage by Sir John Betjeman, who was left the building in an owner's will, it has been restored and new furniture to Burges's design commissioned by its recent owners.

Map 1 C3

76
London Oratory

BROMPTON ROAD, SW3

1876–96
Herbert Gribble

The Brompton Oratory, one of the principal Roman Catholic churches in London, is remarkable as an important building in a style which was anathema to High Victorian Goths, but the clients knew what they wanted.

The Oratory of St Philip Neri was set up in England in 1848 by John Henry Newman and Frederick William Faber, two recent and important converts from the Anglican Oxford Movement. Newman was to stay at the Birmingham Oratory; Faber established the London Oratory in Brompton in 1854. The temporary church, by J. J. Scoles, was demolished in 1880 to make way for the present building, the result of a characteristically mismanaged Victorian competition.

In the competition of 1878 an important condition was that "the style is to be that of the Italian Renais-sance", and J. D. Sedding, E. W. Godwin, Temple Moore and G. G. Scott, Junior were among the thirty architects who tried their hand in the style which Ruskin characterised as "the foul torrent of the Renaissance" and Pugin as "Revived Paganism". But Pugin was alone in being "blown into a change of religion by the whine of an organ-pipe; stitched into a new creed by the gold threads on priests' petticoats"; Newman and his followers had left the Gothic Protestant north and wanted the architecture and style of the centre of their new religion: Rome.

The assessor, Alfred Waterhouse, thought that "most of the competitors appear to have adhered so closely to the style of the Italian Renaissance as scarcely to have made sufficient allowance in point of fenestration for the difference between the amount of sunshine obtained in Rome and London", and particularly praised Scott's design. But the Fathers of the Oratory had not committed themselves to be bound by the assessor's views and they placed Scott fourth, Gordon and Flockhart third, Henry Clutton second and chose a design by the unknown outsider Herbert Gribble, a design that they had had on approval since 1876 and one which Waterhouse thought, although good in plan, "embellished with so much extraneous ornamentation as to be almost vulgar and commonplace".

Gribble (1847–94) was an obscure convert from Plymouth who had worked for J. A. Hansom and was possibly the protégé of the Duke of Newcastle. Despite

The Brompton Oratory; perspective of the original design drawn by Gribble (Courtesy of the London Oratory)

complaints from the architectural profession, work on his design began in 1880 and it was consecrated in 1884. The façade was erected in 1890–3, without its flanking towers, and the outer dome in 1895–6, but this was to a heightened and much better design by George Sherrin who was asked to be architect after Gribble's early death. The vigorously modelled lantern was drawn out by Edwin Rickards while working for Sherrin: it is a fore-taste of things to come from that master of Edwardian Baroque.

Gribble gave the Oratorians what they wanted: a building which would not be out of place in Rome. The plan is roughly that of the Gesù, except with a nave of three bays rather than four, and the elevations, in their executed more than their original design, redolent of late 16th-century Rome. However, unlike many Roman Churches, the Oratory is properly treated on all four sides and its façade is not on one plane but set back above the porch recessed behind coupled columns: a touch of St Paul's.

The interior is even more Italian, of the 17th century, and, as Gribble wrote, "those who had no opportunity of going to Italy to see an Italian church had only to come here to see the model of one". As it now stands it is more richly Italian than Gribble intended, as many of his designs, particularly that for the great Baldacchino, were not executed and real Baroque furnishings installed, such as the Lady Altar, the Altar of St Wilfrid and the marble statues of the Twelve Apostles (by the Sienese G. Mazzuoli). By Gribble are the Altars of St Philip Neri (paid for by the Duke of Norfolk) and the Altar of the Seven Doulours Chapel. The pair of seven-branched candle-sticks by the sanctuary rails were designed by William Burges and given by his patron the 3rd Marquess of Bute. The Altar of the English Martyrs in St Wilfrid's Chapel was painted by Rex Whistler in 1938. The pulpit is of 1930 by Commendatore Formilli, who was responsible for much of the mosaic work in the church. The memorial statue to Cardinal Newman outside the main entrance was designed by Thomas Garner in 1896 and modelled by L. J. Chavalliaud.

In the earlier Oratory buildings designed by J. J. Scoles (1798–1863), the architect of the Roman Catholic churches in Duncan Terrace, Islington, N1 and Farm Street, W1, is the library, one of the most beautiful rooms in London. The extension—St Wilfrid's Hall—is of 1910 by Leonard Stokes.

Map 2 B4

77
Church of the Ascension
LAVENDER HILL, SW11

1876–83
James Brooks & J. T. Micklethwaite

This church is a fine example of the grandness of effect the best mid-Victorian Gothic architects could achieve by using the simplest of means. Brooks here continues the redbrick, lancet window style of Gothic he used in his east London churches. Here, however, the east end is not square ended but apsidal. The building tells particularly well from the east; the roofline is unbroken and the narrow lean-to aisles carried right around the curve of the apse roof is echoed by the chapel and vestry on the north-east side. The projected tower above the south porch was (as usual) never executed.

The site is dramatic, and slopes steeply down towards the Thames. Poor Brooks had to pour most of the available funds into the foundations, to the alarm of his clients, who entrusted the completion of the job to J. T. Micklethwaite (1843–1906) the architect and antiquary, pupil of Gilbert Scott, who carried out Brooks's design. The church was consecrated in 1883.

The interior was never finished: the short stone col-

The Church of the Ascension, Lavender Hill, in 1944 (National Monuments Record, Crown copyright)

umns which support the massive naked brick arcades never had their capitals carved in the nave. The interior effect, of mass and proportion, does not at all suffer for this. However, the church is furnished as neither Brooks nor, probably, Micklethwaite intended: a wooden rood and screen were designed by George Wallace in a late mediaeval style: the rood was installed in 1910, the screen in 1914. The difference in style is the difference between the High Victorian ideal of muscularity and the later Victorian desire for refinement. The glass is by Kempe and Tower. Brooks's design for a bellcote on the roof was not executed; its unworthy substitute was destroyed by fire in 1979.

Map 1 E5

The Royal Bank of Scotland in Bishopsgate; woodcut published in the Builder, *1877 (Royal Institute of British Architects, London)*

78
Royal Bank of Scotland
5 BISHOPSGATE, EC2

1877
Thomas Chatfield Clarke

This building is an interesting essay in the solution of that problem which faced Victorian and Edwardian architects and for which, very occasionally, answers were arrived at worthy of comparison with Renaissance precedent: that is, how to adapt the Classical system of articulation to a tall frontage of a commercial building with large ground floor windows. One answer was the *palazzo* style of façade, with the windows on each floor of slightly different size and shape. In this building the architect attempted to unify the façade by bringing all the four floors into a logical and expressive Classical design.

The ground floor, with large windows, and the first floor are contained under an arcade of five bays supported on bold Ionic columns. The upper two floors rest on this satisfactorily solid base. The bays are separated by Corinthian pilasters, the stonework has horizontal bands of rustication, like an early 19th-century building, but even here the windows of the two floors are linked together in an elongated vertical frame. Above the principal cornice are dormer windows. The façade is of Portland stone, with a plinth of Aberdeen granite. Behind, the structure is of wrought-iron girders and tile arches. The façade is not only ornamented but embellished with suitably allegorical sculpture by Anstey. It must be admitted that the cherubs in the spandrels of the arches are embarrassingly mediocre.

Thomas Chatfield Clarke (1829–95) was a successful City architect responsible for a number of substantial office buildings. He was surveyor to the Fishmongers and Cordwainers Companies, President of the Surveyors Institution, a magistrate and, as an important and established architect with City connections, attempted to follow in the footsteps of Sir William Tite and become a Member of Parliament (as a Liberal), but failed.

Map 2 H2

79
House for Frank Miles
44 TITE STREET, SW3

1878–9
Edward William Godwin

"Sir William Tite, the architect, was chairman of the Metropolitan Board of Works, and in honour of him the Board named one of their new streets, opening upon the Chelsea Embankment. A deputation of painters, by whom the street was principally inhabited, waited upon the Board to remonstrate. 'If one told a cabman', they represented, 'at 12 o'clock at night, to drive one to Tite Street, he only laughed in one's face'", recorded G. G. Scott, Junior, in his notebook of not very funny stories. Tite Street soon became much more associated with the most advanced of artists, and with a certain notoriety; today it is rather sad, as the best houses have gone or have been mutilated.

In Victorian London, the best artists tended to live in Georgian houses in either Chelsea or Hampstead. Would-be Academicians put on an architectural display in the Melbury Road ghetto and the second-rate with pretentions gravitated to Artistic Bedford Park (good artists got out of there as quick as they could). The tone of artistic Chelsea was first set by Rossetti in Cheyne Walk; he was followed there by others of similar calibre. As Girouard observes, "Whistler, Wilde, Sickert, and Sargeant make even the best of Bedford Park seem second or third rate. Bedford Park liked to think of itself as rather daring; but what a squawking in aesthetic drawing rooms there would have been if the morals of Tite Street had been practised in Bedford Park, or if Godwin's raw-boned studios had been introduced among Shaw's sweetly pretty little houses. Late Victorian society made fun of Bedford Park, but had no difficulty in digesting it. Tite Street was more than it could stomach. Artistically it made Whistler a bankrupt; architecturally it emasculated Godwin's designs; morally it sent Miles to a lunatic asylum and Wilde to prison".

In the 1870s the scandals and bankruptcies lay in the future and the perfect architect for the truly *avant garde* was Edward William Godwin (1833–86) who had actually been sacked from Bedford Park after designing the first houses there. He had started as a hard Gothicist in the orbit of William Burges; in the 1870s he showed himself as one of the most imaginative and daring of domestic architects. He produced designs for houses which were tinged with Japanese exoticism and which demonstrated a logical economy in detail which distanced them from the conventional Queen Anne, and which was found to be unacceptable to the Metropolitan Board of Works, who controlled the development of their estate. Godwin was also, perhaps, the perfect architect for the like of Whistler and Wilde: his private life was

a *Godwin's original design for the house for Frank Miles in Tite Street, plans, section and elevation, 1878 (Victoria and Albert Museum, Crown copyright)*

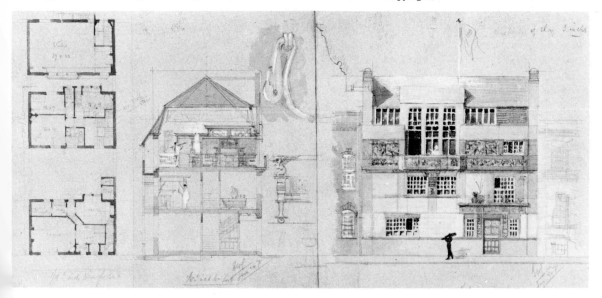

somewhat *louche.* He had in 1865 run off with the young Mrs G. F. Watts—Ellen Terry, the future actress—and lived with her for several years, and had two children by her; one was Edward Gordon Craig. Possibly Godwin's unconventional private life partly accounts for the decline in his professional career; before his early death he was principally occupied with stage and costume design.

Some of Godwin's designs for houses in Tite Street were more conventionally Queen Anne and met with no opposition—and survive. These include 4, 5, and 6 Chelsea Embankment (1876–8) on the corner of Tite Street, and the ungainly Tower House, 46 Tite Street (*c.*1884), with big studio windows. The controversial house was 35, the "White House" for James McNeil Whistler. The first design for this was prepared in 1877 and proposed a vast expanse of green slate roof and a redbrick and plaster wall broken by carefully arranged windows. The Board of Works, who had not been asked for their approval, objected that this rather austere elevation was "of an ugly and unsightly character". Architect and client were obliged to compromise; decorative panels and brick surrounds were proposed, but not added by the time of Whistler's bankruptcy in 1879. The house was then bought by "'Arry" Quilter, altered and scandalously demolished in the 1960s.

The design for No 44 was prepared in 1878. Its street elevation was almost an abstract pattern of rectangles, relieved by terra cotta ornament; balconies were prominent, and designed for flowers; the prominent raised bay had a severe straight parapet. The whole conception was Japanese in inspiration and a remarkably original composition in both form and colour. It was too much for the Board of Works.

What happened is best recounted by Godwin himself:

When the first elevation was sent to the Board of Works our respected friend, Mr. Vulliamy, said 'Why, this is worse than Whistler's,' that it would be useless to lay before the Board, and that it would not do, and yet I consider it the best thing I ever did. I grant you there was no cornice, no parapet and no string course. But is architecture a matter of string courses and parapets . . . Because I choose to do something different to the conventional, because I was not in fashion, and because the Board and its Officers knew nothing by experience of the nature of my work, the Board refused to let my design be carried out.

Well, I made a second design, in which I introduced a number of reminiscences of Holland, the thing was pronounced charming. This is very sad.

I am bold enough to say that I am a better judge than the Board of Works as to what is right in architecture. There is no chance for art or originality when such things as that go on at Spring Gardens.

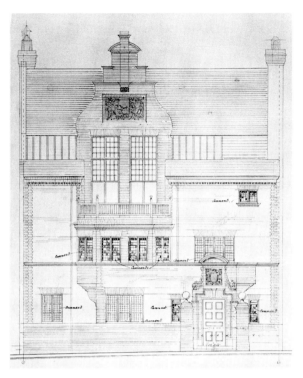

b *44 Tite Street as built; elevation drawn by Godwin, 1878 (Victoria and Albert Museum, Crown copyright)*

A revised design was approved in 1878; the "reminiscences of Holland" included the big Dutch gable and the surround to the front door. The house as built, in red and yellow brick, is still a fine thing, a bold and careful composition with a masterly balance between bare wall and the principal bay; it is very different from a design by Shaw.

Godwin's client, Frank Miles (1852–91), was a rich young man with decidedly Artistic tastes, who had shared rooms with Oscar Wilde after coming down from Oxford. He soon ended up in a lunatic asylum, for reasons open to easy conjecture.

Map 2 B5

80
St Michael

CAMDEN ROAD, NW1

1880–94
George Frederick Bodley & Thomas Garner

This was Bodley and Garner's first London church. The nave and aisles were built in 1880–1; the chancel in 1893–4. According to Edward Warren, the design was more Garner's than Bodley's, but they worked in perfect sympathy and harmony.

After his apprenticeship to Scott, George Frederick Bodley (1827–1907) rather reacted against his master and produced a series of brilliant tough designs in the most vigorous 13th-century Gothic. In the 1860s another Scott pupil, Thomas Garner (1839–1906) had a strong influence on Bodley in turning him back to English styles from Continental precedents. They became partners in 1869 and remained so until Garner became a Roman Catholic in 1896. From the seminal St Augustine, Pendlebury, of 1870–4, Bodley strove for refinement in his architecture and worked to continue the development of English Gothic as it might have proceeded if not cut off by the Black Death.

The stone and stock brick exterior of St Michael does not at first look prepossessing, and is not enhanced by the adjacent ABC factory, although the reticent forms of the masonry and the handling of the flying buttresses show a master-hand. It is the interior which matters, and its dignity is enhanced by the floor being several steps below the level of Camden Road. The typical continuous waggon roof from east to west is broken by stone arches, which require the external flying buttresses; the tracery is of the favoured Flowing Decorated form. The church never received a worthy reredos. For Francis Bumpus,

a *St Michael, Camden Town; perspective drawing of exterior showing unexecuted design for tower published in the* Building News, *1881*

b *The interior of St Michael; perspective drawing published in the* Building News, *1880*

author of that useful compendium of plagiarisms, *London Churches, Ancient and Modern* (1907), "St. Michael's evinces an austere reserve of ornament, a scholarly and refined proportion, and a delicate and fastidious taste in colour that stamp it as one of the most beautiful churches built, not in London alone, but in England since the Reformation". The "simple white interior" of the nave made the young Ninian Comper turn to architecture; he later became a pupil of Bodley. Comper observed that "in the writings of Bodley and still more in his work there is a trace of a slight preciousness, an affinity perhaps with Pater, or a more delicate expression of the aesthetic side of William Morris, and certainly with the Pre-Raffaelites of whom he was actually an associate".

In London, Bodley also designed the mission church of St Mary of Eton, Hackney Wick (1890), and Holy Trinity Church, Prince Consort Road, Kensington (1902–3).

Map 1 E2

Alliance Assurance Company's first building in St James's Street; perspective drawn by Lethaby and published in the Building News, *1882 (Royal Institute of British Architects, London)*

81
Alliance Assurance Offices
88 ST JAMES'S STREET, SW1

DESIGNED 1881
R. Norman Shaw
BUILT 1882–3

This was Shaw's second commercial building; the first, the striking City façade of New Zealand Chambers (1871–3), was destroyed in the Second World War. As with the earlier building, Shaw used the current redbrick domestic style of architecture and demonstrated complete indifference to the immediate environment of Classic stone, brick and stucco.

On each façade Shaw raised the tall elevation of a brick house of the Low Countries, each with tiers of windows separated by pilasters, decorative panels in rubbed brick and, of course, an elaborate gable. But because the building is on the important junction of St James's Street and Pall Mall (and, incidentally, opposite St James's Palace), Shaw placed an octagonal tower with a capped tile roof on the corner.

Less domestic are the broad-arched windows on the ground floor, which both look commercial and give a satisfactorily firm base to the elevations above. This was not common at the time. Shaw was later to employ large ground floor arches in the rebuilding of the Quadrant where the window encompasses not one but two storeys, a device which, as Andrew Saint points out, was used by Cockerell earlier in the century to articulate and to properly proportion his bank façades.

As at Scotland Yard (86), Shaw here employs the High Victorian motif of prominent banding of stone in the red brick, and the alternate voussoirs of brick and stone in the ground floor arches is a particularly happy feature.

There is no better illustration of the change which came over English architecture at the end of the 19th century than to compare this building with the one directly opposite on the west side of St James's Street, designed for the same firm by the same architect twenty years later.

Number 88 St James's Street was designed in 1901 by Shaw, in conjunction with his pupil Ernest Newton, and erected in 1904–5. Red brick has given way to Portland stone; the picturesque and illiterate northern Renaissance of the 17th century to the Grand Manner. Here is a symmetrical façade raised on three massive rusticated arches (containing *two* floors) of a mannered composition of pedimented windows, a bold cornice and a pediment. The Queen Anne was a half-way stage between High Victorian Gothic and full-blooded Renaissance Classicism, but in all styles Shaw displayed subtlety, originality and wit.

Map 2 D3

82
Town Houses

20–26 AND 35–45 HARRINGTON GARDENS, SW7
AND 1–18 COLLINGHAM GARDENS, SW5

BEGUN 1881
Ernest George & Harold Peto

These are the most calculatedly picturesque of Victorian street houses. Ernest George continued the "Pont Street Dutch" style of town houses set by Norman Shaw in Cadogan Square, but made them much more Flemish and embellished the red brick with terra cotta. Their inspiration was the street houses of Bruges or Amsterdam which were a good model as they were tall and thin as well as being infinitely varied in outline and fenestration; their illiterate early Renaissance detail was highly attractive to Gothic renegades who feared the full panoply of the Classical Orders. In these houses George was much more literally Flemish than Norman Shaw; he was also much more concerned to make each house utterly different from its neighbour and, by the design of its gable and its materials, to make each seem by a different hand. This supreme individualism is the furthest possible remove from the uniformity of the Georgian terrace which the Victorians so hated. When George's drawing of Harrington Gardens was exhibited at the Royal Academy in 1883, the *Builder*'s critic commented on "the sham anti-

Houses in Harrington Gardens; perspective drawing by Ernest George, exhibited at the Royal Academy in 1883 (Victoria and Albert Museum, Crown copyright)

que collection of buildings . . . Old streets do occasionally assume this kind of appearance of pieces of buildings in ever so many different manners all muddled together, and they have a picturesque suggestiveness then, but to go about to make this kind of thing deliberately is child's play".

The first houses in the development, 20–26 Harrington Gardens, were promoted in 1880 and built in 1881–2; these are more conventionally "Queen Anne" in style compared with the extravagant gabled houses on the south side of the street. These were built in 1882–4 for individual clients and, because of the shallow site, have wide frontages which lent themselves to the treatment of Flemish and German street houses. Because of the success of these, the Collingham Gardens development was built in 1883–8 as a speculation by the contractors, Peto Brothers, sons of Sir Samuel Morton Peto and brothers of George's partner. Here the houses manage to be wildly picturesque on both the street and the garden fronts, but the speculation was not immediately successful, as the last house was not leased until 1896.

The quality of the workmanship is throughout superb, whether in brick, terra cotta, stone or tile, and the leaded-light fenestration is worthy of study. The occupants were wealthy. In Harrington Gardens, no 37 was taken by W. R. Cassells, but the most distinguished occupant lived next door in no 39: W. S. Gilbert of Savoy Opera fame. Gilbert moved to Grim's Dyke at Harrow Weald in 1890, where Ernest George made additions and alterations to the "Old English" house by Norman Shaw.

Map 2 A4

83
Whitehall Court & the National Liberal Club

WESTMINSTER, SW1

DESIGNED 1884
Archer & Green and Alfred Waterhouse
BUILT 1885–7

On this huge and important site next to the Victoria Embankment, the Liberator Permanent Building and Investment Society raised a vast block of flats in conjunction with the new building of the National Liberal Club which acquired the north end of the site. The scheme had been first promoted in 1883 by Jonathan T. Carr of Bedford Park (89) but it had run into difficulties and, in 1885, sold to a company run by an even more dubious financier, Jabez Balfour, who was eventually prosecuted for multiple frauds. The Club's architect, Alfred Waterhouse, worked in conjunction with the architects of Whitehall Court, the successful commercial firm of Archer and Green—architects of the Hyde Park Hotel in Knightsbridge (1888) and Cambridge Gate in Regent's Park (1875)—to whose plans there were "modifications effected" by Waterhouse. The Metropolitan Board of Works had also to be satisfied, and their insistence on alterations to the design delayed construction.

Whitehall Court, "a Palace of Flats", consists of luxury flats, originally self-contained suites varying from seven to twenty rooms at rents of £300 to £800 per annum. The building was carefully sound-proofed and had lifts. The pioneer building for a large block of mansion flats with architectural pretentions was Shaw's Albert Hall Mansions of 1881, but here, in view of the important site, the elevations are of Portland stone, not brick, and the style is much less disciplined, if more picturesque.

The style is a sort of French château Renaissance, ungrammatical and coarse, of a sort favoured for commercial and residential blocks after the 1870s. The merits are not in detail but in overall treatment. The long elevations—made more horizontal by the strips of balconies—are relieved by four big projecting bays and by a fantastic skyline of dormer windows, gables and towers. Archer and Green powerfully and imaginatively contributed to the romantic skyline of Westminster when seen

a *The first design for Whitehall Court and the National Liberal Club; perspective view from across the Thames published in the Building News, 1884 (Royal Institute of British Architects, London)*

b *Waterhouse's original staircase inside the National Liberal Club, destroyed during the Second World War (Courtesy of the National Liberal Club)*

either above the trees from St James's Park or across the river: the towers of the Palace of Westminster and the Abbey, then the Italianate tower of Scott's Foreign Office, the Classic pavilions on the roof of Vincent Harris's War Office and then the gables and spires of Whitehall Court all contribute to a most picturesque vista. Summerson suggests that the architects cannot have failed to notice Aston Webb and Ingress Bell's very similar unsuccessful design for the War Office (1884).

Typical of Victorian Classic is that—thanks to the Gothic Revival—absolute symmetry is not only unimportant but is almost undesirable in itself. The elevation to the Victoria Embankment is given rough symmetry by the corner and two central towers, but Waterhouse's end is different in detail and articulation. It does not matter. On the acute corner by Whitehall Place, Waterhouse placed a tower, its drama increased by the fact that it rises through several storeys unbroken by balconies or windows. The alterations asked for by the Board of Works actually increased the height and severity of this corner, which contains a staircase to allow direct entrance from

the street to the Gladstone Library on the second floor.

The interior of the Club shows Waterhouse's obsession with hard efficiency, with many parts covered by glazed and moulded coloured tiles. Although a Goth in origin, style did not matter. Waterhouse became increasingly concerned with designing well-planned, pragmatic buildings all of which have a hardness in texture characteristic of his approach. He seems an odd architect to have chosen for a clubhouse, but the Liberal Party's record in commissioning architecture in the 19th century is not inspiring. Nevertheless, Waterhouse did his best to create richness and comfortable splendour and his triumph was the oval central staircase with paired columns between the flights. Sadly, this Baroque conception, redolent of Bernini, was damaged during the Second World War, but the present oval marble staircase is a fine reconstruction of 1950–1 by Bernard Engle. The Club has survived the recent misfortunes of the Liberal Party with the loss of its library's books and other effects.

Whitehall Court and the National Liberal Club were lit by electricity from the beginning. The Whitehall Electricity Supply Co Ltd was incorporated in 1887 and built a station under the raised terrace on the river front of the building, which had a 135 foot tall stack inside. By the time the station was ready, in 1888, it had been bought by the Metropolitan Electricity Supply Co as part of its expanding system.

Map 2 E3

84
Chelsea Vestry Hall, now Old Town Hall

CHELSEA MANOR GARDENS, SW3

1885–7
John McKean Brydon

1904–8
Leonard Stokes

By the end of Victoria's long reign the stylistic wheel had turned full circle. It was again appreciated that different styles were appropriate for different types of building and Renaissance Classicism was back in fashion. A key and influential building in this return to the Grand Manner was J. M. Brydon's design for the Chelsea Vestry Hall of 1885.

The Queen Anne movement had begun as a reaction against the universality of the Gothic Revival. A free and more vernacular style was needed for urban domestic architecture and Shaw, Nesfield, Bodley, Webb and Stevenson adopted the picturesque redbrick styles of the 17th century, both of Home Counties and Dutch derivation. The Classical style—forbidden to strict Gothicists—was employed but never in a pure form; as Goodhart-Rendel put it, the Queen Anne was "a Gothic Game played with neo-Classical counters". The emphasis was on the picturesque and architects still had a horror of symmetry and the Grand Manner. The weakness of the style was its eclectic nature and lack of discipline; in the hands of a supreme artist like Noman Shaw the style was winning but in the hands of lesser men it could be rather less successful.

After a period of complete freedom in the 1870s, architects in the 1880s seemed again to be needing a greater formality. Domestic architecture began to lose the picturesque gables as it was appreciated that the Georgian town-house was essentially English and vernacular and not to be eschewed as an expression of the "foul torrent of the Renaissance" (Ruskin's phrase). At the same time it was felt that the Queen Anne was too domestic for important buildings; something more formal was required for large buildings, a formality which only the Renaissance seemed to be able to provide.

148

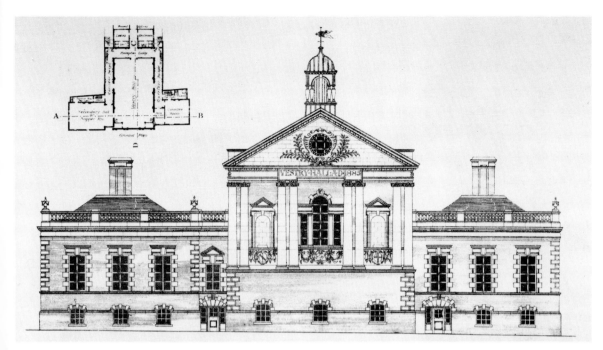

Brydon's original design for the Chelsea Vestry Hall; elevation of Chelsea Manor Gardens front published in the Builder, *1885*

The conscience of these architects of the Queen Anne —almost all of whom had begun life as Gothicists—was squared by the discovery of an *English* Renaissance: the architecture of Inigo Jones and Wren. A growing imperialism in Britain was echoed by a desire for an English style and the answer was the English Renaissance— Wrenaissance. In 1889 Brydon gave a lecture on the subject and in 1893 Reginald Blomfield could speak of "the great architectural age of Wren and Gibbs".

As so often in architecture, the theory was anticipated by a concrete visual statement. Brydon's Vestry Hall design had a façade in the brick and stone manner of the late 17th century. Typical of English architects of the time was the fact that he did not quite follow the rules or get things right, and the elaborately articulated hall inside is full of compromise details which have a Queen Anne flavour. As built, the façade differs slightly from the 1885 design.

Shortly after this building came John Belcher's Institute of Chartered Accountants in Great Swan Alley, EC2 of 1888–93. This was even more in a full-blooded and rich Renaissance manner, and English architecture was launched upon its course towards Edwardian Baroque.

The same tendencies may be seen in Norman Shaw's work in the late 1880s, in his 170 Queen's Gate, SW7 (1887–8) and his big Baroque country houses: Bryanston (1889) and Chesters (1890). John McKean Brydon

(1840–1901) was a Scot who had worked in Nesfield's office and then Shaw's. His earlier work is much more in the Shaw manner. He died before his most important building, the Local Government Board Offices in Parliament Square (1898), was completed; as Goodhart-Rendel remarked of Brydon, "it can leave no doubt in our minds that he thought much more highly of Chambers than Chambers would have thought of him".

In 1899 Chelsea became a borough and the Vestry Hall a town hall. It was extended to the King's Road and given a new front by Leonard Stokes in 1904–8, which continued the style set by his old friend Brydon.

Map 2 B5

85
Brooklyn
8 PRIVATE ROAD, ENFIELD, MIDDLESEX

1886–7
Arthur Heygate Mackmurdo & Herbert Percy Horne

This is one of the most remarkable and yet puzzling works of architecture of the 19th century. With its horizontal lines and flat roof, it has been seen as a pioneer of the Modern Movement; it may also be seen as an idiosyncratic interpretation of Neo-Classicism by one of the most imaginative of Arts and Crafts designers. One cannot help wondering whether the house looked a little different when first built: did it then sport the roughcast which shortly after became the favourite facing material of C. F. A. Voysey, or was that added later?

The architect was Arthur Heygate Mackmurdo (1851–1942) who, in the 1880s, was undoubtedly the most creative and original figure in the world of the Arts and Crafts. As an architect he had been the pupil of T. Chatfield Clarke and then James Brooks. He acquired a social conscience from Herbert Spencer, went to Oxford to attend Ruskin's lectures, toured in Italy with Ruskin and came to know William Morris. With such a background, it is not surprising that Mackmurdo founded the first of the Arts and Crafts guilds, the Century Guild, in

Brooklyn, Enfield; an early photograph

1882. In 1883 he published *Wren's City Churches*, a book as remarkable for its proto-Art Nouveau title page with its most un-Wrenlike swirling lines as for its subject matter (Wren was anathema to the Gothic Revival and Morris only committed the SPAB to the defence of the City churches owing to the advocacy of Thomas Carlyle.) In 1884 Mackmurdo began publishing the *Hobby Horse*, the crucially influential art magazine. At the same time he designed furniture and wallpaper.

Mackmurdo's first house on the Bush Hill Estate at Enfield (6, Private Road, of *c.* 1873) is very much in the tile-hung half-timbered style of Noman Shaw. The later house shows a remarkable transformation in style. All trace of Gothic picturesqueness has disappeared. Instead the design shows a clear horizontality which may owe something to the late Japanesy style of E. W. Godwin (eg his original design for Whistler's White House in Chelsea, 1878). Certainly the inspiration is Classical, and of a more mannered variety than that which permeated the early Queen Anne movement.

The six ground floor sash-windows are separated by piers and pilasters which alternately support sculptured figures and the pilaster theme is continued on the side elevations. There is no attempt at carrying through the horizontal logic of the Orders, and the side elevations seem quite unrelated. The straight parapet was originally enlivened by a series of balls, only two of which survive at the corners.

The design had decorative elements, however: the piers have moulded terra-cotta capitals and the ground floor windows are flanked by naturalistic ornament in terra cotta both of which features, when unpainted, would have made the house more colourful. The front door (at the back) is reached under a covered way supported on typical Mackmurdo columns, ie square wooden piers with flat tops, a characteristic feature which appeared in the influential 1886 Liverpool Exhibition stand for the Century Guild.

The odd Classicism of this house may well reflect the influence of Herbert Percy Horne (1864–1916), who was Mackmurdo's partner and collaborator from 1883 until 1890. Both men worked together on the river front of the Savoy in 1889. When they separated in 1890, the production of both men rather fell off. Horne had always been more literary and went to live in Italy where he devoted himself to writing art history. Mackmurdo continued to practise; he designed interesting redbrick houses in Chelsea, notably 25 Cadogan Gardens, SW3 (1893–4) for Mortimer Mempes but did little good after the turn of the century.

Map 1 F1

86
Metropolitan Police Central Offices, New Scotland Yard

VICTORIA EMBANKMENT, SW1

1887–91; 1898–1907
R. Norman Shaw

a *New Scotland Yard; photograph taken from Westminster Bridge in the 1890s, before the extension was built (Greater London Council)*

In the sad history of the government patronage of architecture during the 19th century, the building of New Scotland Yard is one of the few happy results. On a prominent site Norman Shaw was able to design his only public building and met the challenge of adapting his domestic style to a large metropolitan structure with triumphant success.

His appointment was a tribute to his reputation. Instead of the usual muddle occasioned by open competition—the latest unhappy result being the Liberal Government's appointment of the mediocre Leeming and Leeming to design the Admiralty in 1884—the Tory Home Secretary, Henry Matthews, consulted Shaw on his own authority in 1886. At first he was to act as consultant architect to the Police Surveyor, J. Dixon Butler, as the Receiver to the Metropolitan Police District, Alfred Pennefather, was determined to consult an "architect of standing" so as to erect a worthy architectural monument; by 1887 Shaw was in command.

The site was a splendid one but with a sad history—a site on the Embankment near Westminster Bridge dedicated to a National Opera House which, so typical of England, never got built. It was acquired for the Police in 1886. Shaw had to accommodate himself to several of the Government's proposals. He was happy to use the four-square courtyard plan prepared by Butler, but was less happy about the experiment to use granite and Portland stone from government-owned quarries. The granite was to be quarried free of charge by Dartmoor convicts (which offended trade unions) and was, in the event, employed with great success for the base of the building, but Shaw wished to introduce what was an innovation in a public building, red brick, and he wrote that "it is a serious question whether a building with a grey granite base, a white stone upper part and a slate roof might not look very cold, and whether it would not materially gain by the introduction of a warm material like red brick".

Always adept at handling clients, Shaw had his way: Portland stone was reserved for the window surrounds, cornices and for bands of stone introduced into the brick.

The first design exhibited at the Royal Academy in 1887 did not have the massive gables and high roof, but the general four-square mass, accentuated by the corner turrets—"pendentive towers"—was designed for the magnificent position overlooking the Thames. Although there are rational Puginian asymmetries in the fenestration on the lower granite storeys, the mass of the building did not demand Shaw's usual picturesque arrangements; instead the segment-headed and segmental-pedimented windows are regularly placed. The skyline tells because of the rows of dormer windows, the massive chimneys, the huge gables topped by aedicules and obelisks and the pointed roofs on the towers. These last were possibly intended to suggest the spiked helmets of London "bobbies"; Beresford Pite said each looked like a "pickelhaube".

The inspiration for the overall design would seem to have been Netherlandish (Pite called it "a Dutch-cheese warehouse from the banks of the Dort"), although Albert Richardson thought the details derived from a Renaissance building in Copenhagen. But there was an important English source of influence on the final form of the building, redesigned in 1888–9: the Baroque porches with broken pediments are a response to the design of the Institute of Chartered Accountants in Great Swan Alley, EC2, prepared by John Belcher in 1888, a building which was to have a seminal influence on the revival of 17th-

b *The original main entrance to New Scotland Yard (Greater London Council)*

century Classicism in England in the 1890s.

The design of New Scotland Yard reflects another source of influence which permeates Victorian architecture but is less evident in Shaw's work: Ruskin. Andrew Saint has observed how the pendentive turrets, the hollow square form, the colouring inspired by associated geology and suggesting mass giving way to lightness as the building rises, all correspond with Ruskin's demands for public architecture.

The building was completed in 1891; the previous year the Government had been questioned in Parliament over the design and the appointment of the architect. The repellent Sir William Harcourt, MP, and former Liberal Home Secretary lead the gratuitous attack. In a further attack in 1898, when again in Opposition, Harcourt announced that Scotland Yard "is rather inferior, in my opinion, in architectural beauty to the premises of Messrs. Crosse and Blackwell, which face it on the other side of the river", (by Roumieu and Aitchison, 1884: demolished) and he was answered by a letter to *The Times* in Shaw's defence signed by a distinguished list of architects and artists which achieved nothing but provides further evidence of the curious political fact that during Victoria's reign Liberal governments were conspicuous in their insistence on cheap architecture at the expense of architectural quality, while Tory govern-

ments, perhaps as a legacy from Disraeli's connection with "Young England", attempted to give London worthy public buildings and tended to see the merits of designers in the Gothic Revival tradition. Harcourt's criticism did elicit interesting comment for Shaw to use in the Government's defence. "My aim has been to have less of what I should call 'style', and more of what I should call character. Style gives what we have already got many examples of, viz. dull copies of Italian palaces, mediaeval buildings etc. and they are generally found to be unsuited to their purpose, ill lit, and from an artistic point of view, dead and so failures . . . I dwell on New Scotland Yard being a genuine building, in which we have no sham or shew fronts, all is of the same quality and in the court it is the same. In order to secure this, a quality which I consider essential to good building, I have reduced the ornamental features to a minimum, relying on the bulk and outline to give the desired character. Had I sacrificed what I believe to be a sound principle I might have put more ornament on the shew fronts, and so possibly have made it more attractive to a certain class of mind. But after all the whole matter is a question of taste, on which I fear people never can and never will agree, certainly not for some time." Elsewhere Shaw was reported as aiming at "solidity and sternness to give simplicity. . . . His view of the Metropolitan Police is that it is an essentially stern, and not at all frivolous body", which is certainly suggested by the massive granite base of the building.

The one regret is that the building was ever extended, even though it was done by Shaw himself, as Pennefather was determined he should. A new block was built to the south in 1905–7, having been designed in 1897, along with a new police station in Cannon Row, to the southwest, built in 1900–2. By being in the same style, the extension reduces the impact of the original massive, four-square block which must have once seemed so prominent in contrast to its neighbours.

Shaw's first biographer, Reginald Blomfield, wrote in 1940, "Years ago I ventured the opinion that, leaving the Houses of Parliament out of account, Scotland Yard is still the finest public building erected in London since Somerset House, and that is still my opinion". Andrew Saint, his second biographer, writes that "square is metropolitan might, flanked by four guardians of the Queen's peace (the helmetted turrets), New Scotland Yard keeps its stalwart watch upon London's riverside". How sad that the Police have moved out into their undistinguished tower in Corbusian Victoria Street.

Placed on the wall of New Scotland Yard is the memorial medallion to Shaw, designed by his pupil Lethaby and modelled by Hamo Thorneycroft in 1913.

Map 2 E3

87
Church of the Holy Redeemer

EXMOUTH MARKET, CLERKENWELL, EC1

1887–1906
John Dando Sedding & Henry Wilson

This building erected on the site of the Spa Fields Chapel brought to the shabby terraces of Clerkenwell a convincing piece of Italy—ordinary Italy—and as such is a monument to the Aestheticism of the late Victorian Anglo-Catholics and an expression of the extent to which the revolt against mid-Victorian Gothic was prepared to go.

In the hands of Bodley and G. G. Scott, Junior, that revolt remained largely within the context of the once-forbidden late mediaeval English styles. But John Dando Sedding (1838–91) felt that more needed to be done to bring life into ecclesiastical architecture. This he largely achieved by trying to realise the ideals of Ruskin and Morris in accompanying craftsmanship and freedom in style. Sedding became increasingly involved with the Arts and Crafts Movement, was a master of the Art Workers' Guild and, when he had secured his reputation by dying young, became a hero for younger men. He built comparatively little. His chief work, Holy Trinity, Sloane Street, SW1, although begun in 1888, is really a monument of the 90s. Inside a building of the Perpendicular style, Sedding encouraged a galaxy of artists and sculptors to work and, although the interior was never completed, it is a repository of gorgeous ecclesiastical art objects. The result has no unity, however, and justifies Goodhart-Rendel's comment that Sedding was "a muddly architect; a soft not a hard".

In his first London church, in Clerkenwell, he showed himself more pure in style, but the style is remarkable, possibly because the area had a significant Italian community. Sedding chose the style of a simple Italian Renaissance church. With its façade boldly inscribed "Christo Liberator", it is hard not to take the building as Roman Catholic. Sedding thought he was being stylistically "naughty" at Sloane Street; here he was being even more naughty.

The eaves and simple pediment have the Italian quality of Inigo Jones's St Paul, Covent Garden. The brick walls are relieved on the façade by bands of stone; the other

Church of the Holy Redeemer, Clerkenwell, as originally designed by Sedding; perspective drawing of the interior by Gerald Horsley, 1887, published in the Memorial of the Late J. D. Sedding, *1891*

elevations are composed of bands of coloured brick and broken by the big simple circular windows. (These side elevations seem to exhibit the ultimate affectation of holes in the brickwork as if their coating of marble is absent, as on so many Italian buildings, but the façade is not so treated.)

Sedding managed to keep his eaves and upper walls unbroken on the side elevations (probably never meant to be seen as the church stands in a busy street) which belies the complexity of the interior. This, although articulated by a giant Corinthian order standing on panelled pedestals, is not rectangular but has a sort of cross plan with diminutive transepts. It hints at the sort of game of a cross with a square which Wren played in his City churches. Indeed, the building reminded Walter Pater of Renaissance churches in Venice and Wren's London churches as they must have looked when fresh and clean.

The church was consecrated in 1888 but completed later with differences to the design published in 1887.

This drawing shows changes in level and the baldacchino placed against the east wall; it also shows that the walls were intended to be painted in fresco. Sedding believed that a church should be "wrought and painted over with everything that has life and beauty—in fresh and fearless naturalism covered with men and beasts and flowers". Nothing was done, however, and the interior would probably be best white rather than in Anglican pastel shades of yellow and blue.

As with many of Sedding's jobs, the building was completed by this assistant Henry Wilson (1864–1934), a gifted designer whose work often combined Arts and Crafts excellence with an interest in the Byzantine. Wilson drew up plans for completing the church in 1892. Inspired by Santo Spirito in Florence, Wilson left Sedding's baldacchino free standing and extended the building behind to form a Lady Chapel; the work was carried out in 1894–5.

Wilson also designed the interesting buildings which flank the façade: on the left is the parish hall, on the right the clergy house with its campanile. An appeal was launched for these in 1901 and they were ready for occupation in 1906. These buildings are in a primitive but very subtle Romanesque style, carried out in economical materials: stock bricks and red tiles. Although rugged and apparently commonplace, they are full of clever idiosyncracies, such as that the campanile is not square in plan. Wilson also designed the font (1909) and the Chapel of All Souls (1921), whose reredos, presented by Wilson, is a cast of that in the chapel at Welbeck Abbey (1906).

Map 2 F1

a *Westminster Abbey seen from the Victoria Tower of the Palace of Westminster in c1860 before the restoration of the Chapter House was undertaken (Westminster Abbey Library)*

88
Westminster Abbey
WESTMINSTER, SW1

1849–78
George Gilbert Scott

1878 onwards
John Oldrid Scott

1878–97
John Loughborough Pearson

It may seem perverse to include Westminster Abbey in a guide to Victorian London, but the Abbey, like most of our great mediaeval churches, owes much of its present appearance and splendour to 19th-century restorers and designers. Sir Gilbert Scott, Surveyor to the Abbey from 1849–78, has been much criticised for his activities at the Abbey, but he, as the best-known and most active of Victorian restorers, who was connected with almost every cathedral in the country, has often been blamed for work done by his predecessor, Blore, and his successor Pearson.

Scott succeeded the dull pedant, Edward Blore (1787–1879), noting that "this is an appointment which has afforded me more pleasure than any other which I have had". He continued Blore's refacing of the exterior of the Abbey, a refacing which continued right through the 19th century and which is being resumed today. Much of Scott's work at the Abbey consisted of archaeological investigation, and he poured his enthusiastic researches into his *Gleanings from Westminster Abbey*, first published in 1861.

Some of Scott's activities were possibly ill advised, such as his coating the stone with "shellac dissolved in spirits of wine", which Lethaby claimed was, in fact, French polish, but although this darkened the stone, it stopped it crumbling and hardened it sufficiently to allow future cleaning. Lethaby's conservative use of limewash as a preservative seems to have been eminently satisfactory in the cloisters.

Scott wrote in his *Recollections* that "my own works at the Abbey have not been extensive. They consist of two pulpits, three grilles, an altar rail, the gable and pinnacles of the south transept, sundry tops of pinnacles, a new altar-table in the sanctuary of the church, and another in

Henry's VII's Chapel". Some of his furnishings have since been replaced. In 1866 he tackled the 15th-century reredos of the High Altar, "which I found in plaster, [and] has been restored in alabaster and marble, with great care and precision". The new sculpture was by Armstead, the mosaic by Messrs Salviati of Venice.

Scott's greatest work was the restoration of the 13th-century Chapter House, undertaken in 1866. Long used by the Government, its condition was deplorable. Its interior was "little more than a ruin . . . choked up with presses, chests, galleries, huge sacks of parchment, and every possible obstruction and disfigurement. Its beautiful windows . . . walled up, and its elegant vaulting destroyed" and, as old photographs confirm, the window tracery, buttresses and original roof of the structure had been removed. Scott enjoyed the restoration: "I may truly say that this was a labour of love, and that not a point was raised which would enable me to ascertain the actual design of any part, nor was any old feature renewed of which a trace of the old form remained". He rooted about behind the panelling for fragments of sculpture as evidence of the original design, and exposed the splendid mediaeval floor tiles, and "I know of no parts which are conjecturally restored but the following: the external parapet, the pinnacles, the gables of the buttresses and the roof". Very likely the roof was not originally a pyramid; but even Scott's severe critics of his restoration policy had to admit that the restored Chapter House was better than its previous state.

No so with the north transept, the principle entrance front of Henry III's church. This had much suffered from the addition and the removal of a porch which had abutted against the three great portals. These portals had been covered by a sort of screen by Wren's surveyor, Dickenson, in 1719–22, who had also repaired and Gothickised the rest of the front. Scott attempted to restore these portals. After careful investigations made in 1871 the old design was recovered. Work began on the eastern portal in 1875 and the restoration of the other two was continued by J. O. Scott after 1878. Even Scott's severe critic, the quintessentially "anti-scrape" W. R. Lethaby, had to admit that the restoration was accurate in its design. But for William Morris, founder of the Society for the Protection of Ancient Buildings in 1877, the modern sculpture was hard and mechanical and was just "imitating the inimitable". It was impossible to recapture the work of the mediaeval mason which had been weathered by time: as Ruskin had fulminated in the *Seven Lamps* (1849), "the spirit of the dead workman cannot be summoned up, and commanded to direct other hands, and other thoughts . . . Do not let us talk . . . of restoration . . . the thing is a lie from beginning to end".

But the real mischief on the north transept was wrought, not by Scott, but by his successor as Surveyor,

b *The north transept of Westminster Abbey in c1880 when only the left-hand portal had been restored (National Monuments Record, Crown copyright)*

J. L. Pearson. The present north transept front is virtually a design by Pearson. Anti-scrape critics were alarmed when, in 1884, a close hoarding was erected around the whole transept. They had reason to be alarmed; when the scaffolding came down in 1892 it could be seen that Pearson had entirely rebuilt the transept above the portals. What is extraordinary is that Pearson changed the design. Dickenson's rose window, which available documentary evidence confirmed to be a copy of the old 13th-century window, was replaced by a new one to Pearson's design which eliminated the interesting feature of the glazed spandrels in the bottom corners of the rose which survive in the south transept. Furthermore, Pearson altered the blank tracery of the gable, even though it was undoubtedly 13th-century work, theoretically his favourite period of architecture. As Lethaby pertinently observed, "the restorers seem never to have heard of criticism. They ought, one would think, to know old forms when they see them . . . how could they have thought that such beautiful forms of 1250–60 got up there?"

Scott would never have done this. He was often guilty of "conjectural restoration" in which work of later "debased" periods was replaced, and the results are sometimes not wholly satisfactory. But it is difficult to believe that he would have knowingly altered work of the approved best period, Middle Pointed, as he was too careful and profound an antiquarian. Pearson, however, much more an architect than an antiquarian, maintained ruthless mid-Victorian attitudes to old buildings into a period when, thanks to Ruskin, Morris and others, more conservative views on restoration prevailed. Pearson also showed insensitivity in his work at Peterborough Cathedral. His new west front to Westminster Hall (1888), necessitated by the removal of Kent and Soane's Law Courts (which had survived the fire of 1834) once Street's new Law Courts were finished, also caused much controversy, as did his project to restore the interior of the Abbey in 1892.

Pearson was succeeded as Surveyor by two much more sympathetic restorers: Scott's pupil, J. T. Micklethwaite (who held the appointment from 1897 to 1906) and then W. R. Lethaby (1906–28)

Westminster Abbey, as the national Valhalla, continued to be filled with monuments in the 19th century, although lovers of Gothic architecture felt that these often huge and inappropriate memorials interfered with the dignity of the architecture. Unexecuted projects for a separate building, a Gothic "Campo Santa" were drawn up both by Scott (1854) and Pearson (1890) as a receptable for monuments.

The Victorian memorials and monuments in the Abbey are too numerous to mention, but several may be singled out. In the north transept are the Victorian statesmen: Disraeli (d. 1881) by Boehm; Gladstone (d. 1898) by Thomas Brock; Peel (d. 1850) by John Gibson. In the south aisle of the nave is the Fawcett monument (d. 1884) by Alfred Gilbert, and the Brunel window, designed by Norman Shaw and Henry Holiday in 1868. Another engineer, Robert Stephenson (d. 1859), is commemorated by a brass by Scott on the floor of the north side of the nave. Nearby are brasses of architects: Sir Charles Barry (d. 1860); Scott (d. 1878), a brass by Street; G. E. Street (d. 1881), by Bodley, 1884; and Pearson (d. 1897) by W. D. Caroe, 1898.

In front of the west end of the Abbey is the Memorial to the dead of Westminster School in the Crimean War, by Scott (1859–61). By Scott also are the adjacent Dean's Yard buildings (1854).

Map 2 E4

89
Bedford Park
TURNHAM GREEN, W4

1875–7
Edward William Godwin

1877–86
R. Norman Shaw

1880 onwards
E. J. May, Maurice Bingham Adams and others

When, in 1882, the American humanist, Moncure Daniel Conway, revisited the site of the Battle of Turnham Green (1642) he was not, apparently, prepared for what he found. "Angels and ministers of grace! am I dreaming! Right before me is the apparition of a little red town made up of quaintest Queen Anne houses . . . Surely my eyes are cheating me; they must have been gathering impressions of by-gone architecture along the riverside Malls, and are now turning them to visions, and building them by ideal mirage into this dream of old-time homesteads! . . . Their gables sometimes fronting the street, their doorways adorned with various touches of taste, the windows surrounded with tinted glass, the lattices thrown open, and many comely young faces under dainty caps visible here and there, altogether impressed me with a sense of being in some enchanted land . . . For those who dwell here the world is divided into two great classes—those who live at Bedford Park, and those who do not" (Travels in South Kensington).

The extraordinary thing is how little Bedford Park has changed—the "front garden suburb", with its Queen Anne houses, survives in all its preciousness and insularity.

The genius of the property speculator who created Bedford Park, Jonathan T. Carr (1845–1915), was that he combined avant-garde architecture with a middle-class ideal. The idea that the inhabitants of Bedford Park were cultured aesthetes reacting with horror against "high Victorian vulgarity of mahogany, wax-fruit, gilt-frames, crinolines and stucco" is probably a myth of the Kind Hearts and Coronets vintage, but it probably is true that for many middle-class families with artistic pretensions and

a *View of the Co-operative Stores and Tabard Inn in Bedford Park published in Moncure Conway's* Travels in South Kensington, *1882*
b *Queen Anne's Gardens, from the same source*

adopting progressive views, the choice between the stuccoed houses of Bayswater or the Gothic villas of Norwood was not attractive. In Conway's words, "the people who most desired beautiful homes were those of the younger generation whom the new culture had educated above the mere pursuit of riches, at the same time awakening in them refined tastes which only through riches could obtain their satisfaction".

A whole cult of the "House Beautiful" had emerged, a greater interest in art and decoration, inspired by the writings of Eastlake and Mrs Haweis, in reaction to High Victorian muscular Christianity, seriousness and Gothic. Carr bought twenty-four acres near Turnham Green station on the London and South-Western Railway's Richmond line (1869) and, in 1875, asked E. W. Godwin to design some houses. Godwin's credentials for being Artistic were impeccable; he had not only designed Aesthetic Japanesy furniture but had run off with Mrs G. F. Watts, that is, the future actress, Ellen Terry, and had lived in sin with her. Unfortunately, the planning of Godwin's houses was unsatisfactory (notably 1 and 2 The Avenue) and in 1877 Carr turned to the doyen of house architects, the creator of the Queen Anne Style, Norman Shaw, who really created the image of Bedford Park.

By 1883 the estate comprised 113 acres and 490 houses had been erected in the irregular, tree-lined streets. In 1880 Shaw ceased to be connected directly with Bedford Park and he was succeeded by his assistant E. J. May (1853–1941). Most houses are in the manner of Shaw set in several alternative designs, but often designed by May, or another assistant, Maurice B. Adams (1849–1933) or by W. Wilson, or Coe and Robinson.

For a precise survey of all the Bedford Park houses, T. Affleck Greeves's *Bedford Park, the First Garden Suburb* must be consulted. Two buildings in particular, however, must be mentioned here, two of the community buildings which create the essential social centre of the suburb; the church and the pub, both designed by Shaw.

It is difficult to know how serious Shaw was in his design for St Michael and All Angels. Normally a serious, if imaginative, Tractarian in his churches, Shaw here employs the Queen Anne which gives the building a certain levity. The essence is Gothic, that is, the arcades, but it is the Gothic of the 17th-century; debased, with echoes of St John, Leeds, which Shaw, with Scott, helped to preserve. Perhaps at this period, Classicism was acceptable if it was provincial and illiterate, and therefore not too formal. Hence the screen and the galleries and the odd dormer windows. An Aesthetic touch is given by the elegant benches and the panelled dados to the walls and columns (a motif derived from G. G. Scott, Junior's St Agnes, Kennington, of 1874–7). The abnormally elevated chancel was a fashion of the 1870s. The Queen Anne prettiness of the exterior is achieved by the 17th-century lantern and entrance porch. Shaw later wrote to J. D. Sedding, "Why you should *pretend* (yes Sir, pretend) to care anything about the Church at Bedford Park I can't conceive . . . You know I am not a Church man, I am a house man, and soil pipes are my speciality", but Shaw designed many distinguished churches and, by 1886, he seems to have fallen out with Carr (the year Bedford Park Ltd went bankrupt).

The church was designed in 1878, and built in 1879–82. The north aisle and hall were added in 1887 by Adams, who later designed the south-east All Souls chapel in 1909. The inner south porch is by Martin Travers. The vicarage was designed by E. J. May in 1881.

The church was a social centre for some (those who were not left-wing agnostics were usually High Church), the pub opposite for others. The Tabard is at the end of a terrace which also contained the co-operative stores (all very *News from Nowhere*); this is a composition of gables, but considerable variety is created to differentiate the buildings. The inspiration was Staple Inn in Holborn, then (like all old houses) plastered with the timber not exposed. Inside the Tabard are tiles by William de Morgan, and reliefs by Walter Crane, and the design for the original inn sign was by T. M. Rooke.

Shaw's Tower House for Carr was demolished in the 1930s and Adams's School of Art was bombed. The most discordant note in the suburb, however, was deliberate, the house designed by Voysey: 14 South Parade (1891), which, with its white stucco and archaic leaded lights, was just juvenile rebelliousness against the comfortable domesticity of Queen Anne redbrick and white paint.

Curiously, Bedford Park did attract the cultured aesthetes Carr wanted, although the best artists tended to move on to Chelsea once they were successful. In the first few decades, Cecil Aldin, G. K. Chesterton, Sidney Cockerell, Moncure Conway, Edward Gordon Graig (Godwin's illegitimate son), William Nicholson, H. P. Horne (Mackmurdo's partner), A. W. Pinero, Lucien Pissarro, Martin Travers, Stepniak (the tame anarchist) and John B. Yeats all lived there for a time.

Social life—the club, tennis matches, progressive politics, emancipated women, and fancy dress parties—was rather self-consciously successful. Little would seem to have changed. As the writer of the "Ballad of Bedford Park" recounted

> With red and blue and sagest green
> were walls and dado dyed,
> Friezes of Morris there were seen
> and oaken wainscot wide
>
> Thus was a village builded
> for all who are aesthete
> Whose precious souls it fill did
> with utter joy complete
>
> For floors were stained and polished
> and every hearth was tiled
> And Philistines abolished
> by Culture's gracious child.

Map 1 B3

90, 91, 92
Kew Gardens
KEW, SURREY

Palm House
1845–8
Decimus Burton & Richard Turner

Temperate House Lodge
1866–7
William Eden Nesfield

Marianne North Gallery
1882
James Fergusson

Among the many interesting structures dotted about the Botanical Gardens at Kew are several remarkable Victorian buildings.

The Palm House, of 1844–8, is rightly famous and praised by Pevsner as "one of the boldest pieces of 19th-century functionalism in existence—much bolder indeed, and hence aesthetically much more satisfying, than the Crystal Palace ever was". The possibilities of iron and glass are exploited to the full, and the result is much lighter and more elegant than any contemporary railway station shed, although, doubtless, for railway trains the curved forms would not have been suitable. The success of the Palm House is due to the fact that it is not just the work of an engineer but that its symmetrical masses, with lower wings, and clerestory tops, were composed by an architect.

The engineer was Richard Turner of Dublin, the architect Decimus Burton (1800–81), a Classicist, who is best known for the Screen and Arch at Hyde Park Corner (1825–46) and the Athenaeum in Pall Mall (1827–30). It is significant that he collaborated with Joseph Paxton, the designer of the Crystal Palace, on the details of the Great Conservatory at Chatsworth (1836–40). Turner was more than an engineer. He had designed elegant glasshouses for the Botanic Gardens in both Belfast and Dublin. After Burton's first design had been turned down in 1844, Turner produced a Gothic scheme for Kew which Burton then modified.

The Palm House at Kew in 1979 (photograph by Martin Charles)
The Marianne North Gallery at Kew in 1979 with the North Lodge to the right (Photograph by Martin Charles)
Nesfield's Lodge at Kew in 1979
(Photograph by André Goulancourt)

It is depressing to find that Burton was also responsible for the very pedestrian Temperate House (1859–62); as Pevsner truthfully observes "so rapidly then did the pride in engineering pure and simple collapse which had blazed the victories of the early Victorians. The naked beauty of the Palm House could no longer be tolerated and fussy stone piers and roofs had to be introduced to make the buildings look like architecture".

Burton also designed the Museum No 1 (1856–7), in minimal brick Classical, the main gates (1848) and the Campanile (water tower and chimney).

As pioneering in its own way as the Palm House is the Temperate House Lodge, by Kew Road. It was designed in 1866 by Norman Shaw's partner, William Eden Nesfield (1835–88), and is often described as one of the first buildings in the Queen Anne style. But this lodge is not Queen Anne in the manner of Shaw; it is a highly formal but deliberately idiosyncratic composition, with its outsized coved cornice, roof and chimneys. It is beauti-

fully detailed: leaded-lights and glazing bars in the dormer windows—which have a sunflower motif embossed in the lead sides—and rubbed brick pilasters and decorations on the chimneys. This was doubtless inspired by the Palace or Dutch House, in Kew Gardens, a gabled redbrick building of 1631 which was being studied by young architects looking for something different from Gothic.

Nesfield designed several remarkable buildings, Cloverley Hall (1866–8) and Kinmel Park (1871–4), usually touched by a Japanese aestheticism as well as the urbanity of the 17th-century, before he declined into inactivity and alcohol, and died prematurely. Nesfield and Shaw were only in partnership from 1866–9 and they never did any work jointly. Nesfield's father, William Andrews Nesfield, was a landscape gardener who altered Regent's Park (the Broad Walk), St James's Park and remodelled the gardens at Kew.

Nesfield's Lodge looks very advanced and sophisticated compared with the nearby Marianne North Gallery; it is hard to believe that this building is over a decade later, and that it is the one work carried out by James Fergusson, the architectural historian and critic. Fergusson (1808–86) was the author of the *Illustrated Handbook of Architecture* (1855), the *History of the Modern Styles of Architecture* (1862), and the *History of Indian and Eastern Architecture* (1865–7). He was an inflential critic of the Gothic Revival and was generally in favour of a rational but ornamental Italianate Classicism.

His confused and miserable little building is proof that—in architecture especially—actions speak louder than words. It is also proof that those 19th-century architects who did not conspicuously attempt to find a "new style" were those who often produced the most successful and sophisticated buildings. He devoted much research to the original method by which Greek temples were lit, and he tried out his discoveries here—the gallery is top lit by a clerestory filled with opaque glass.

The Gallery was designed to house 848 flower paintings by Marianne North, an intrepid explorer who travelled twice around the world. Her paintings were done between 1871 and 1890.

Map 1 A4

93, 94
Merchant Seamen's Orphans' Asylum, now Snarebrook Hospital
HERMON HILL, WANSTEAD, E11

1861–3
George Somers Clarke, Senior

Infant Orphans' Asylum, now Council Offices
HOLLYBUSH HILL, WANSTEAD, E11

1843–5
George Gilbert Scott & William Bonython Moffat

The semi-rural calm of Wanstead, where once stood Colen Campbell's famous Palladian mansion, would seem to have been a particularly favoured spot for the care of those unfortunate children, celebrated in Victorian novels, who had managed to lose both of their parents.

In 1861 the Prince Consort, in one of his last public duties, laid the foundation stone for an institution to house and educate 400 girls and boys whose fathers had perished at sea. The resulting building was a most successful essay in the secular use of fashionable Venetian Gothic by the architect of that other Venetian building, 7 Lothbury in the City (46). Two such imaginative designs from the elder Somers Clarke are, perhaps, rather surprising from a man who was an assistant to Sir Charles Barry. Clarke had certainly studied his *Stones of Venice*, for what is impressive about this building is the unfussy integrity of the brick walls, which are pierced by the window openings rather than being elaborated with much projecting detail. The brick walls are given a polychromatic treatment by horizontal bands of darker brick among the red, arranged so as to link the regularly spaced windows on each storey on the rather classically composed elevations. However, the essentially romantic and picturesque nature of the Venetian Gothic style is evident in the

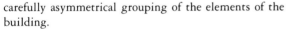

a *The Merchant Seamen's Orphans' Asylum at Wanstead; wood-cut published in the* Building News, *1862 (Royal Institute of British Architects, London)*

b *The Infant Ophans' Asylum at Wanstead; woodcut published in the* Builder, *1843 (Royal Institute of British Architects, London)*

carefully asymmetrical grouping of the elements of the building.

Many aspects of the design would look strange even in Venice, particularly the dormer windows and the excellent tower, which is a most imaginative composition: it contains water-tanks and servants' bedrooms. At the base of the tower, which rises firmly from the ground as Ruskin demanded, is the main entrance porch, and over the door is a relief of a shipwreck carved by Thomas Earp, who was responsible for all the architectural sculpture. When opened in 1863 the Asylum was only partially complete as the architect designed it to be built in stages.

Also in Wanstead, in Hollybush Hill, is the former Infant Orphans' Asylum, now Council Offices. It was won in competition in 1843 by Scott and Moffatt, ie George Gilbert Scott (1811–78) and William Bonython Moffatt (1812–87) who were in partnership until 1845, and chiefly engaged in the design of cheap Union Workhouses, built as a result of Edwin Chadwick's cruelly utilitarian Poor Law Amendment Act 1834.

Scott later recalled that "nothing could exceed the energy with which Moffatt threw himself into this competition, the most important by far into which we had then entered, nor the pains he took in thoroughly mastering its practical requirements. The planning was chiefly his, the external design, which was Elizabethan, mine. We succeeded and from that moment Moffatt's head was turned! He used to boast that he could 'afford' to make a fool of himself. His talent, energy and industry remained, but he was an altered man. He cared not who he offended either by direct annoyance, or indirectly by his strange ways of conducting himself". Moffatt became embroiled in speculation during the great railway mania of 1846 and later ended up in a debtors' prison. Scott fortunately terminated the partnership in 1845 and went from strength to strength. The Asylum was opened in 1845 by Leopold I, King of the Belgians: Queen Victoria's Uncle and confidant.

Map 1 H1

95
Harrow School

HARROW-ON-THE-HILL, MIDDLESEX

1818 ONWARDS
Charles Robert Cockerell, Charles Foster Hayward, George Gilbert Scott, William Burges, Basil Champneys, Edward Schröder Prior, Herbert Baker and others

Like most public schools, Harrow is almost entirely a Victorian creation and the school buildings and boarding houses dominate the village. What is remarkable is that the school boasts a concentration of 19th-century buildings of particularly high quality.

Even what appears to be the old core of the school (the Old School) is partly 19th-century as, in 1818–20, C. R. Cockerell (1788–1863) inaugurated his career as a fastidious Classicist by reproducing a twin of the 1611 Speech Room building and adding crow-stepped Tudor gables to both. It is a totally convincing pastiche. His chapel, of 1838, gave way to a new one by G. G. Scott.

Scott designed both the new chapel and the adjacent Vaughan Library. The two buildings illustrate the accepted 19th-century idea of "propriety": the Chapel being the more important is in flint and stone; the Library in polychromatic redbrick.

The Chapel (1854–7) has an odd plan, with a nave and a south aisle of approximately the same height, but the nave has a polygonal apse and eastern transepts added in 1902–3. The style is Scott's favourite Geometrical Decorated Gothic. The interior seems to have been designed chiefly for the rows of memorial tablets. The reredos was designed by A. W. Blomfield. The original glass, by Wailes, Hardman, Clayton and Bell, and A. Lussor, has unfortunately been "improved" by lightening.

Scott, in his *Secular and Domestic Architecture* of 1857 was determined to show, like all mid-19th-century Revivalists, that Gothic was adaptable and suitable for any purpose, but, although the Vaughan Library (1861–3) is clearly not a church, the windows are limited to ecclesiastical types, including a rose window.

The Headmaster's house is by Decimus Burton (1840, enlarged 1845–6) but the architect who did most at Harrow as Charles Forster Hayward (1830–1905), who designed most of the gaunt dark red polychromatic brick boarding houses in Peterborough Road and Grove Hill. He had a strong connection with Harrow, designed the school laboratories (1874) and the sanatorium (at the end of Mount Park Avenue) and the old gymnasium (1864) as well as the Public Hall in the village.

Much more interesting and much more successful as an

Harrow School in the early 20th-century before the construction of the War Memorial Building; from left to right there is the Old School, the Speech Room, and the Chapel (National Monuments Record, Crown copyright)

example of secular Gothic than Scott's Library is the new Speech Room, first designed by William Burges in 1871 and built in 1874–7 to an altered design. Its plan is remarkable—a D shape based on that of a Greek theatre. On the exterior, the severe 13th-century Gothic Burges liked was wrapped cheerfully around the curved wall, while along the straight entrance front the arcaded façade has something of the quality of Venetian Gothic Ruskin admired. The north tower was only finished in 1919, the carving completed in 1923. The south tower was added by Herbert Baker in 1925. The interior painting and glass was by C. F. Ball (1924–5).

Inside, the space could not be more rational. The elaborate wooden roof is supported on three iron columns and the shape of the domes and the decoration echoes the curved shape of the banked seats below.

If the Speech Room is a fine example of the uncompromising heavy Gothicism of the mid-Victorian, the Butler Museum, the other side of the High Street, is a fine example of the elegance and flexibility of late Victorian Queen Anne. It was built in 1884–6 and designed by Basil Champneys, architect of the quintessential example of "Sweetness and Light", Newnham College, Cam-bridge. On its sharply sloping site, the museum boasts fine Flemish gables, tiny oriel windows, superb rubbed-brick detail and, at one corner, an open arcaded staircase which announces its purpose with unashamed Gothic sincerity, but in redbrick Renaissance style. The design of this elevation is a masterly exercise in asymmetry within symmetry.

Later Victorian buildings at Harrow were designed by an erudite Old Harrovian, best known for his extremely wayward Arts and Crafts buildings: Edward Schröder Prior (1852–1932). He designed the laundry superin-tendent's house in Alma Road (Northolt Road) (1887) and the New Music Room, below the Butler Museum, in 1891, and the Billiard Room (1889), as well as some of the later boarding houses.

Among later buildings may be mentioned the War Memorial Building between the Speech Room and the Old School (1921) by Herbert Baker; an excellent example of the synthesis of Classical and Arts and Crafts and his subtle response to the shape and nature of the site. It replaced a house by T. G. Jackson.

Map 1 A 1

Postcript: Demolished Buildings

The greater part of Victorian London still survives. The shape and texture of the London which developed in Victoria's reign—streets, public buildings, railways and suburban housing—remained the essential fabric which the 20th-century has occasionally enhanced and usually spoiled. The Edwardians tried to make London more imperial and grand; subsequent generations tried to replan London for the motorcar and replace the usually grimy legacy of chaotic private enterprise by the apparently efficient style of "our day and age", and, of course, bombs fell. Georgian London began to fall to modern redevelopment in the years between the wars but not until the 1960s was there a concerted attack on the material remains of Victorian London. Although many inner London suburbs were first razed by the LCC post-war idealists, it was in the 1960s that Victorian villas began to give way to modern maisonettes, and, incred-ibly, buildings like St Pancras and King's Cross stations and the Foreign Office were threatened with demolition in that actively self-confident and meretricious decade. Nevertheless, for better or for worse, much of Victorian London is still with with us, and seems adequately to represent to the public the essence of an urban fabric rather better than the arid spaces, the concrete, glass and Formica of recent redevelopments. And, miraculously, almost all of the principal architectural monuments of Victorian London stand still, whether because of their utility or sheer durability is often difficult to say.

Very few interesting and important buildings which ought to be in this guide have disappeared. The principal loss is undoubtedly that of the most optimistic and symbolic product of Victorian Improvement, the Crystal Palace. Sir Joseph Paxton's pre-fabricated glass and iron hall for the Great Exhibition which had been enlarged and re-erected on the top of Sydenham Hill in 1854, where it stood for the delight of Londoners until 1936 when tragically destroyed by fire.

In the threatening years of the late 1930s this conflagration seemed ominously prophetic and with good reason. The Second World War took a severe toll of architecture. The principal victims, perhaps because of their size and vulnerability in the primary target areas, were churches, first those by Wren, and then the Vic-torian ones. The saddest losses were perhaps, Pugin's St George's Roman Catholic Cathedral, Southwark; But-terfield's St Clement, City Road; Burges and Brook's St Faith, Stoke Newington; Teulon's St Thomas, Agar Town; Pearson's St John, Red Lion Square and the younger Scott's All Hallows, Southwark. Many more damaged churches would have gone if it had not been for the enthusiastic efforts of parishes in the face of the philistine indifference of the church authorities towards Victorian buildings.

Losses among Victorian secular buildings were much fewer; possibly the worst was Norman Shaw's New Zealand Chambers, that highly inventive Queen Anne building which first rebelled against the staid architectural tradition of the City (see p. 16). It is sad that Shaw's other work in the City of London, Baring's Bank, had to give way in 1974 to silly and destructive road widening.

Bombs fall, time decays; what is outrageous is the number of excellent Victorian monuments which have been demolished since 1945 *for no good reason*. The following are buildings which deserve inclusion here and which could still be visited and enjoyed by users of this guide if not for the cynical indifference of the paramount authorities.

a *The Euston Arch in 1961, shortly before demolition (National Monuments Record, Crown copyright)*

96
Euston Station: Propylaeum and Great Hall
EUSTON ROAD, NW1
1836–7; 1846–8
PHILIP & PHILIP CHARLES HARDWICK

Possibly there was some excuse for the demolition of the Great Hall—the booking hall—at Euston as part of British Railways redevelopment plans in connection with electrification even though it was one of the best Classical rooms in London, but there was none for the destruction of the so-called Arch. It could have been moved nearer the Euston Road, or, indeed, left where it was, where today it might succeed in redeeming the unmitigated banality of the airport-style new station building. The Euston Arch—a Greek Doric propylaeum—was a monumental architectural expression of man's triumph over the elements: that is, it marked the beginning of the first trunk mainline railway in the world, the London and Birmingham Railway, opened in 1837. As it was a symbol of the great railway age, perhaps it was inevitable that the forward-looking mediocrities of BR's management should be determined to destroy it in their pathetic attempt to create a modern image for the railways. In this aim they were aided by the LCC and, ultimately, the Prime Minster, Harold Macmillan, who allowed the Arch to go after the heated controversy of 1960–1, a battle for architecture which blooded and strengthened the newly formed Victorian Society for future fights.

b *The Great Hall at Euston; photograph published in A. E. Richardson's* Monumental Classic Architecture, *1914*

97
Sun Life Assurance Building
THREADNEEDLE STREET, EC3
1841–3
CHARLES ROBERT COCKERELL

a *The Sun Life Assurance Building; perspective drawing published in* Monumental Classic Architecture, *1914 showing original design*

It may seem incredible that the last surviving building by Cockerell in London was demolished as recently as 1971, but so it was.

Cockerell's first design was made in 1839, but road widening proposals forced him to redesign the building in 1841 on a smaller site and with a chamfered corner on the junction of Threadneedle Street and Bartholomew Lane. The executed building was immensely rich and subtle in its elevations, the different floors expressed with an eclectic architectural treatment and Mannerist idiosyncrasy typical of this fastidious and scholarly architect: Greek Doric columns, varieties of Mannerist rustication, superbly cut Renaissance detail. The ground floor windows would seem to have been the prototype for the haunched segmental arch type so typical in Victorian commercial and domestic architecture.

In 1890 the painter Frederick Leighton was discovered by Phené Spiers and the Baron de Geymüller gazing at the building; he explained that "whenever he wanted to revivify himself with the sense of the beauty of Greek work he used to come down and look at Cockerell's works". In 1895 the building was enlarged with extraordinary sensitivity by F. W. Porter, who put in extra floors above the first floor and re-erected Cockerell's top storey and cornice above. The building still retained all the character and complexity of Cockerell and was excellent in itself, yet the fact that the original design had been altered was used as an excuse by the fastidious experts on the Historic Buildings Council not to resist the proposal to redevelop the important site behind the Bank of England, a site on which Cockerell's Portland stone building stood and harmonised so well with the surrounding Classical architecture.

b *The Sun office in 1962 (National Monuments Record, Crown copyright)*

<table>
<tr><td>

98
Coal Exchange
LOWER THAMES STREET, EC3
1847–9
JAMES BUNNING

</td><td>

99
Columbia Market
BETHNAL GREEN, E2
1866–8
HENRY DARBISHIRE

</td></tr>
</table>

Professor Hitchcock called the Coal Exchange "the prime City monument of the early Victorian period". It was remarkable less for its Classical exterior than for its domed circular hall. This rotunda was of iron, and as an example of iron construction was comparable with Labrouste's libraries in Paris. Not content with naked construction, Bunning, the architect to the City of London, moulded the stanchions and railings of the circular galleries in the forms of cables and ropes; other mining themes were developed in the murals by Frederick Sang.

In 1958 the City of London proposed demolishing the building for commercial development; they were assisted in this resolve by the Ministry of Transport's intended widening of Lower Thames Street. A four-year battle for its preservation ensued which, like the concurrent one for the Euston Arch, reached the highest authorities. The Exchange was demolished, hastily, in 1962, notwithstanding proposals to re-erect it elsewhere. The site is still empty, and stands next to the hateful urban motorway which Thames Street now is.

The Columbia Market was a huge folly, but London needs a few follies and the monuments of LCC totalitarianism which now stand on the site of this preposterous Gothic fantasy are not an acceptable replacement.

The Market was built by the great philanthropist Baroness Burdett-Coutts who, knowing that the East Enders were cheated by sharp traders, spent £200,000 on a free market where fair exchange might take place. It failed within six months, more owing to the boycott of powerful traders than because of its didactic and inappropriate architecture. The City then attempted to run it as a fish market, but it was given back to the Baroness in 1874 and closed in 1885. Such elaborate architecture was unusual for Darbishire, best known as the designer of the serviceable but gloomy blocks of working-class tenements erected all over London by the Peabody Trust. He was the architect of the four grim blocks which comprised Columbia Square, built in 1860–2, which was next to the Market, and which the Baroness had earlier paid for. Dickens had found the site for this remarkable and generous woman, who had bought it (despite local opposition) in 1857.

The interior of the Coal Exchange in 1961 (Architectural Press)

The Columbia Market, Bethnal Green, shortly before demolition (National Monuments Record, Crown copyright)

Pevsner, in 1952, called the Market "one of the great follies of the Victorian Age" and added "the building should be preserved at all cost and made some reasonable use of". Columbia Square and Market were demolished between 1958 and 66 by the LCC and replaced by flats.

100
St Agnes
KENNINGTON PARK, SE11
1874–91
GEORGE GILBERT SCOTT, JUNIOR

The interior of St Agnes, Kennington Park, in 1890 (National Monuments Record, Crown copyright)

In his short and tragic career George Gilbert Scott, Junior (1839–97) built comparatively little, and much of that has been destroyed. St Agnes, Kennington was his masterpiece, and recognised as such by his contemporaries. It was the principal example in London of that rejection of the High Victorian Gothic in favour of an architecture more catholic and refined which occured in the 1870s. St Agnes was daring in being in a late Decorated style which tended towards the forbidden, debased Perpendicular. The church had an austere exterior but a rich, numinous interior, with furnishings designed by Scott and his pupil Temple Moore. It contained the finest set of glass windows by C. E. Kempe. For over half a century St Agnes was an influential model for church architects who visited its spacious elegant interior, either to admire the refined mouldings, the screens and other fittings, all with a definite flavour of the Renaissance, or perhaps to participate in the Anglo-Catholic ritual in the English tradition, for which the church was renowned.

In 1941 an incendiary bomb destroyed the roof; all the furnishings and most of the glass was preserved. After the war, S. E. Dykes Bower prepared plans for a full restoration, estimating that 75% of the cost of the complete structure was still extant. In 1953 the Diocese of Southwark determined upon the demolition of the church so as to erect a smaller building. Despite the availability of a full War Damage grant for restoration and strenuous opposition—particularly from the Council for the Care of Churches, who considered St Agnes "the most important 19th-century building to have been damaged in the late war"—the building was demolished in 1956, having been left open to the weather for fifteen years. The reredos and cut-down screen were retained in the miserable new building placed on the site; other furnishings were used by Dykes Bower in his restoration of the Church of the Holy Spirit, Southsea.

Imperial Institute
IMPERIAL INSTITUTE ROAD, SW7
1887–93
THOMAS EDWARD COLLCUTT

Inspired by the Colonial Exhibition of 1886, the winning design for the Imperial Institute was published in the year of Victoria's Golden Jubilee and the foundation stone laid in the same year by the Queen, Empress herself. The Institute was the principal architectural expression of the rising tide of late Victorian imperialism and a fine and colourful monument in the centre of the South Kensington complex of public buildings. Tennyson, Poet Laureate, had celebrated the Jubilee with the lines:

> Raise a stately memorial
> Some Imperial Institute
> Rich in symbol and ornament
> Which may speak to the centuries

Thanks to London University, the building only spoke to seventy years; it went soon after the end of the Empire and only the tower is left, elegant but forlorn, protruding from the litter of the concrete cubes of Imperial College which have been growing like a cancer in recent decades, destroying all interesting architecture in the vicinity. A Norman Shaw house, a Fairfax Wade college and Collcutt's masterpiece are included in the dons' tally so far.

Thomas Edward Collcutt (1840–1924) was one of the great eclectics of the later 19th-century; he used bric à brac from any sources, but particularly from the French and Spanish Renaissance, and he handled them with a picturesque wit. He was also, like Waterhouse, a master in terra cotta and liked colour in his buildings. He designed Wakefield Town Hall (1877) and, in London, the Palace Theatre in Cambridge Circus (1890) and much of the Savoy (1889, 1903–4). The Midland Bank in Ludgate Hill (1890) is like a little piece of the Imperial Insitute.

Collcutt got the Institute in a limited competition. His design was symmetrical but, like the Law Courts by his old master, Street, it was interesting in small sections as a long building in a narrow street should be. The Institute was conspicuous for the combination of Portland Stone and redbrick. Detail was concentrated in the upper parts, as Ruskin recommended, with a forest of gables, towers and domes, some with an almost oriental flavour. Above all floated the great campanile: a sheer square tower of stone breaking into a complex dome at the top, a form

inspired by Segovia. Summerson has written that the Institute "was perhaps *the* representative public monument of late Victorian London—not only because of its size and the sentiment it embodied, but because it so obviously issued from a tradition more concerned with domestic ease than with monumental display".

The Institute served several functions and housed parts of London University for many years. Nevertheless, in their expansion plans of 1953, the Imperial College of Science and Technology could find no use for it. One might have thought that London University would have been content with destroying half of Bloomsbury, but dons are the worst of vandals, combining naked philistinism with intellectual superiority and an unshakable conviction of the importance of their own priorities and the excellence of their own taste. Considerable public opposition, including, for once, the Royal Fine Arts Commision failed to prevent the destruction of the centre of "Albertopolis" and only succeeded in saving the beautiful tower.

All the rest along with Fairfax Wade's Royal College of Needlework was needlessly torn down between 1957 and 1965. It could have been used as a Museum of Empire—which Britain needs—or to house the considerable Indian collections in the country, and the India Office Library, dislodged from Whitehall and grudgingly housed in an early Siefert tower in Waterloo. The loss of the Institute is an unnecessary tragedy.

The Imperial Institute shortly after completion (National Monuments Record, Crown copyright)

List of Architects and their Principal Buildings

Numbers in bold after an entry refer to the number of the study in the book. Former names of buildings are given if they have been renamed, and the present names are given in the heading to the study.

All these buildings—the Institute, Scott's beautiful church and the great Doric Propylaeum—were needlessly destroyed in the dark days of the 50s and early 60s. Perhaps the scandal of their destruction would not occur today. Yet even now masterpieces of Victorian architecture are threatened. Several of the buildings discussed in this guide may not be standing in a few years time—St Stephen, Rosslyn Hill (**58**), for instance—and at the time

of writing the Government is determined upon destroying part of the Natural History Museum. In this new decade an appalling number of good church buildings may become redundant and their futures uncertain.

Architecture is never safe: that most subtle and useful of the arts, so expressive of personality, history and national character, so vital in a civilised society, is all too subject to the vagaries of economics and taste, and the ever-strong forces of English philistinism. If this book ensures that more people look at the best of Victorian architecture, take it seriously and, perhaps, regard it with affection and delight, so that our architectural legacy from the past is made a little safer, then the authors' objective will have been achieved.

Maurice Bingham Adams 1849–1933

Houses in Bedford Park, W4 (**89**)	1880 onwards
Additions to St Michael, Bedford Park, W4 (**89**)	1887, 1909
Additions to St Peter, London Docks, Wapping Lane, E1 (**41**)	1884–94
Passmore Edwards Art Gallery, Peckham Road, SE5	1896–8
Passmore Edwards Library, Peckham Road, SE5	1909
London School of Economics, Houghton Street, WC2	1899

George Aitchison 1825–1910

59–61 Mark Lane, EC3 (**33**)	1864
Leighton House, 12 Holland Park Road, W14 (**47**)	1865–79
Founders' Hall, St Swithin's Lane, EC4	1877–8
Royal Bank of Scotland, formerly Drummonds, 49 Charing Cross SW1	1885

Archer and Green

Cambridge Gate, Regent's Park, NW1	1875
Whitehall Court, Victoria Embankment, SW1 (**83**)	1885–7
Hyde Park Hotel, Knightsbridge, SW1	1888

Sir Charles Barry 1795–1860

St John the Evangelist, Holloway Road, N7	1826
St Paul, Essex Road, N1	1826
Holy Trinity, Cloudesley Square, N1	1827–8
St John's National Schools, Holloway Road, N7	1830
Travellers' Club, Pall Mall, SW1	1830–2
St Peter, St Peter's Street, N1	1834
Royal College of Surgeons, Lincoln's Inn, WC2 (altered)	1835–6
New Palace of Westminster, Westminster, SW1 (**1**)	1835–60
Reform Club, Pall Mall, SW1 (**2**)	1839–41
Terrace and Steps, Trafalgar Square, SW1	1840
Façade of the Treasury, Whitehall, SW1	1845
Bridgewater House, Cleveland Row, SW1 (**7**)	1845–54
12, 18–19 and 20 Kensington Palace Gardens, W8	1845–7
Pentonville Prison, Caledonian Road, N1 (altered)	1847
Additions and alterations to St John's Lodge, Regent's Park, NW1	1847

Charles Barry, Junior 1823–1900
with Robert Richardson Banks 1813–72

Dulwich College, College Road, SE21 (**44**)	1866–70
St Stephen, College Road, SE21	1868–75
Piccadilly façade to Burlington House, W1	1869–73
Great Eastern Hotel, Liverpool Street, EC2	1884

Edward Middleton Barry 1830–80

Royal Opera House, Bow Street, WC2 (**19**)	1857–8
Floral Hall, Bow Street, WC2	1858–60
St Giles-in-the-Fields, National Schools, Endell Street, WC2	1860
Charing Cross Station Hotel (roof altered), The Strand, WC2	1863–4
Temple Gardens Building, Middle Temple Lane, EC4	1878

Thomas Bellamy 1798–1876

St Anne, Brookfield, Highgate West Hill, N6	1852–3
Emmanuel Church, Camberwell Road, SE5	1841–2
Law Fire Insurance Office, Chancery Lane, WC2 (**21**)	1857–8 and 1874–6

John Francis Bentley 1839–1902

St Francis of Assisi, Pottery Lane, Notting Hill, W11 (additions) (**25**)	1861–3
235 Lancaster Road, W11	1863
Sunnydene, 108 Westwood Hill, Sydenham, SE26 (**55**)	1868–70
Ellerslie, Sydenham Hill, SE26	1870
Church of Corpus Christi, Brixton Hill, SW2 (unfinished)	
St Thomas's Seminary, Hammersmith, W6 (**73**)	1876–88
St Mary, Cadogan Street, SW3	1877–82
Our Lady of the Holy Souls, Bosworth Road, Kensal Green, W10	1881
Redemptorist Monastery Buildings, Clapham Park Road, SW4	1891–3
Cathedral of the Most Precious Blood, Westminster, SW1	1894–1902

Edward Lushington Blackburne 1803–88

The Tower of St Mark, St Mark's Rise, Dalston, E8 (**34**)	1877–80

Edward Blore 1787–1879

Survey and repair work at Westminster Abbey (**88**)	1827–49
St George, Nine Elms Lane, SW8	1828
St James the Great, Bethnal Green, E2	1842–3

George Frederick Bodley 1827–1907 and
Thomas Garner 1839–1906

River House, 3 Chelsea Embankment, SW3 (**74**)	1876–9
St Michael, Camden Road, NW1 (**80**)	1880–94
St Mary of Eton Mission Church, Hackney Wick, E8	1890
Holy Trinity Church, Prince Consort Road, Kensington, SW7	1902–3

John Raphael Brandon 1817–77
Church of Christ the King, Gordon Square, WC 1 (13)	1850–4
1 Clement's Inn, WC 2	1874

James Brooks 1825–1901
St Michael, Mark Street, Shoreditch, EC 2 (redundant)	1863–5
St Andrew, Barking Road, Plaistow, E 13 (redundant)	1867–70
St Columba, Kingsland Road, Haggerston, E 2 (redundant) (56)	1868–9
St Chad, Dunloe Street, Haggerston, E 2 (57)	1868–9
St John the Baptist, Holland Road, W 14	1872
Church of the Ascension, Lavender Hill, SW 11 (77)	1876–83
Church of the Transfiguration, Algernon Road, Lewisham, SE 13	1880–6
Church of the Holy Innocents, Paddenswick Road, Hammersmith, W 6	1889–1901
All Hallows, Savernake Road, Gospel Oak, NW 3 (completed by Giles Gilbert Scott in 1913–15)	1892–1901

John McKean Brydon 1840–1901
Chelsea Vestry Hall, Chelsea Manor Gardens, SW 3 (84)	1885–7
Chelsea Polytechnic and Library, Manresa Road, SW 3	1891–5
Local Government Board Offices, Parliament Square, SW 1	1898–1912

William Burges 1827–81
Speech Room, Harrow School, Harrow-on-the-Hill, Middlesex (85)	1874–7
Tower House, 29 Melbury Road, Kensington, W 14 (75)	1876–81

Decimus Burton 1800–81
Villas, etc in Regent's Park	1819–30
Screen and Arch, Hyde Park Corner, SW 1	1824–5 and 1827–8
Athenaeum Club, Waterloo Place, SW 1	1827–30
Palm House, Kew Gardens, Kew, Surrey (90)	1845–8
Temperate House, Kew Gardens, Kew, Surrey	1860–99

William Butterfield 1814–1900
All Saints, Margaret Street, W 1 (11)	1849–59
St Matthias, Matthias Road, Stoke Newington, N 16	1851–3
St John, Glenthorne Road, Hammersmith, W 6	1858–9
Sir Walter St John's School, High Street, Battersea, SW 11	1859
Former St Michael's Vicarage, Burleigh Street, Covent Garden, WC 2	1859–60
St Alban, Brooke Street, Holborn, EC 1 (altered) (24)	1861–2
Alterations, Christ Church, Albany Street, NW 1	1867
St Augustine, Queen's Gate, SW 7 (61)	1870–7
St Mary, Brookfield, Dartmouth Park Hill, N 19	1876

Richard Cromwell Carpenter 1812–55
Lonsdale Square, Islington, N 1	1842–5
St Mary Magdalene, Munster Square, NW 1 (10)	1849–52

Basil Champneys 1842–1935
St Luke, Oseney Crescent, Kentish Town, NW 5 (51)	1868–9
Oak Tree House, Redington Gardens, Hampstead, NW 3	1872–3
42 (Hall Oak) Frognal Lane, NW 3 (own house)	1881
Butler Museum, Harrow School, Harrow-on-the-Hill, Middlesex (95)	1884–6
St Bride's Vicarage, Bridewell Place, EC 4	1885
Fawcett Memorial, Victoria Embankment, SW 1	1886
19–27 Copthall Avenue, off London Wall, EC 2	1890
St Andrew and St Michael, Blackwall Lane, Greenwich, SE 10	1900–2
Bedford College, Regent's Park, NW 1	1910–13

Chester Cheston, Junior
St Mark, St Mark's Rise, Dalston, E 8 (34)	1864–6

George Somers Clark, Senior 1829–82
Merchant Seamen's Orphans' Asylum, Hermon Hill, Wanstead, E 11 (93)	1861–3
General Credit Company, 7 Lothbury, EC 2 (46)	1866

Thomas Chatfield Clarke 1829–95
25 Throgmorton Street, EC 2	1869
Royal Bank of Scotland, Bishopsgate, EC 2 (78)	1877
66–67 Cornhill, EC 3	1880
77–78 Gracechurch Street, EC 3	1897

Henry Clutton 1819–93
St Francis of Assisi, Pottery Lane, Notting Hill, W 11 (25)	1859–60
Bedford Chambers, Covent Garden, WC 2	1877–90

Charles Robert Cockerell 1788–1863
Old Speech Room building (the old school) Harrow School, Harrow-on-the-Hill, Middlesex (95)	1818–20

Thomas Edward Collcutt 1840–1924
Imperial Institute (only tower remains), Kensington SW 7 (101)	1887–93
Savoy Hotel, The Strand, WC 2	1889–1903
Palace Theatre, Cambridge Circus, WC 2	1889–90
Midland Bank, Ludgate Hill, EC 4	1890

Lewis Cubitt 1799–1883
Houses on the south side of Lowndes Square, SW 1	1841–3
King's Cross Station, King's Cross, N 1 (14)	1851–2

Thomas Cundy, Junior 1790–1867
St Paul, Knightsbridge, SW 1	1840–3
St Michael, Chester Square, SW 1	1846
St Barnabas, Pimlico Road, SW 1 (with Butterfield) (9)	1847–50
St Gabriel, Warwick Square, SW 1	1852–3
St Mark, Hamilton Terrace, St John's Wood, NW 8	1846–64

Henry Darbishire
Early Peabody Trust Buildings, working class flats, good examples in Blackfriars Road, SE 1 and Commercial Street, Spitalfields, E 1	1864 onwards
Holly Village, Swain's Lane and Chester Road, Highgate, N 6 (37)	1865

Samuel Daukes 1811–80
St Andrew (formerly in Wells Street, Marylebone, NW 1), Old Church Lane, Kingsbury, NW 9 (8)	1845–7
Colney Hatch Mental Hospital, Friern Barnet, Herts	1847–51
Christ Church, Cannon Place, Hampstead, NW 3	1852

James Fergusson 1808–86
Marianne North Gallery, Kew Gardens, Kew, Surrey (92)	1882

Francis Fowke 1823–65
South Kensington Museum, Cromwell Road, SW 7 (26)	1856 onwards

Frederick John Francis 1818–96 and **Horace Francis** 1821–94
Christ Church (tower only survives), Lancaster Gate, W 2	1854–5
City Offices Company Building, 39–40 Lombard Street, EC 3 (52)	1868
Former Grand Hotel, Charing Cross, SW 1 (now Grand Buildings)	1878–80

Sir Ernest George 1839–1922 and **Harold Peto** 1828–97
Messrs Goode, 17–21 South Audley Street, W 1 (70)	1875–91
Bee-Hive Coffee House, now Cow Rubber Works,	

Streatham High Road, Streatham Common, SW16   1878–9
20–26, 35–45 Harrington Gardens, SW7 and 1–18
Collingham Gardens, SW5 (82)   1881–96
Houses in Mount Street, W1   c1885–90
St Andrew, Guildersfield Road, SW16 (with Yeates)   1886–7
Claridges Hotel, Brook Street, W1   1894–7
Golders Green Crematorium, Hoop Lane, NW11   1905
Royal Exchange Buildings, EC3 (with Yeates)   1907–8
Royal Academy of Music, Marylebone Road, NW1
(with Yeates)   1910–11
Southwark Bridge   1913–21

John Gibson 1814–92
Central Baptist Chapel, Bloomsbury Street, WC1   1845–8
National Provincial Bank, 15 Bishopsgate, EC2 (32)   1863–5
Former SPCK Building, Northumberland Avenue,
WC2   1876–9
Child's Bank, Fleet Street, EC4   1879

Edward William Godwin 1833–86
Houses at Bedford Park, Turnham Green, W4 (eg 1 and
2 The Avenue) (89)   1875–7
4, 5 and 6 Chelsea Embankment SW3   1875–7
44 Tite Street, Chelsea, SW3 (79)   1878
46 Tite Street, Chelsea SW3   c1884

Harry Stuart Goodhart-Rendel 1887–1959
North aisle and entrance porch, St Mary, Bourne Street,
SW1 (68)   1926–34
Hay's Wharf, Tooley Street, SE1   1931

Philip Hardwick 1792–1870
Goldsmiths' Hall, Foster Lane, EC2   1829–32
City Club, Old Broad Street, EC2   1832–3
Lincoln's Inn Hall and Library, Lincoln's Inn, WC2
(with P. C. Hardwick) (6)   1843–5

Philip Charles Hardwick 1820–90
Great Western Hotel, Paddington Station, Praed
Street, W2 (15)   1851–3
2 Palace Gate, W8   1873–6

Charles Forster Hayward 1830–1905
Buildings at Harrow School: Old Gymnasium (1864);
School Laboratories (1874); Boarding Houses,
Peterborough Road, Grove Hill; Harrow Village   1864
Public Hall, Harrow-on-the-Hill, Middlesex (95)   onwards

Edward I'Anson 1812–88
British and Foreign Bible Society, 146 Queen Victoria
Street, EC4 (45)   1866–7
65 Cornhill, EC3 (64)   1871
School of Medicine for St Bartholomew's Hospital,
Giltspur Street, EC1   1878–9
Corn Exchange Chambers, 2 Seething Lane, EC3   1879
Central Library, Walworth Road, Southwark, SE17   1893

James Thomas Knowles 1806–84
Cedar Terrace and Thorton Terrace, Clapham Common,
SW4   1860
Grosvenor Hotel, Victoria Station, SW1 (with Sir
James Thomas Knowles 1831–1908) (27)   1860–2
Thatched House Club, 76 St James's Street SW1 (with
Sir James Knowles)   1862

Edward Buckton Lamb 1806–69
St Martin, Vicar's Road, NW5 (40)   1865–6
St Mary Magdalene, Canning Road, Addiscombe,
Surrey   1868

Arthur Heygate Mackmurdo 1851–1942
6 Private Road, Enfield, Middlesex   1873
Brooklyn, 8 Private Road, Enfield, Middlesex (with

Herbert Percy Horne 1864–1916) (85)   1886–7
25 Cadogan Gardens, SW3   1893–4
12 Hans Road, SW3   1894

William Moseley 1799–1880 and **Andrew Moseley**
City Bank, Threadneedle Street, EC2 (18)   1856

William Eden Nesfield 1835–88
Temperate House Lodge, Kew Road, Kew, Surrey (91)   1866

Charles Octavius Parnell d. 1865
Whitehall Club, 47 Parliament Street, SW1 (35)   1864–6

Joseph Peacock 1821–93
St Simon Zelotes, Milner Street, SW3 (22)   1858–9
St Stephen, Gloucester Road, SW7   1864
Church of the Holy Cross, Cromer Street, WC1   1887–8

John Loughborough Pearson 1817–97
St Peter, Kennington Lane, Vauxhall, SE11 (28)   1863–4
St Augustine, Kilburn Park Road, NW6 (62)   1871–98
St John the Divine, Sylvan Hill, Upper Norwood, SE19   1875–87
Catholic Apostolic Church, Maida Avenue, Maida Vale,
Paddington, W2   1891–3
Astor Estate Office, Victoria Embankment, WC2   1892–95

James Pennethorne 1801–71
Public Record Office, Fetter Lane, EC4   1850–1
West façade of Somerset House, Lancaster Place, WC2   1852–6
Ballroom wing, Buckingham Palace, SW1   1853–5
10 Buckingham Gate, SW1   1854
Stables, outbuildings, attic storey Marlborough House
Mall, SW1   1861–3
London University buildings, Burlington Gardens, W1
(43)   1866–9

Frederick Hyde Pownall born 1825
2–4 Brook Street, W1   1860
St Peter, London Docks, Wapping Lane, E1 (41)   1865–6
Highgate Police Court, Archway Road, N6   1897
Corpus Christi RC Church, Maiden Lane, WC2   1873–4

Augustus Welby Northmore Pugin 1812–52
House of Lords, etc, at the New Palace of Westminster,
SW1 (with Charles Barry) (1)   1840–60
St George's Cathedral, Southwark, SW1 (mostly
destroyed)   1841
St Peter, Woolwich New Road, SE18 (incomplete)   1842–50
St Thomas, Rylston Road, Fulham, SW6   1847–9

Edward Robert Robson 1835–1917
Board School, Bonner Street and Green Street, Bethnal
Green, E2 (71)   1875
The People's Palace (now Queen Mary College, London
University), Mile End Road, E1   1885–90
Many other London Board Schools
Institute of Painters in Watercolour, (now PanAm),
Piccadilly, W1   1882

Robert Lewis Roumieu 1814–77
Literary Institute, Almeida Street, N1   1837
Tollington Park Estate, Hornsey, N8   1860–70
French Hospital, Victoria Park Road, Hackney, E9   1865
The Priory, Roehampton, Middlesex   1866
33–35 Eastcheap, EC3 (53)   1868
Milner Square, Islington, N1   c1840

Joseph John Scoles 1798–1863
St John the Evangelist, Duncan Terrace, N1   1843
Church of the Immaculate Conception, Farm Street,
W1   1844–50
Library and other buildings for the London Oratory,
Brompton Road, SW3 (76)   1876–96

Sir George Gilbert Scott 1811–78

St Giles, Camberwell Church Street, SE5 (with W. B. Moffatt) (5)	1842–4
Infant Orphans' Asylum, Hollybush Hill, Wanstead, E11 (with W. B. Moffatt) (94)	1843–5
Dean's Yard Buildings, Westminster, SW1	1854
Harrow School Chapel and Vaughan Library, Harrow-on-the-Hill, Middlesex (95)	1854–7
Porch of St Michael, Cornhill, EC3	1857–60
Government Offices, Parliament Street, Downing Street, St James's Park and King Charles Street, SW1 (29)	1863–74
Albert Memorial, Kensington Gore, SW7 (31)	1864–75
The Midland Grand Hotel, St Pancras Station, Euston Road, NW1 (36)	1865–77
St Mary Abbot, Kensington High Street, W8 (59)	1869–79
Addition to Library, Lincoln's Inn, WC2 (6)	1871–3

Henry Young Darracott Scott 1822–83

Royal Albert Hall, Kensington Gore, SW7 (42)	1867–71
Huxley Building (now part of Victoria and Albert Museum), Exhibition Road, SW7 (with J. W. Wild) (26)	1867–71

John Oldrid Scott 1841–1913

Greek Orthodox Cathedral of Aghia Sophia, Moscow Road, Bayswater, W2 (69)	1874–82

John Dando Sedding 1838–91

Church of the Holy Redeemer, Exmouth Market, Clerkenwell, EC1 (with Henry Wilson) (87)	1887–98
Holy Trinity Church, Sloane Street, SW1	begun 1888

R. Norman Shaw 1831–1912

Grims Dyke, Harrow Weald, Stanmore, Middlesex	1870–72
Lowther Lodge, Kensington Gore, SW7 (67)	1873–5
196 Queen's Gate, SW7	1874–6
8 and 11 Melbury Road, W8	1875–6
6 Ellerdale Road, NW3	1875–6
Old Swan House, 17 Chelsea Embankment, SW3 (72)	1875–7
Bedford Park, Turnham Green, W4: church, Tabard public house, etc (89)	1877–80
Farnley House, 15 Chelsea Embankment, SW3	1877–9
Clock House, 8 Chelsea Embankment, SW3	1878–80
Albert Hall Mansions, Kensington Gore, SW7 (67)	1879–86
Alliance Assurance Offices, 1–2 St James's Street, SW1 (81)	1882–3
39 Frognal, Hampstead, NW3	1884–5
Holy Trinity Church, Latimer Road, W11 (altered)	1887–9
Metropolitan Police Central Offices, New Scotland Yard, Victoria Embankment, SW1 (86)	1887–91 and 1898–1907
Alliance Assurance Offices, 88 St James Street, SW1 (with Ernest Newton) (81)	1901–5
Piccadilly Hotel, Piccadilly, W1	1905

Sydney Smirke 1798–1877

King's College, The Strand, WC2	1830–1
Oxford and Cambridge Club, Pall Mall, SW1 (with Sir Robert Smirke)	1836–7
Additions to Royal Bethlem Hospital, Lambeth, SE1 (now Imperial War Museum)	1838–46
Paper Buildings, King's Bench Walk, EC4	1838–48
Conservative Club, St James's Street, SW1 (with George Basevi)	1843–5
British Museum Reading Room, Great Russell Street, WC1 (16) (Museum begun by Sir Robert Smirke, 1823, who worked on it until 1845)	1854–7
Additions to Burlington House, Piccadilly, W1	1867–74

John James Stevenson 1831–1908

Board Schools with E. R. Robson	1872–5
8 Palace Gate, W8	1873–5

42–48 Pont Street, SW1	1876–8
1–2 Lowther Gardens, SW7	1877–8
63–73 Cadogan Square, SW1	1881–6
1 Fitzjohn's Avenue, NW3	1883
Houses in Kensington Court, W8	1883–90

George Edmund Street (1824–81)

St Paul, Herne Hill, SE24	1858
St James-the-Less, Lillington Gardens, Vauxhall Bridge Road, SW1 (23)	1859–61
St Mary Magdalene, Rowington Close, W2 (50)	1867–78
St John the Divine, Vassall Road, Kennington, SW9 (65)	1871–4 and 1887–8
All Saints, Lower Common, Putney, SW15	1873–4
Royal Courts of Justice, The Strand, WC2 (60)	1874–82
4 Cadogan Square, SW1	1879
St James, Sussex Gardens, W2 (except tower and entrance)	1881–2

Samuel Sanders Teulon 1812–73

St Mark, Silvertown, North Woolwich Road, E16	1859
"Restoration" of Ealing Parish Church, St Mary's Road, Ealing, W5	1866–73
St Stephen, Rosslyn Hill, Hampstead, NW3 (58)	1869–76

Sir William Tite 1798–1873

Mill Hill School, Middlesex	1825–7
Chapels at the South Metropolitan Cemetery, West Norwood	1839
Royal Exchange, City, EC3 (4)	1841–4

George Truefitt 1824–1902

St George, Tufnell Park Road, N7 (48)	1866–8

Thomas Verity 1837–91

Criterion Theatre, Piccadilly Circus, W1 (63)	1870–84
Comedy Theatre, Pantin Street, Haymarket, SW1	1881

Alfred Waterhouse 1830–1905

17–18 Lincoln's Inn Fields, WC2 (54)	1871–2
Natural History Museum, Cromwell Road, SW7 (66)	1873–80
Prudential Insurance Offices, High Holborn, WC1	1878–1906
1 Old Bond Street, W1	1880
Congregational Church, Lyndhurst Road, NW3	1883
National Liberal Club, Westminster, SW1 (83)	1885–7
King's Weigh House Chapel, Duke Street, W1	1889–91
University College Hospital, Gower Street, WC1	1897–1906

Philip Webb 1831–1915

91–101 Worship Street, Shoreditch, EC2 (30)	1861–2
1 Holland Park Road, W14	1864–6
35 Glebe Place, Chelsea, SW3	1868–9
1 Palace Green, Kensington Palace Gardens, W8 (49)	1868–70
19 Lincoln's Inn Fields, WC2 (54)	1868–70

William White 1825–1900

All Saints, Talbot Road, Notting Hill, W11	1852–5
St Saviour, Aberdeen Park, Highbury, N5 (39)	1865–6
St Mark, Battersea Rise, SW11	1873–4
St Peter, Plough Road, Battersea, SW11	1875–6
St Mary-le-Park, Albert Bridge Road, Battersea SW11	1881
St Stephen, Battersea Park Road, SW11	1886–7

James William Wild 1814–92

Christ Church, Christchurch Road, Streatham, SW2 (3)	1840–1
Work at South Kensington Museum with H. Y. D. Scott (26)	1867–71
Bethnal Green Museum, façade, Bethnal Green, E2 (17)	1872

Robert Jewell Withers 1823–94
Lavers and Barraud's stained glass works, 22 Endell
Street, WC2   1859–60
St Mary, Bourne Street, SW1 **(68)**   1873–4

Sancton Wood 1816–86
Queen's Assurance Company, 42 Gresham Street, EC2
(12)   1850–2

Lancaster Gate houses, Bayswater, W2   1857

Matthew Digby Wyatt 1820–77
Paddington Station, Praed Street, W2 (with Isambard
Kingdom Brunel) **(15)**   1851–4
Durbar Court of the former India office, Whitehall,
SW1 (now the Foreign and Commonwealth Office **(29)**   1864–7

Index

Numbers in **bold** refer to the main discussion of a building

174